Poverty in the Histo[ry]
of Economic Thougl[t]

Poverty in the History of Economic Thought: From Mercantilism to Neoclassical Economics aims to describe and critically examine how economic thought deals with poverty and the poor, including its causes, consequences, reduction, and abolition.

This edited volume traces the economic ideas of key writers and schools of thought across a significant period, ranging from Adam Smith and Malthus through to Wicksell, Cassel, and Heckscher. The chapters relate poverty to income distribution, asserting that poverty is not always conceived of in absolute terms, and that relative and social deprivation matter also. Furthermore, the contributors deal with both individual poverty and the poverty of nations in the context of the international economy. By providing such a thorough exploration, this book shows that the approach to poverty differs from economist to economist, depending on their particular interests and the main issues related to poverty in each epoch, as well as the influence of the intellectual climate that prevailed at the time when the contribution was made.

This key text is valuable reading for advanced students and researchers of the history of economic thought, economic development, and the economics of poverty.

Mats Lundahl is Professor Emeritus of Development Economics at the Stockholm School of Economics, Sweden.

Daniel Rauhut is Associate Professor and holds a PhD in Economic History. He works as senior researcher at the University of Eastern Finland in Joensuu, Finland.

Neelambar Hatti is Professor Emeritus in the School of Economics and Management at Lund University, Sweden.

Routledge Studies in the History of Economics

Ordoliberalism and European Economic Policy
Between Realpolitik and Economic Utopia
Edited by Malte Dold and Tim Krieger

The Economic Thought of Sir James Steuart
First Economist of the Scottish Enlightenment
Edited by José M. Menudo

A History of Feminist and Gender Economics
Giandomenica Becchio

The Theory of Transaction in Institutional Economics
A History
Massimiliano Vatiero

F.A. Hayek and the Epistemology of Politics
The Curious Task of Economics
Scott Scheall

Classical Liberalism and the Industrial Working Class
The Economic thought of Thomas Hodgskin
Alberto Mingardi

English Economic Thought in the Seventeenth Century
Rejecting the Dutch model
Seiichiro Ito

Poverty in the History of Economic Thought
From Mercantilism to Neoclassical Economics
Edited by Mats Lundahl, Daniel Rauhut and Neelambar Hatti

For more information about this series, please visit www.routledge.com/series/SE0341

Poverty in the History of Economic Thought

From Mercantilism to Neoclassical Economics

Edited by
Mats Lundahl, Daniel Rauhut and Neelambar Hatti

LONDON AND NEW YORK

First published 2021
by Routledge
2 Park Square, Milton Park, Abingdon, Oxon OX14 4RN

and by Routledge
52 Vanderbilt Avenue, New York, NY 10017

Routledge is an imprint of the Taylor & Francis Group, an informa business

British Library Cataloguing-in-Publication Data
A catalogue record for this book is available from the British Library

Library of Congress Cataloging-in-Publication Data
A catalog record has been requested for this book

ISBN: 978-0-367-35423-7 (hbk)
ISBN: 978-0-429-33129-9 (ebk)

Typeset in Bembo
by codeMantra

To the memory of Carl–Axel Olsson

Contents

Contributors

Benny Carlson is Professor Emeritus of Economic History at the Lund School of Business and Management, Lund University, Sweden. His fields of interest include the history of economic ideas, the spread of economic and social ideas, mainly between the United States, Germany, and Sweden, and the economic and social integration of immigrants in a comparative perspective, mainly involving the United States, Canada, Great Britain, and Sweden.

Martin Dribe is Professor of Economic History and Director of the Centre for Economic Demography at the Lund University School of Economics and Management, Sweden. His research interest is in economic and historical demography, and he has published widely on mortality, fertility, marriage, migration, and social mobility. His research has appeared in leading journals of economic history, demography, epidemiology, and sociology.

Christian Gehrke is Associate Professor at the Department of Economics of the University of Graz, Austria, and co-director of the Graz Schumpeter Centre. He has published several papers, mostly on classical economics, in the main journals on history of economic thought and has edited and co-edited a number of books, including *Sraffa and Modern Economics* (two volumes, jointly with Roberto Ciccone and Gary Mongiovi, Routledge 2011). He is co-editor of the *Centro Sraffa Working Papers Series* and serves on the editorial boards of *Metroeconomica*, the *Bulletin of Political Economy*, and the *European Journal of the History of Economic Thought*. He is currently also a member of the Executive Committee of the European Society for the History of Economic Thought.

Neelambar Hatti is Professor Emeritus, School of Economics and Management, Lund University, Sweden. His research interests include gender issues, institutions, growth, trade, decentralization, poverty, and corruption. Among his publications are 25 volumes on the new world order (1987–2007), jointly edited with Hans Singer and Rameshwar Tandon. His other publications include *Unwanted Daughters; Gender Discrimination* *in Modern India* (2010; coedited with T.V. Sekher) and *Politics and Poverty of Politics* (2018; coedited with Daniel Rauhut). More recently, he has co-authored several studies with Rameshwar Tandon and S.V. Hariharan: *Control of Resources* (2017), *Globalization Syndrome* (2017), *Third World Perspectives on Technology* (2018), *Trade Policy for the Third World* (2018), *International Monetary Interdependence in the New Century* (2019), and *Trade in Services in the New Century* (2020).

Johan Lönnroth is a former MP and deputy leader of the Swedish Left Party. He is also an MPhil in mathematics and Associate Professor of Economics. He has published books and articles, mainly on the history of economic thought. Among his publications in English, the following can be mentioned: 'Before Economics' (in *The History of Swedish Economic Thought*, edited by Bo Sandelin, Routledge 1990), 'Swedish Model Market Socialism 1870–1930' (in *Socialism and Marginalism in Economics*, edited by Ian Steedman, Routledge 1995), 'Political Economy Textbooks and Manuals and the Origins/Roots of the Scandinavian Model' (in *The Economic Reader: Textbooks, Manuals and the Dissemination of the Economic Sciences during the 19th and Early 20th Centuries*, edited by Augello Massimo and Guidi Marco, Routledge 2011) and 'Who Came First: Politicians or Academic Economists?' (*History of Economic Theory and Policy*, 2013).

Mats Lundahl is Professor Emeritus of Development Economics at the Stockholm School of Economics, Sweden. Among his research fields are development economics, international economics, agricultural economics, economics of discrimination, economic history, political economy, economic biography, history of economic doctrines, and music. Lundahl has written or edited seventy-one books. He is the author of *Knut Wicksell on Poverty: 'No Place Is Too Exalted for the Preaching of These Doctrines'* (Routledge, 2005).

Lars Magnusson is Professor and Chair of Economic History, at the Uppsala University, Sweden. His main fields of interest are general European economic history, Swedish economic history, and the history of economic thought. He served as Vice President of Uppsala University 2005–2008 and Dean of the Faculty of Social Sciences in Uppsala, 2012–2017. Magnusson has held fellowships at Max Planck Institute for History, Institute des Hautes Études in Paris, the European University Institute in Florence, and Keio University, Tokyo. He is member of the Swedish Royal Academy of Sciences and served as Chair of the Swedish Collegium of Advanced Study (SCAS) from 2004 to 2017. His is currently working on European economic thought from the seventeenth to the nineteenth century. On this subject, he has published several monographs including *Mercantilism: The Shaping of an Economic Language* (Routledge, 1994), *The Tradition of Free Trade* (Routledge, 2003), and *The Political Economy of Mercantilism* (Routledge, 2014).

The late **Carl-Axel Olsson** was Professor Emeritus of Economic History, School of Economics and Management, Lund University, Sweden. His main research interests were the history of economic thought and questions pertaining to methodology, particularly those concerning the borderline between economics and history. His publications include *Alfred Marshall and Economic History* (1991) and *The Cobweb Theorem, Equilibrium and Counter-finality* (1997).

Daniel Rauhut is Associate Professor and holds a PhD in Economic History at Lund University, Sweden. Rauhut has worked as Senior Lecturer of Social Work at three Swedish universities and is currently Senior Researcher at the University of Eastern Finland in Joensuu. His research interests cover issues related to ideas on poverty and social welfare, as well as economic thought. Among his publications are *Den besvärliga fattigdomen* [The Troublesome Poverty] (2011) and the co-edited volume (together with Neelambar Hatti and Carl-Axel Olsson) *Economists and Poverty: from Adam Smith to Amartya Sen* (2005).

Preface

The present volume, the first of two planned volumes, began to see the light of day in the course of discussions between three scholars some years ago at the Department of Economic History, Lund University. These discussions resulted in a realization that there was an urgent need for a study dealing with how economists have looked upon the causes of and solutions to poverty. This volume covers the views of selected economists from the mercantilist to the neoclassical period who have paid particular attention to this issue.

Our grateful thanks to the contributors for their original and erudite papers. It has been a stimulating learning experience working together, with so many illuminating discussions. We hope this volume will constitute an accessible introduction for students and scholars interested in history of economic thought, especially how economists in the past have dealt with the issue of poverty and its consequences.

Finally, we would like to mention that Professor Carl-Axel Olsson, a dear friend and an esteemed colleague, was a member of the original group, which initiated the discussions concerning the issue of poverty among the economists of the past. Sadly, Carl-Axel is no more, and we dedicate this volume to his memory.

Lund and Stockholm, 1 February 2020
Mats Lundahl
Daniel Rauhut
Neelambar Hatti

Introduction

Economic thought and poverty

Mats Lundahl, Daniel Rauhut and Neelambar Hatti

Throughout history, poverty has been the constant companion of mankind. One of the earliest authors to discuss this was Aristotle (1999), in his *Politics*. According to him, hungry men caused revolutions; poverty and starvation went hand in hand. Aristotle also held that one of the worst forms of poverty was to be without children. A person without children would have no family to ask for help when sick, old or poor. Needless to say, after Aristotle, the causes and cures of poverty have then been discussed in many disciplines.

The determinants of poverty are complex. On the most basic level, for millennia, the humans have had to devote most of their resources to ensure survival—mainly to agriculture. As argued by Walt Rostow in a classic text, before the development of what he calls 'pre-Newtonian science and technology' in the late seventeenth and early eighteenth century, production functions were 'limited' and 'a ceiling existed on the level of attainable output per head' (Rostow 1960, p. 4). It was only with the systematic application of modern science in the production process that it proved possible to break through this ceiling.

However, the use of new technologies was just a necessary condition for increasing incomes, but not a sufficient one. As Douglass North has reminded us, in another classic text, for maximum exploitation of superior methods to be feasible, an efficient organization of the economy is essential (North 1981, p. 17):

> The stock of knowledge and the stock of technology set upper bounds to human well being but do not themselves determine how successful human beings are within those bounds. It is the structure of political and economic organization which determines the performance of an economy as well as the incremental rate of growth in knowledge and technology. The forms of cooperation and competition that human beings develop and the systems of enforcement of these rules of organizing human activity are at the very heart of economic history. Not only do these rules spell out the system of incentives and disincentives that guide and shape economic activity, but they also determine the underlying distribution of wealth and income of a society.

It is not self-evident that the political and economic organization of a society is efficient. On the contrary, 'the fact that growth has been more exceptional than stagnation or decline suggests that "efficient" property rights are unusual in history' (North 1981, p. 6). Inefficient property rights serve to keep the wealth of a society below the technologically determined maximum, and 'in a world of non-market decision making inefficient forms of political structure do persist for long periods of time' (North 1981, p. 7). North's argument is clearly related to the issue of poverty. The organization of society determines both how much there is to distribute in a society and who gets what, that is, both the average income and who will be rich and who will be poor, and hence what society does or ought to do in order to reduce poverty. As will be emphasized, above all, in our second volume, different societies also interact in ways which may be conducive to riches in one part of the world but rags in another part. The analysis of political and economic organization extends across national borders.

The foregoing amounts to a very general statement of why societies and in-dividuals within societies may be poor. It provides a framework for concrete analysis. As both the present book and its companion volume will demon-strate, this is a task tackled by economists in very different ways over the centuries.

Throughout history, the 'poor' have been considered some sort of residual group to be taken care of by the society. Both individual and structural fac-tors have been used to explain poverty and its incidence. Economic theory aims at the analysis and solution of, for example, allocation and distribution problems. It attempts to provide answers to what goods and services a soci-ety should produce, how they should be produced and how much should be consumed and by whom. Regardless of whether poverty is determined by individual or structural factors, it is linked to the fundamental problems of allocation and distribution.

Many path-breaking studies by distinguished economists have dealt with poverty. Nevertheless, the absence of broad, systematic research of this issue until after the Second World War, and the rise of development economics, is a bit puzzling. Economists long before Adam Smith men-tioned poverty and various aspects connected with it. However, schol-ars interested in the history of economic theory and poverty are, almost without exception, still restricted to the individual original writings of different economists.

The present study aims to describe and critically examine how economic thought, representing different theoretical schools, has historically dealt with poverty and the poor. In this context it also tries to explain how the process of social and economic change has been addressed. This volume will focus on the period from the early seventeenth century to the early twentieth century, discussing how mercantilism, classical and neoclassical economics viewed the causes of and cures for poverty.

Definitions of poverty

The research on poverty has dealt mainly with three different definitions of poverty: absolute poverty, relative poverty and poverty where both absolute and relative aspects are included. Absolute poverty relates to the physical existence of a person; there is a clear break point where poverty begins (Andreβ 1998). The Malthusian subsistence level is a good example of absolute poverty (Malthus 1992). The 'primary poverty' of Seebohm Rowntree, that is, lack of resources enough for survival, also falls into this category (Rowntree 1902). In recent decades, the concept of absolute poverty has begun to gain more supporters (e.g. Joseph and Sumption 1979), but it has been considered to be applicable mainly to Third World countries. Using an absolute definition of poverty is, however, not without problems, since not every individual requires the same amount of energy and persons living in different climates have different needs for clothing and so on. The subsistence level is also dependent on which items are deemed essential as well as on the price of the items. In fact, the definition of poverty as absolute is, indeed, relative.

During the second half of the twentieth century, poverty came to be defined in relative terms. The situation of an individual has been compared to an average, generally accepted standard of living (Townsend 1979, Halleröd 1997). Poverty cannot be constant over time and space, and the needs of different persons are different (Townsend 1995). Income and consumption are important tools for measuring poverty (Townsend 1979, Halleröd 1993, Ringen 1988). The 'secondary poverty' of Rowntree, that is, the lack of resources needed for a functioning social life, also falls into this category (Rowntree 1902, 1942).

Amartya Sen has shown that poverty is dependent not only on a core of absolute poverty but also on social functions, that is, poverty has *both* absolute and relative constituents (Sen 1982, 1983, 1997, 1999a). Such a view of poverty is not entirely new. Both Georg Simmel and Rowntree divided poverty into one absolute ('primary') and one relative ('secondary') component (Simmel 2019, Rowntree 1902, 1942). Although Sen has been heavily criticized for involving absolute aspects when analyzing poverty (see, e.g. Townsend 1985, Piachaud 1987), the criticism has not convincingly shown any flaws or misconceptions of this approach to poverty. For instance, according to the conceptualization of relative poverty as relative deprivation, a homeless person is poor because he or she feels socially inferior relative to others. According to the social exclusion approach to poverty, on the other hand, a homeless person is poor because he or she is no longer attached to the moral order in society. The consensual approach, in turn, asserts that the homeless person is poor because his or her lifestyle is far inferior to what a majority of the population considers a 'normal' consumption standard. It is, however, worth noting that the homeless person also has a low income and a low consumption standard. All these three approaches ignore the fact most homeless persons have to struggle for their physical existence. A homeless person also faces absolute poverty.

Poverty is also cumulative: '[P]eople on low incomes generally also experience poor housing, educational facilities, transport and communications' (Hantrais 1995, p. 156). Linda Hantrais argues that the poor are 'persons, families and groups of persons whose resources (material, cultural and social) are so limited as to exclude them from the minimum acceptable way of life in the [country] in which they live' (Hantrais 1995, p. 157). Her definition is *not* confined to just income poverty. To understand modern poverty the definition must be broader and focus on more than just income poverty.

Social exclusion can be seen as the result of the cumulative effects of poverty (Walker 1995), denying the individual participation and membership of a moral, social, economic or political community. Graham Room (1995, p. 6) argues that the Anglo-Saxon poverty research tradition

> is closely associated with the liberal vision of society, under which society was seen by the relevant and political elites as a mass of atomized individuals engaged in competition within the marketplace. The goal of social policy was to ensure that each person had sufficient resources to be able to survive in this competitive arena.

The moral aspects of poverty

The age-old view that the poor are themselves to be blamed for their situation and that only the deserving poor should be supported continues to exist today. Being poor means that a person is considered different in one way or another. Robert Walker argues that the non-poor who do not face any risk of becoming poor themselves 'are likely to have little concern for poor people or policies to help them' (Walker 1998, p. 36). This is due to the social affinity structure in society (Rauhut 2002). In the research tradition of social exclusion (Room 1995, p. 6),

> society is seen by intellectual and political elites as a status hierarchy or as a number of collectivities, bound together by sets of mutual rights and obligations that are rooted in a broader moral order. Social exclusion is the process of becoming detached from that moral order.

That persons struggling with poverty become detached from the moral order in society is true not only today but even more so for the period discussed in the present volume.

Already some mercantilist thinkers were deeply concerned about the low morality of the working class and their corrupt behaviour, which they assumed led to poverty (see Chapter 1). According to Malthus, high fertility and immoral values caused poverty (Chapter 3). Ricardo, Mill and Wicksell held similar views (Chapters 3, 4, 5 and 8). Mill and Marshall considered the educational level of the poor to be too low, which, in turn, made them unable to understand what was best for them (Chapters 3 and 7). To Marx the exploitation of the workers by the capitalists was immoral (Chapter 6).

Adam Smith had a somewhat different view. The poor have not chosen their misery themselves, and hence by looking down at them, we show corrupted sentiments. For Smith, it was unethical to worship the rich and loathe the poor (Chapter 2). Amartya Sen stresses Smith's words that all men should be able to appear in public without any feeling of shame (Sen 1999b). The poor need to be empowered, and this, according to Smith, is attained through education (Chapter 2). Eli Heckscher also considered it important that all have access to education, regardless of the economic situation of their parents (Chapter 10).

One reason why moral aspects in poverty have been considered important in economic thought may be related to the idea that social ideas are considered inferior to economic laws and economic efficiency. Free riding of any kind is immoral, and if people are unable to feed themselves, this implies that somebody else has to do it for them. If an able-bodied person asks for poor relief, many economists during the period analyzed in this volume have considered him or her as an 'undeserving poor'. A 'deserving poor' is someone who has tried everything possible to feed himself or herself, but failed. Who is a 'deserving' or 'undeserving' poor is, however, open to moral interpretation and influence of social ideas.

The contributions

The contributions to the present volume include ideas on the causes and cures of poverty from mercantilist to neoclassical economic thought. They span the period from the early seventeenth to the early twentieth century.

Mercantilism and classical economic thought

Many students of mercantilist political economy have pointed to the contradiction between, on the one hand, the emphasis of labor as a source of wealth and, on the other hand, the endeavor to reduce the income share of this factor of production to the lowest possible level. In his contribution, Lars Magnusson, in Chapter 1, notes that a common strand in the literature on mercantilism has been to stress that mercantilist writers themselves held that the wealth of a country was dependent on the existence of poverty. The mercantilist attitude has been labelled cynical because it held that the working classes sought nothing but immediate physical rewards. It also contained the notion of a 'backward-sloping supply curve of labor': Higher wages would not be conducive to an increased work effort. What was needed was stern discipline and a risk of starvation. 'Good times' for the workers, with high wages, meant 'bad times' for the national economy.

Magnusson's essay questions this stereotypical view of mercantilism and contrasts it with the view of those mercantilists who contended that the wealth of a nation was due not to mass poverty but to a high level of employment. Of course, it was possible to argue that low wages made a country internationally competitive. However, they should be above the subsistence level, and trade liberalization and cheap provisions, not least from the colonies, mattered more, and so did the improvement of English agriculture. Magnusson sets the ideal of the 'honest worker' earning a good living against the view which stressed the importance of poverty for the wealth of nations.

Daniel Rauhut (Chapter 2) discusses Adam Smith's views on poverty. Contrary to what one may think, they do not represent the thinking of a laissez-faire liberal. Smith's views were complex; he was well aware that poverty can be both absolute and relative. The former was the most serious variety, since in the worst scenario it bordered on starvation. This called for government intervention in the form of poor relief, which is nothing but a short-term measure. Economic growth was essential for reducing poverty in the long run.

Relative poverty, in turn, was a matter of subjectively perceived social inferiority. This, according to Smith, the moral philosopher, was a result of the corrupted moral sentiments in society. Rauhut raises the question whether Smith also regarded social inequalities as a positive force in society—a tool that could serve to mitigate poverty—since the feeling of social inferiority might spur a poor person to work harder in order to advance on the economic and social ladder and in the end become somebody admired by his or her fellow citizens.

Social inequality is often linked with social injustice. Smith dealt with the latter phenomenon as well. In his view, in all societies, the existing laws and institutions favored the richer strata and disfavored the poor. Frequently, government regulations were directly conducive to poverty—not least to obstacles to the free movement of workers. Smith saw their removal as an important step toward both increased production and the improvement of the economic situation of the poor.

Thomas Robert Malthus is most known for his *An Essay on the Principle of Population*, which appeared for the first time in 1798. Martin Dribe, in Chapter 3, emphasizes how Malthus, in a systematic way, presents a theory of the relationship between economy and population. According to this theory, it is the availability of food that will determine the size and growth of the population. The population is forced to grow pari passu with the availability of food by the operation of either 'preventive' checks, reducing the number of births, or, ultimately, 'positive' checks, serving to increase death rates.

In the situation where, without checks, the population tends to grow faster than the means of subsistence, poverty and starvation are never far away. Technical progress can improve the lot of the poor, but only temporarily, for, unless birth rates are checked, higher wages will simply serve to lower the death rate and increase the birth rate. The population increases and wages are pressed back to the subsistence level.

In his *An Essay on the Principle of Population* Malthus devoted much energy to the criticism of the English Poor Laws. In his view such a system did nothing to increase the means of subsistence of poor families. It simply served to increase birth rates, since it encouraged the poor to marry. This, Malthus argued, was the case not least with the peasantry, who became dependent on parish assistance. The Poor Laws, furthermore, made people less thrifty and more prone to live from hand to mouth. As Malthus saw it, the solution to the poverty problem lay not in welfare measures but in improved moral standards among the poor: entering a marriage only when the resources necessary for providing for a family existed and implementing voluntary restraint on childbearing within the family.

Christian Gehrke's essay on David Ricardo (Chapter 4) demonstrates that the latter was engaged in the poverty problem in three different capacities: as an economic theorist, as a member of parliament and as a private citizen. Ricardo, the economist, argued that a robust reduction of poverty would require economic growth: a lower rate of population growth in combination with increased capital formation. His well-known campaign against the Corn Laws grew from a desire to improve the lot of the poor through cheaper foodstuffs. Gehrke also discusses Ricardo's changing views of the effect of introduction of machinery on the wage level.

Ricardo's interest in poverty was not only theoretical. On the contrary, he was a practical man who was actively engaged in social issues. As a member of parliament, he attacked the outdated English Poor Laws, arguing that this relief scheme reduced the work effort of those covered by them and that they were conducive to higher birth rates. He also opposed public works since, in his view, the latter simply diverted funds from other uses and hence did not increase employment. Gehrke further provides an account of Ricardo's position with respect to a number of social issue bills presented in Parliament.

Ricardo, the private citizen, was engaged in a number of charitable projects for poverty reduction. Gehrke discusses two types of such ventures: educational institutions aiming at the provision of instruction to working-class children and the creation of savings banks for the poor. (At the time, British banks, in general, did not accept small deposits.)

Daniel Rauhut (Chapter 5) examines John Stuart Mill's analysis of the poverty problem. Mill considered the Malthusian theory of population an axiomatic truth. Accordingly, he argued in favor of education that would allow the poor working class to reduce its fertility pattern. Mill thought that it was the duty of the government, in general, to impose measures that made it possible to control the growth of the population. Those unwilling to keep their family size down should be made to emigrate with the aid of government subsidies. Mill held out a carrot for those from the working classes who, through education, had supposedly improved their 'cultivation' and moral standards and reduced their fertility rates: They would have plural votes in elections, while those who had failed to do so would have to be content with a single vote.

Rauhut concludes that John Stuart Mill was a radical. Advocating reforms of the poor relief system, subsidization of emigration and education to achieve fertility reduction among the poor was not a strategy in line with the conventional wisdom of the time.

Johan Lönnroth's chapter on Marx and his followers (Chapter 6) deals both with the poverty of the workers as a prerequisite for the enrichment of the capitalists in the grand theoretical scheme of Marx and with specific empirical instances of poverty as they appear throughout his writings. The exploitation of the working class goes hand in hand with the development of capitalism, which would not have been possible without it. The role of the lumpenproletariat for keeping wages down as well as other possible uses of the lumpenproletariat by the ruling class is examined.

Marx also deals with concrete instances of poverty, as prevalent among English factory workers, in his inaugural address to the First International, where he also emphasized that poverty had been the perennial companion of the vast majority of mankind. Another episode that attracted his attention was the Irish famine in the mid-1840s. Lönnroth also stresses that, contrary to what is commonly alleged, Marx did not hold that labor was the only creator of wealth and that the development of capitalist society actually created preconditions that made it possible for workers to break out of their poverty.

Lönnroth also briefly examines the views of Lenin and Rosa Luxemburg. Lenin called for the poor peasants of Russia to join forces with the revolutionary industrial workers to overthrow the existing capitalist society, since abolishing poverty by gradual reforms was impossible. Luxemburg, in turn, paid attention to the homeless families in Berlin. Charity, for her, began at home. But her concerns also extended abroad. As capitalism expanded across the globe, looking for new markets, it also looked for new workers to exploit, a perspective which she shared with Lenin.

Lönnroth finishes his essay with an account of how Marx's ideas have been diluted both in the communist countries and in the West. Poverty, by definition, could not exist in Stalin's Soviet Union, whereas in Western Europe, it was reduced by the creation of the welfare state.

The neoclassics

In his essay on Alfred Marshall, Carl-Axel Olsson, in Chapter 7, shows that Marshall devoted himself to the academic discipline of political economy motivated by a desire to understand poverty as a social phenomenon and thus to investigate how it could be combated. Marshall, who epitomized the neoclassical economist and the deductive approach to economics, was a man deeply concerned with the social problems of his day.

Marshall argues that inadequate wages cause poverty. Poverty means that children are forced to grow up with too little food, insufficient clothing, bad housing and incomplete education due to the need to start working at an early age to make some money, insufficiently nourished bodies and low mental capabilities. This makes poverty cumulative and creates a vicious circle of it. Marshall considered that poverty was a question of distribution which economic theory did not deal with adequately.

Society is characterized by an unequal distribution of prosperity. This is true regardless of the dimension under investigation: material living standard, individual freedom, opportunities or moral stature. Marshall objected to this and argued that it had to be shared by all. The differences are due to social, not genetic, circumstances. Here, society has a responsibility for initiating action to reduce poverty and increase the opportunities of disfavored groups. The influence of Mill can be clearly seen in Marshall's ambitions to fight poverty.

Mats Lundahl (Chapter 8) examines Knut Wicksell's views of what causes poverty and how poverty should be dealt with. The cause was to be found in the growth of the population—a fact that Wicksell stressed all his professional life. Too many children made for poor families. Diminishing returns everywhere characterized the economy. This, in the end, would be conducive to a Malthusian situation unless the surplus population emigrated. The optimum population was the one maximizing the per capita income. As Wicksell saw it, the remedy, in turn, was early marriages combined with the use of contraceptive methods within the family.

For a long time, the conventional wisdom was that Wicksell's analysis of poverty was the one area where he was not original; he was simply considered a follower of Malthus. Lundahl, however, shows that Knut Wicksell's views on population growth, diminishing returns and poverty constitute a full-fledged general equilibrium system of population growth, production, consumption, international trade and migration in a framework that was later recognized as the specific factors model of international trade. In his analysis of how the combination of population growth and diminishing returns served to stimulate emigration in Europe in the late nineteenth century, Wicksell gradually pulled together all the factors needed to build a system which lends itself to formalization within a latter-day framework. In the end his originality extended into his analysis of poverty and population as well.

It is not surprising that the critics failed to see the originality of the Wicksellian approach. First, Wicksell's views on population and poverty have to be synthesized from a large number of sources, mainly his Swedish pamphlets. Second, the specific factors model was not formalized until 1971, long after Wicksell's death. Thus, it is no wonder that Wicksell failed to spell out his model explicitly so that his contemporaries could appreciate his originality.

Gustav Cassel is known mainly as a distinguished scholar in the field of monetary economics. However, as Benny Carlson (Chapter 9) stresses, he also had a profound interest in, and frequently wrote about social issues, not least in Swedish newspapers. Cassel considered that social policy was an essential ingredient in the promotion of economic growth. Unless the social and economic position of the workers was improved, their productivity would not increase. Wages had to be high enough to prevent poverty, cover sickness and old age and serve as a buffer in case of unemployment. This could be achieved in different ways, for example via the state or the trade unions.

Cassel, however, stressed the importance of avoiding welfare dependency. As time went by, his stance against what he termed the 'degeneration of assistance policy' gradually hardened. He fought what he saw as a 'claimant spirit', maintained that the trade unions were prone to exploiting unemployment benefits and condemned the 'social security state'. All his life, Cassel was convinced that the road out of poverty was that of economic growth, not that of dependence on state welfare measures.

Eli Heckscher changed his ideological beliefs from social conservatism to economic liberalism around 1910. This shift of emphasis away from confidence in the capacity of the state for wise and forcible intervention towards the conviction that the individuals have the capability to take responsibility for themselves ought to have had an influence on his views on poverty and inequality. However, Benny Carlson (Chapter 10) does not find any major changes over time in Heckscher's view of the causes and cure of poverty.

According to Heckscher, varying aptitude, talent and different starts in life, for example inheritance and education, as well as random chance, cause wealth and poverty. The responsibility for avoiding poverty rests with the private individual: An adult individual who is intelligent enough to act in his or her own interest does not need the state, or anyone else, as a guardian. If too much responsibility is laid on society, there is a risk of breeding welfare dependency. Heckscher also stresses that poverty is related to the distribution of income.

Sometimes, individuals do not act in their own interest, and therefore the state must compel them to save through the medium of social insurance so as to provide against future risk. Heckscher accepted a leveling of income and wealth by progressive taxation and inheritance taxes, but he was also aware that it will not take very long before this will compel the state to tax 'the broad masses'. The cure against poverty, according to Heckscher, is genuinely liberal, for example free education to reduce the impact of a poor start in life, vocational training to raise the value of the workforce and employment services to improve the efficiency of the labor market. These measures are aimed at increasing economic growth, which is needed if poverty is to be reduced in the long run.

Many path-breaking studies by economists have dealt with aspects related to poverty. The contributions to the present volume describe and critically examine how selected economists from the mercantilist period to the classical and neoclassical periods have analyzed the causes of and cures for poverty. Its companion volume will extend the perspective to cover the period from Keynes to the present.

References

Andreβ, H.J. (1998). Empirical Poverty Research in a Comparative Perspective: Basic Orientations and the Outline of the Book. In H.J. Andreβ (ed.), *Empirical Poverty Research in a Comparative Perspective* (pp. 1–26). Aldershot: Ashgate.

Aristotle. (1999). *Politics*. Kitchener: Batoche Books.

Halleröd, B. (1993). Preferenser och fattigdom. In B. Halleröd, S. Marklund, A. Nordlund, and M. Stattin (eds), *Konsensuell fattigdom – en studie av konsumtion och attityder till konsumtion* (pp. 65–80). Umeå Studies in Sociology No. 104. Umeå universitet, Sociologiska institutionen.

Halleröd, B. (1997). Forskning om fattigdom, relative deprivation och social exkludering. In J. Vogel (ed.), *Välfärd och ojämlikhet i 20-årsperspektiv 1975–1995* (pp. 137–147). Stockholm and Örebro: SCB.

Hantrais, L. (1995). *Social Policy in the European Union*. London: MacMillan.

Joseph, K. and Sumption, J. (1979). *Equality*. London: John Murray Publishers.

Malthus, T. (1992). *An Essay on the Principle of Population*. Oxford: Oxford University Press.

North, D.C. (1981). *Structure and Change in Economic History*. New York and London: W.W. Norton and Company.

Piachaud, D. (1987). Problems in Definition and Measurement of Poverty. *Journal of Social Policy, 16*(2), 147–164.

Rauhut, D. (2002). *Fattigvård, socialbidrag och synen på fattigdom i Sverige 1918–1997*. Stockholm: Almqvist & Wiksell International.

Ringen, S. (1988). Direct and Indirect Measures of Poverty. *Journal of Social Policy, 17*(3), 351–365.

Room, G. (1995). Poverty and Social Exclusion: The New European Agenda for Policy and Research. In G. Room (ed.), *Beyond the Threshold* (pp. 1–9). Bristol: Polity Press.

Rostow, W.W. (1960). *The Stages of Economic Growth: A Non-Communist Manifesto*. Cambridge: Cambridge University Press.

Rowntree, B.S. (1902). *Poverty – A Study of Town Life*. London: Macmillan & Co.

Rowntree, B.S. (1942). *Poverty and Progress*. London: Longmans, Green & Co.

Sen, A. (1982). *Poverty and Famines – An Essay on Entitlement and Deprivation*. Oxford: Clarendon Press.

Sen, A. (1983). Poor, Relatively Speaking. *Oxford Economic Papers, 35*(1), 153–169.

Sen, A. (1997). *On Economic Inequality*. Oxford: Clarendon Press.

Sen, A. (1999a). *Commodities and Capabilities*. Oxford: Oxford University Press.

Sen, A. (1999b). *Development as Freedom*. Oxford: Oxford University Press.

Simmel, G. (2019). *Der Arme*. Milan: MIM Edizioni Srl.

Townsend, P. (1979). *Poverty in the United Kingdom*. London: Allen Lane and Penguin Books.

Townsend, P. (1985). A Sociological Approach to the Measurement of poverty – A Rejoinder to Professor Amartya Sen. *Oxford Economic Papers, 37*(4), 659–668.

Townsend P. (1995). The Need for a New International Poverty Line. In K. Funken and P. Cooper (eds), *Old and New Poverty* (pp. 29–54). London: River Oram Press.

Walker, R. (1995). The Dynamics of Poverty and Social Exclusion. In G. Room (ed.), *Beyond the Threshold* (pp. 102–128). Bristol: Polity Press.

Walker, R. (1998). Rethinking Poverty in a Dynamic Perspective. In H.J. Andreβ (ed.), *Empirical Poverty Research in a Comparative Perspective* (pp. 29–49). Aldershot: Ashgate.

1 Were good times really that bad?

Mercantilist views on poverty and employment

Lars Magnusson

In a highly influential study from 1920, *The Position of the Laborer in a System of Nationalism*, the American economist Edgar Furniss presented what he felt was a paradox in a mercantilist political economy: '… on the one hand, the importance of the laborer as a source of wealth was considered supreme; on the other, there were few to question the justice of reducing the laborer's share to its lowest possible terms' (Furniss 1965, p. 24). Perhaps more forcefully than anybody else, he emphasized that mercantilist writers in general—particularly in Britain during the seventeenth and eighteenth century, but also elsewhere—had argued for that a country's richness lay in the poverty of its poor. Accordingly, its wretched lot became soulless instruments—cogs in the wheels of a machinery of production—in a 'system of nationalism'. By replacing mercantilism with 'system of nationalism', his aim was to point at the similarities between seventeenth- and eighteenth-century economics, and the kind of war economy that had been introduced during World War I, but also, with what he called 'the gem of the socialist theory', the labor theory of value (Furniss 1965, p. 25). Hence, in this system, the interest of the state served as the motive power of policy and thinking, he argued.

Moreover, it implied the 'right' but also the 'duty' to work, both of which did not exist in an individualist society built on utilitarian moral philosophy (Furniss 1965, pp. 78, 84). As a representative example, he cites from John Cary, the early eighteenth-century Bristol merchant and writer: 'When the nation comes to see that the labor of its people is its wealth it will put us on finding out methods to make every one work that is able' (Furniss 1965, p. 79). Furniss's presentation of the well-known mercantilist writer Sir William Temple, who wrote in the 1660s, illustrates his general opinion: '… his attitude toward the labouring class was not merely sever, it was bitter and cynical, established upon a belief that the lower classes of society were actuated by no impulse higher than that of immediate physical gratification' (Furniss 1965, 124). Some ten years after Furniss, Eli Heckscher (1995, p. 297) followed suit and depicted the 'cynical' world view of the mercantilist writers. Moreover, contemporary troubled economic writers argued that the poor preferred idleness after working only a couple of days in a week. In more recent times, it has been taken for granted by economic historians and historians of economic doctrine that mercantilist writers and politicians of the seventeenth and eighteenth century, in general, believed in the existence of a 'backward-sloping supply of labor' according to which workers went to work only in order to keep up a meagre subsistence wage (Coats 1992). Only the naked force of strict discipline in a workhouse (and/or punishment for idleness) or the threat of starvation would tempt the poor to work. Hence, the conclusion was drawn that 'good times' when workers could support themselves more easily were 'bad times' for the national economy.

In contrast to earlier interpretations of mercantilism harking back to Adam Smith's famous definition from 1776—as a (failed) doctrine of a favorable balance of trade leading to an inflow of specie—Furniss had a different approach. Certainly, the mercantilist writers were concerned about the balance of trade and supported both *dirigisme* and protective measures. However, he insisted that they had argued that labor and production—not a trade surplus in itself—were the sources of wealth. He frequently referred to authors who argued that every new laborer put to work meant a net contribution to the 'common stock', for example William Hay in 1751: 'I suppose 100,000 unemployed capable of labor ... if employed would ... amount to 1,300,000 pounds which would be so much addition to the common stock' (Furniss 1965, p. 111). Hence, to the extent that the mercantilists were fallacious, it was not because they confused gold and silver with wealth, but instead that they saw addition of labor units as a positive contribution to growth, disregarding objections (made by modern economists) that there might exist declining returns to labor and, even more so, comparative advantages in foreign trading. He stated that, in general, mercantilist writers of nationalist stance always preferred domestic production and industrial protection. By achieving full employment and fencing off imports, a nation could maximize its wealth (stock). Contemporary economists seldom spoke in favor of autarky, but rather argued that foreign trade should be organized in a 'profitable' way which meant that a country in order to prosper should work up its domestic, but also imported, raw materials and sell value-added manufactures to the foreigners.

That economic writers in the seventeenth and eighteenth century did not believe that money (gold or silver) was identical with wealth can be directly inferred from the contemporary literature (Magnusson 2015, p. 100f.). This even goes for British mercantilists who generally held foreign trade in high esteem; Roger Coke described it in 1670 as a lady '... more Courted and Celebrated than any former by all the Princes and Potentates of the World' (Coke 1995, p. 305) and by others it was denoted as a 'precious Jewell' (Roberts 1995, p. 264), or for Thomas Mun (1995 p. 49) in 1621, it was simply 'the very Touchstone of a kingdom's property'. Moreover, in 1699, Charles Davenant (1995, p. 12) wrote,

> Gold and Silver are indeed the Measure of Trade, but that the Spring and Original of it, in all nations is the Natural or Artificial Product of the Country; that is to say, what this Land or what this Labour and Industry Produces.

It is quite clear that a majority of writers from Thomas Mun and Edward Misselden in the 1620s, by and large, agreed with this statement. Moreover, they would argue that to have abundance of money in a country was of great importance for its economic progress and wealth. But this did not imply at all that money was identical with wealth. Rather, a net inflow of money could be used as a 'barometer' signaling whether a nation won or lost in its trade with other countries. Others would say that abundant money would help to speed up intercourse in the marketplace and stimulate growth and development. Thus, a net inflow of money could be a means to enhance wealth; but wealth itself was always the result of production and work (Magnusson 2015, p. 100f.).

At the same time, it is true that references to a positive balance of trade were repeated in much of the economic literature until the middle of the eighteenth century, when the specie-flow mechanism introduced by David Hume and others became generally accepted. However, what economic writers most often referred to was *not* that wealth existed in the form of gold and silver in the prince's coffer. Some were critical to the theory simply because 'overplus' seemed to be an impractical policy goal; it was too complicated to caliber whether a nation had a plus or not in its foreign affairs. However, others found problems on a more theoretical level arguing that an inflow of money might only mean a change in the value of money (inflation). Hence, especially the American economist E.A. Johnson in the late 1930s emphasized that from the 1690s English mercantilists such as Josiah Child, Charles Davenant and Nicholas Barbon developed a new idea which alternatively has been called the theory of 'foreign-paid incomes', the 'labor balance of trade' or the 'export of work' doctrine (Johnson 1937, p. 301f.). By exporting wares with as much value-added content as possible, England could reap a profit, they thought; customers in Spain, Portugal or other countries would not only pay England for its raw materials but also for its workers. The profit would thus appear in the form of wages to an enlarged workforce ('number of hands'). Such increased employment was expected to have important dynamic effects admitting a higher population (based on a lower age of marriage, but also on immigration of foreign workers) and rising consumption. However, the profit would also lay in more sailors employed, rents to collect, freight charges and other so-called invisibles. It was argued that the value of land would arise due to an increasing demand for agricultural goods as well as a general lowering of interest rates—Holland was here mentioned as an exemplary case.

Johnson agreed with Furniss that a 'primitive' theory of production could be extracted from this literature emphasizing that wealth was a consequence of work and labor. Moreover, much of the mercantilists calculations of how wealth could be increased built on the notion of a direct correlation between numbers of employed workers and an increase of the national 'stock'. Johnson also emphasized that although a higher population was seen as a clear asset—note that a pre-Malthusian optimism not to fear overpopulation still prevailed—we must recognize that only an employed person was a net contribution to the national stock. Idleness was a direct loss. To the extent that involuntary unemployment existed, it should be combated by public efforts. Most often, it was taken for granted that pauperism, begging and so on were an effect of inborn laziness, indolence and corruption that could only be remedied by hard disciplinary measures.

Against this backdrop, the aim here is to clarify some of the misunderstandings which still prevail concerning the alleged view that mercantilists, in general, held work and production as a cornerstone of national wealth while at the same time 'reducing the laborer's share to its lowest possible terms' (Furniss 1965, p. 1f.). Concentrating on the English writers, we ask whether all of them were cynical. Or can we find other attitudes and viewpoints? Did they really propose that a nation's richness lay in its number of poor? What might they have meant when they said so?

Poverty or good livelihood?

In the foreword to one early eighteenth-century tract *The System or Theory of the Trade of the World* (1720) authored by Isaac Gervaise, the seminal American historian of economic doctrine Jacob Viner noted that when his author used the word 'the poor' he rather referred to 'producers' (Viner 1954, p. 7). Gervaise was the son of a French Huguenot who had emigrated to London and argued in his tract that a country in the long run cannot have an 'overplus of its proper proportion of the grand denominator' (specie money)—foreshadowing David Hume's famous specie-flow argument. Also, when late seventeenth-century economic authors such as Josiah Child or Sir William Temple talked about the 'poor', they rather referred to number of 'hands' or workers. Hence, a rich nation is a nation with an abundance of employment—not many poor in our modern sense of the term. Authors such as Temple were especially impressed and envious of the Dutch miracle—William Temple wrote an extremely influential tract on it published in 1673, *Observations on the United Provinces*—not the least because it seemed to bring more welfare (higher real wages) also to the poorer strata.

Hence, in the long run, a leading commercial country abounding with manufactures and trade would be more beneficial for the workers. Certainly, such a view became much more common in the beginning of the eighteenth century, but we should not be surprised to find it even earlier. The main problem, according to Child (1995, p. 57) in 1693, was,

> ... [t]hat our Poor in England, have always been in a most sad and wretched condition, some Famished for want of Bread, others starved with Cold and Nakedness, and many whole Families in all our Parts of Cities and great Towns, commonly remain in a languishing, nasty and useless Condition, Uncomfortable to themselves, and Unprofitable to the Kingdom ....

In this respect, Holland had performed much better, Child argued. The task must be to study their example and increase the employment of the poor in England. In the same manner, Samuel Fortrey in 1663 regarded the establishment of manufactures at home as a sure way for a nation to become richer: '… the people furnished at home with all things both of necessity and pleasure' (Fortrey 1995, p. 287).

We can certainly multiply our examples. In 1641, Lewes Roberts (1995, p. 238) argued that 'work-men and Arts-masters' should 'be kept well' in order to produce good 'merchandize'. The skillful should in every manner be 'cherished, encouraged and rewarded' (but the 'lasie and sluggish punished'). Henry Robinson, in 1650, argued that those who are poor are the unemployed in contrast to those employed 'relieved' by work. A little later, he even proposed that 'well-being' of workers in the form of security, food and 'Rayment' was a proper goal for society (Robinson 2008, p. 67f.). When the pseudonym 'Philanglus' in the famous *Britannia Languens or A Discourse of Trade* (1680)—regarded as a central piece of mercantilist writing usually ascribed to one William Petyt—talks about 'a sweet Harmony in a Nation which hath property when every one's Hand and Head is employed', that might sound like a cynicism. However, he adds that introduction of manufactures which means 'the support of hundreds of thousands of Families' allow that they receive a 'good livelihood'. Moreover, in another place, he says that it is by no means an advantage to have people who are 'poor and miserable' as this 'weakens their Bodies, Courages, or Faith' (Petyt 1995, p. 294, 300). In fact, many writers do not draw a distinction—as argued by Furniss as we saw—between the interest of the state and its workers.

Employment was a key also for the improvement of the lot of the poor. Here we can again refer to John Cary, regarded by Furniss as one of the leading proponents of the 'national system'. Most certainly, Cary maintains, labor is 'the curse under which Man first fell' and that 'by the Sweat of his Brow he should eat his Bread'. However, he immediately continued that to be employed is 'a state of Happiness, if compared to that which attends Idleness …' Moreover, in general, an idle man takes 'more pain' walking the streets of London' than 'an honest Man doth at his Trade, and yet seem not to get bread' (Cary 2008, p. 233). Cary is without doubt harsh in his views, ready at any moment to confine beggars and unemployed to the workhouse. Simultaneously, he propounds that it is in his self-interest that an unemployed should seek a steady position in a trade or manufacture. At the same time, he as well as others argued in favor of low wages. Moreover, he would have been skeptical toward William Hay, a justice of the peace and a Whig politician, who in a small tract, *Remarks on the Laws Relation to the Poor*, from 1735, stated that 'A better Provision for the Poor is so much wanted that I earnestly wish it may be no longer delayed' (Hay 2008, p. 332). According to Cary (2008, p. 233), this might be too extreme and promote laziness and wickedness. On the other hand, to keep 'honest workers' on the brink of starvation was not the best means to increase the riches of a nation. Look at the Dutch example, he says. In that country, workers had good provisions and full employment, and there were no beggars.

Low wages

There is no doubt that mercantilist writers in general agreed on the benefits of low wages. That this did not mean wages below the subsistence level we have already made clear. Nor did this necessarily mean low *real* wages, as we will soon come back to. How they defined a subsistence wage was as unclear as often still today. A 'good livelihood' or the wage for an 'honorable worker' implied that the latter would be able to procure for himself and his family. This standard was also custom-based, on the individual's standing in the social hierarchy and the 'rights' which followed from that (Magnusson 2020, p. 23f).

Still, it was certainly supposed during the second half of the seventeenth and the first half of the eighteenth century that England was involved in a life-and-death struggle of international competition, especially with the Dutch who, according to Thomas Mun and many others, had outcompeted the English for example in the North Sea fishing (Mun 1995, p. 137f.). To be able to sell at low relative price to foreigners was of utmost importance in order to keep up or even more so increase the market share of a specific country. This implied low labor costs but also that other costs should be minimized. Referring to the fishing industry, Thomas Mun (1995) argued that Dutch fishermen had far more cost-effective boats than the English. With regard to the important trade in wool cloths, Charles Davenant said in 1696, 'The only beneficial way to England making wool yield a good price, is to have it manufactured cheaply'. Moreover, 'to make England a true gainer by the woollen manufacture, we should be able to work the commodity so cheap, as to undersell all comers to the markets abroad' (Davenant 1995, p. 221). For this purpose, the cost of labor was the most strategic factor. However, England was a high-cost country and there was no reason to expect that this would change, at least not in short-run perspective.

There were several reasons for this state of affairs. Petyt (1995, p. 314f.) in his *Britannia Languens* talked about a number of 'clogs' which held back the English export trades and made them less competitive. In general, they were characterized as 'bad' laws and institutions (duties, charges, monopolies, etc.) which made trade and navigation expensive. Davenant (1995, p. 236) pointed especially to the high duties, excise duties and taxes put on consumption: '... for if Malt, Coals, Salt, Leather and other things bear a great Price, the Wages of Servants, Workmen and Artificers will consequently rise, for the Income must bear some proportion with the Expence'. However, there were also other problems involved, Davenant (1995, p. 237) believed. To begin with, the many idle persons who could not support themselves but needed relief was a burden to society: '... for want of which, these miserable Wretches must perish with Cold and Hunger'. More employed was a necessity if England should be able to increase its competitive edge, he thought. However, Davenant was not very optimistic regarding England's chances to reach this goal. In order to succeed it must develop a radically new strategy, he believed. Instead of producing cheap woolen cloth for a mass market, it would be better if England as a high-cost and high-wage country would develop manufactures of finer qualities and sorts. Instead, it should encourage the import of coarser sorts from abroad, especially from East Asia. Hence Davenant—as well as a number of other writers around the turn of the seventeenth century who belonged to the group of 'Tory free traders' (Ashley 1966)—supported an enlarged East India trade (including the company with the same name). To buy unfinished and therefore cheaper wares and sell more worked-up ones would on balance be a gain to England, Davenant argued.

However, in a seminal contribution to our understanding of the mercantilist discussion in England around 1700, Istvan Hont (2005) stressed other voices also could be heard in this discussion. For example, John Pollexfen disagreed completely with Davenant and warned that an inflow of cheap materials to England might bring 'our Working people to Poverty', he predicted (Hont 2005, p. 242). Instead, Pollexfen developed an argument for increased protection. Only by keeping out the cheaper imports from abroad would Britain be able to gain. We must protect ourselves from the low cost and wage countries, this true protectionist argued. Without doubt, after 1700, this became the dominant position. By and large, an identical argument was developed by the Bristol merchant we have already met, John Cary, when he intervened in the discussion on the East India Trade. This trade, he claimed, 'for many Reasons I take to be mischievous to the Kingdom'. The East India Company enriched certain men but impoverished the country as a whole, he stated. It takes off only very little of our own Manufactures but imply an import of cheap calicoes and silk from the far East. The aim of such intervention, he says right on (Cary 1995, p. 9),

> … is to persuade the gentry of England to be more in Love with our own Manufactures, and to encourage the wearing them by their Examples, and not of choice to give Employment to the Poor of another Nation whilst ours starve at home.

By and large, such writers argued for what we would call import substitution as a main national economic strategy and shared a view which later has been developed by adherents of the infant-industry argument.

The need for cheap supplies

That the mercantilists saw the agricultural sector as a most important sector when it came to making a nation rich is often forgotten today. Given the fact that the English mercantilists were focusing mainly on the role of foreign trade for national wealth, this can perhaps be easily understood. However, this is without doubt a mistake. Instead, most mercantilists shared the same general view concerning the role of land as William Petty (1986, p. 68) when he called it 'the mother' of wealth which ought to be combined with 'the father'—labor—in order to create national wealth. In the same manner, Lewes Roberts (1995, p. 236) emphasized that the 'natural' yield from land was the 'fontaine of all the riches and abundances of the World' – which is often forgotten, he added. Hence, agriculture produces 'natural commodities or wares' or the 'natural riches'. Especially when worked upon by 'art' and sent abroad, such natural riches would be especially profitable, he of course argued, as a good mercantilist (Roberts 1995, p. 235f.). Moreover, Roberts saw a general benefit for a kingdom to be furnished by 'corn at cheap rates'. This had been the case for Holland which during a dearth had received millions of pounds of corn from England, which, in turn, had been 'impoverished' by the exports (Roberts 1995, p. 262). Hence, agriculture was important for at least two reasons. First, it provided food and other necessities in order to keep up a working population. Second, it brought forward raw materials that could be worked up and exported.

The argument that cheaper provisions could be a positive factor which made English manufactures more competitive becomes increasingly frequent as we move into the beginning of the eighteenth century. Basically, two means for such a purpose have been highlighted in the literature. First, the role of colonies—the so-called plantations—were stressed. Second, improvement in agriculture in order to raise productivity and thus allow more production was seen as a possibility. In both cases, the effect would be to lower the price of consumption goods which, in turn, meant that wages could be reduced or kept at a competitive level. Views differed about to what extent this would keep wages at a subsistence rate or even allow for a certain increase of living standard for workers through rising real wages.

Plantations

Concerning the 'plantations', early eighteenth-century mercantilist writers focused mainly on the possibilities for England to grab new territories on the other side of the Atlantic Ocean; the Caribbean islands and the east coast of present-day United States. Asia was mainly there to trade with and Africa in order to grab slaves. In America, plenty of land was open and ripe for exploitation and cultivation. One of the first mercantilists who explicitly mentioned the plantations in this manner was Samuel Fortrey in his anti-French tract *England's Interest and Improvement* from 1673 (Fortrey 1995, p. 297):

> I conceive, no forein Plantation should be undertaken, or prosecuted, but in such countreys that may increase the wealth and trade of this nation, either in furnishing us, with what we are otherwise forced to purchase from strangers, or else by increasing such commodities, as are vendible

abroad; which may both increase our shipping, and profitable employ our people; but otherwise, it is always carefully to be avoided, especially where the charg is greater than the profit, for we want not already a countrey sufficient to double our people, were they rightly employed; and a Prince is more powerful that hath his strength and force united, that he that is weakly scattered in many places.

Hence, according to contemporary observers, the plantations could bring three kinds of services to the motherland. In the first place, the colony could provide her with all sorts of necessities and luxuries. Moreover, the English consumers would have the exclusive right to what could be grown or otherwise procured in the plantations. Imports from the plantations could consist of raw materials to be worked up in the English manufactures. Malachy Postlethwayt in 1757 referred to such imports when he wrote, 'Whatever materials our capital manufactures we shall not be capable of raising among ourselves, we may easily do by wise encouragement in our plantations' (Postlethwayt 1968, p. 177). Josiah Gee referred to both these imports in his widely read treatise on British trade from 1729. Hence, for example, the transports from the sugar plantations (Barbados, Jamaica, etc.) to England would consist of sugar and ginger but hopefully in the future also cinnamon, cloves, mace and coffee—precious consumer items which England had to buy with expensive money from Asia 'by way of Holland'. Moreover, the plantations in Virginia would supply tobacco, which could be partly resold to other countries (according to Josiah Gee such re-exportation was, in general terms, especially gainful and the 'surest way of enriching this Kingdom'. From Carolina—a province which 'lies in as happy a Climate as any in the World'—rice, olives, silk, indigo and many other items would be sent into England. Gee (1969, p. 29f.) also looked ahead to a future when Carolina would provide England with hemp and flax, but also raw iron. It was more problematic with the colonies in the North (Pennsylvania, New Jersey and New York), he thought. Not so generously equipped by nature, they could, nevertheless, be a source for England's much needed masts, timber, tar and so on.

A second option was Ireland, which had fallen in English hands during the seventeenth century and could more directly contribute to lower food prices and raw materials for the motherland's manufactures. As an agricultural colony, Ireland could contribute especially with cheap wool sent freely. Irish cattle and corn, on the other hand, should not be allowed to reach English shores as lower food prices hurt its landowners. Josiah Child, for instance, felt that the Irish marketing of meat and corn could be pernicious to English interests, especially as such goods could be sold 'at cheaper rates than we can afford to the beating us out if those trades' (Lipson 1943, p. 197). However, cheaper food prices could still contribute to English manufactures as it kept wool at a low price which made English worked-up wool competitive and less expensive (Lipson 1943, p. 197f.).

Perhaps the keenest propagandist of the use of plantations for such purposes was Charles Davenant (1656–1714) (Wadell 1959, pp. 179–188, Pocock 1985, Hont 2005, p. 20f., Magnusson 2015, p. 200f.). Being an excise commissioner and an MP for St. Ives in Cornwall, he lost all his official positions during the 'Glorious revolution' (1688), unfortunately (for him) supporting the wrong political masters. In 1695, his first major economic tract work appeared, *An Essay Upon the Ways and Means of Supplying the War*, a work which gained him some reputation. Another tract in defense of the East India Company – where he was on the salary list—followed in 1696: *An Essay on the East India Trade*. After the succession of Queen Anne in 1702, Davenant was back in public service again, as a stern Tory, and he was made inspector general of exports and imports. Supporting infant-industry tariffs, he was, nevertheless, quite liberal in his economic views which has made some authors include him among the 'Tory free traders' (Ashley 1966, p. 3, Magnusson 2015, p. 63) and as a 'free trade imperialist' believing in the role of international competition (Hont 2005, p. 201f.). However, Davenant was, indeed, also favoring a formal empire under the English flag. He made it explicitly clear which role plantations would play for England:

> Our plantations (if we take care to preserve them from foreign insults and invasions) … produce commodities indispensably necessary to this part of the world, and not to be produced elsewhere, and with industry and conduct, may be made an exhaustible mine of treasure to their mother kingdom.

Without doubt, he also saw the plantations as a major consumer of English wares in the long run: '… as further as they increase in people, will consume more of our home manufactures than we have hands to make' (Davenant 1995, p. 225). Taking a possibly partisan view in the interest of the East India Company, he also spoke about the future role of particularly India as an exporter of cheap silk, which could be worked up in England.

Improvement of agriculture

As mentioned, improvement in agriculture in order to raise productivity and thus allow for more production was increasingly seen as a possibility in mercantilist literature during the eighteenth century. The effect would be to lower the price of consumption goods and keep wages in the manufacture sector at a competitive level. Such views were voiced even earlier, but they appeared in their mature form with Malachy Postlethwayt (c. 1697–1767). His most important works were *Britain's Commercial Interest Explained and Improv'd* and *Great Britain's True System* (both published in 1757). However, he was mostly known during his lifetime as the author of the encyclopedic handbook, *The Universal Dictionary of Trade and Commerce* (1751–1755). Postlethwayt regarded agricultural improvements in Britain combined with Plantations as the main pillar of Britain's future wealth.[1]

Already at the very beginning of his *Britain's Commercial Interest*, Postleth-wayt (1968, p. 2f., 177) argues that the polity 'of this nation' must see to that old agricultural lands are improved and virgin acreage exploited in order to increase the 'universal plenty'. He goes on to argue that this will make 'the price of the necessaries of life no more than one half, or even one third what it is at present'. Moreover, he states, 'This will inevitably reduce the general price of labour, that being regulated by the price of the necessaries of life ...' In fact, most of the first volume of his voluminous work on British commerce is dedicated to the issue how 'the necessaries of life' could be achieved more cheaply. Especially, the third 'dissertation' is devoted to a discussion of the 'various general principles of agriculture, founded on experience, for the improvement of lands ...' (Postlethwayt 1968, p. 74). He points specifically to how 'art' could improve agriculture but also to the necessity to apply 'the science of husbandry and agriculture' (Postlethwayt 1968, p. 88). Always on his mind is how new methods and technology could be applied in order to make 'the necessaries' cheaper and support an even larger population. 'Hath not experience sufficiently manifested what advantage other nations have received, by their keeping of their bread at a reasonably stated price through the year', he asks, talking approvingly of public granaries and storehouses. Would not their introduction in England make 'the workman's wages, and the value of his goods most fixt and certain?', Postlethwayt (1968, p. 89) asks. Without doubt, from this, he also makes a political point when he then discusses '... in what manner country gentlemen and planters may promote the benefit of their estates, in conjunction with that of the nation'. Moreover, he seeks to convince the reader that the landed and trading interests must be 'connectively considered' (Postlethwayt 1968, p. 45).

Work discipline

Besides low wages and/or provisions, strict work discipline was also highlighted during this period by mercantilist writers. As we have noted, the most important argument for increased labor discipline was an alleged irregularity in manners of workers in manufactures and the putting-out trades, especially a slack time discipline and the existence of a backward-bending supply curve of labor (Thompson 1991). From Furniss onwards, such fears have pictured the mercantilist economists as harsher and more cynical than what they perhaps deserve. With horror, Furniss (1965, p. 103f.) cites from writers who presented a dismal picture in black, especially a Wiltshire clothier-master William Temple (not Sir William Temple, the seventeenth-century English ambassador to Holland), who wrote a number of tracts in the middle of the eighteenth century and who was clearly obsessed by the corrupt nature and low morality of the British workforce. Furniss admits that Temple was 'always an extremist' but still cites him frequently. Most economic writers at the time (including James Steuart, William Tucker, Postlethwayt and indeed also Adam Smith), no doubt, found Temple's outcries in moral panic in the

1770s too extreme. This included his recommendation that all poor workers' children should be placed in workhouses (or houses of correction) at the age of four, which many economic writers by this time disagreed with Temple (Furniss 1965, p. 114f., Coats 1992, p. 63f.).

Still, that, for example, John Cary was ready to apply harsher methods in order to put idle or unregular laborers to work is quite clear: '... here I find that nothing but good laws will do it, such as may provide work for those who are willing, and force them to work that are able' (Cary 2008, p. 83). Cary was certainly a leading propagandist of workhouses in which idle hands could be turned into productive workers. Working for the city administration in Bristol, he believed that his city's workhouse system was so superior that it should be introduced everywhere in England. Charles Povey, Charles Davenant, William Temple and many others also proposed schemes of the same kind. However, it is easy to draw anachronistic conclusions from such proposals. We must not immediately define the wealthy director of the English East India Company, Josiah Child, as a hypocrite when he argued for increased 'relief and employment of the poor' as a means to combat poverty leaving 'our Children of Poor' suffering both physically and morally. Charity is not enough, he says. Instead, 'those Poor Creatures' must be put to work. The main obstacle is bad laws and practices, he thinks. Like Adam Smith and his disciples almost a 100 years later, Child (1995, p. 59) regarded the contemporary Poor Law system as the most formidable problem:

> The sad radical Error I esteem to be leaving it to the care of every Parish to Maintain their own Poor only; upon which follows the shifting off, sending or whipping back the poor Wanderers to the Place of their Birth.

Instead of keeping them out, city authorities should encourage poor people to move in, he argues. This will create more employment followed by the betterment of the situation of the poor.

Moreover, in 1699, Charles Davenant proposed the establishment of a public works system to be implemented throughout England. In order to better maintain 'the Impotent Poor and for buying Commodities and materials to employ and set at Work the other Poor', he suggested that a joint stock company with a capital of 300,000 pounds should be set up through public initiative. Instead of paying large sums for poor relief, the parishes should be obliged to buy shares in this new company or Corporation. Hence, it shall provide a stock to employ idle poor in all kinds of productive work: 'the Corporation are to provide Materials and labour for all that can work'. In order to guarantee that the Corporation will not outcompete private employers it shall pay the laborers less: '[f]or example, if another Person would give one of these a Shilling, the Corporation ought to give but Nine Pence'. On the other hand, the person employed by the Corporation would be guaranteed a job: '... the Corporation will be oblig'd to maintain them and their Families in all Exigencies which others are not oblig'd to ...' (Davenant 1995, p. 243). Such schemes were anathema for nineteenth-century laissez faire economists who tried to prove the perils of the 'mercantile system'. However, their often paternal and moralistic language should not make us jump to the conclusion that none of them was sincere when they pitied the poor and suggested remedies to make their lives easier.

Labor encouraged

Already during the seventeenth century, in the English mercantilist discussion it was common to speak in favor of immigration, especially of skilled handicraftsmen; specifically, how to encourage Huguenots to move from French territories after the Edict of Fontainebleau (1685), which had revoked the liberal Edict of Nantes from almost a century earlier, was at the forefront of the discussion. The new edict, which among other things led to the eviction of the protestant Huguenots from public service and schools, led to a mass flight of hundreds of thousand artisans and workers to protestant countries such as Holland and England. Settling in Spitalfields in London, many textile weavers and workers set up their own manufactures or alternatively became employed by domestic masters. In general, most economic writers at the time looked on this emigration with approval. Especially in relation to France, the employment of skilled workers was looked on as favorable in the international competition. For example in 1673, Samuel Fortrey (1995, p. 279) argued that

> ... to increase the people of this nation, permission would be given to all people of foreign contryes, under such restrictions as the state shall think fit, freely to inhabit and reside within this kingdom, with liberty to buy or sell lands or goods, to import or export any commodities, with the like privilege and freedom that English men have.

This would be most advantageous as '... those people that would come from other countries to inhabit here, would also bring their riches with them' (some were, indeed, wealthy, but not the majority). Moreover, especially the manufactures would bloom with the arrival of many industrious people (Fortrey 1995, p. 279). To a country with freedom of religion, a free constitution, a 'pleasant' and 'temperate' climate (!) and every possibility for a thriving man to become rich, it would be easy to recruit many new hands in order to enrich the nation, Fortrey stated. For many others, the Dutch example proved the advantages of having 'a free constitution' and good government. Was it not because of this that the Dutch had become so rich and able to outcompete the rest of the world, they argued?

Certainly, everybody was not ready to draw the conclusion that it was a particularly good idea to treat also the domestic workforce more favorably. However, in contrast to those who argued that only cheap provisions and thus low wages could be a competitive factor, others came to the conclusion that because workmen in England, in general, were treated better than elsewhere—and had an elevated living standard—it was unlikely that lowering the wage could serve as a realistic one-for-all strategy to increase national wealth. However, such arguments, which became commonplace in the middle of the eighteenth century, was not unknown even earlier. In 1701, a John Martyn, who also took part in the discussion on the East India company, presented a novel strategy: to increase productivity as a means to elevate the competitive edge in English and to sell at a low price.[2] Like, for example, Davenant, in contrast to Pollexfen, Martyn was willing to accept more foreign competition in textiles: 'free trade'. In contrast to Davenant, however, he argued that a better competitive position could only be achieved by means of a more efficient industry. Only by increasing productivity through the introduction of new and better methods of production could the high-cost and high-wage country compete in the longer run. Moreover, Martyn (1701) argued that a reduction of 'English Manufactures' could be reduced without abating the workmen's wages. If production of for example textiles could be carried out in less time or with less labor, he argued 'the Wages of should be as high as ever' (Hont 2005, p. 281). Increased mechanization by machinery was already at this time sometimes mentioned as a way of increasing productivity (Anonymous 2008, p. 103). However, the main method proposed was to increase the division of labor. Martyn mainly talks about the merits of labor-saving through increased division in work. He points to shipbuilding in Holland as an example to imitate. Here, he states, with its 'order and regularity of work', there are 'as many Artists, as there are several different Parts of Ships of different dimensions' (Martyn 1701, p. 270f.).

Concluding remarks

We have argued here against the stylized picture of mercantilist thinking and writing that contends that the latter necessarily implied the view that wealth in a country presupposed a multitude of poor people. Most certainly, English economic writers during this period often believed in the existence of 'a backward-sloping supply curve of labor' and they often depicted workers as lazy by nature. They were paternalistic in their attitudes. At the same time, they did not speak in favor of poverty (or even less so degradation) in general. Rather, their emphasis was on employment: A rich country was one in which a majority was employed in a regular manner. Many economist writers shared the view that wages should be low in order to create a competitive position for England in the international competition for markets at this time. However, others were, in fact, willing to consider increasing the competitive position of English manufactures and industry through cheaper provisions, which could even lead to a rising real wage. Also, other economist writers argued that English workers had a higher living standard than workers in other countries and they were even ready to defend this factum. Still others held that increased productivity especially though a more extended division of labor was the future for English industry in a world of international trade rivalry.

Increasingly, during the eighteenth century, many came to argue against *dirigisme* and stated that protection of home manufacture and high duties on import would not suffice in the long run. The argument was that this would only lead to a race to the bottom and a loss for all trading parties. For example, a writer such as Malachy Postlethwayt (1968, p. 397) would argue that duties could provoke protectionist counter-measures: 'For if it be natural for a nation to make as little use as possible of foreign manufactures, it is certain, that foreigners have a reciprocal right to lay the manufactures of that nation under equal restrictions'. This would rather discourage English workers—just like migrants—to work harder and more productively. A higher output could only be achieved when the workmen felt they could get a better deal. No workhouse or harsh disciplinary methods could do this job. After Bernard Mandeville's (1988) *The Fable of the Bees* (published in 1714) provokingly stated that 'public benefits' could arrive from 'private vices', a new emphasis was placed on the role of popular consumption, questioning, for example, the relevance of sumptuary laws. Increasingly, it was thought (at least until Malthus) that the possibility of increased consumption would trigger the worker to greater regularity and productivity in work. Better times could, in fact, imply better times for the national economy. Hence, Postlethwayt, in 1757, argued for the superior strategy to enhance the 'art of seducing, or pleasing to higher degree the consumer of every kind' (1968, p. 398). Even before that, Jacob Vanderlint (1954, p. 82) had written that '... the working people can and will do a great deal more work than they do, if they were sufficiently encouraged'. He added, 'I take it for a maxim, that the people of no class will ever want industry, if they don't want encouragement'. To conclude, we seem to be very far from the stereotype version of mercantilism and the view of poverty as a precondition for national wealth.

Notes

1 On Postlethwayt, see the entry in *Oxford Dictionary of National Biographies* and *New Palgrave's Dictionary of Economics* (2018).
2 The little we know on Martyn is summarized by Hont (2005, p. 245f.). See also Thomas (1926, p. 171f.).

References

Anonymous ([1690] 2008). A Discourse upon the Necessity of Encouraging Mechanic Industry. In L. Magnusson (ed.), *Mercantilist Theory and Practice, Vol. IV* (pp. 99–140). London: Pickering & Chatto.
Ashley, W.J. (1966). The Tory Origin of Free Trade Policy. In W.J. Ashley (ed.), *Surveys. Historic and Economic* (pp. 268–303). London: Longmans.

Cary, J. ([1695]1995), *A Discourse Concerning the East India Trade* (1695), in L. Magnusson (ed.), *Mercantilism: Critical Concepts in the History of Economics, Vol. II*. London and New York: Routledge.

Cary, J. ([1717] 2008). An Essay Towards Regulating the Trade, and Employing the Poor of this Kingdom. In L. Magnusson (ed.), *Mercantilist Theory and Practice, Vol. IV* (pp. 225–254). London: Pickering & Chatto.

Child, J. ([1693] 1995). A New Discourse of Trade. In L. Magnusson (ed.), *Mercantilism. Critical Concepts in the History of Economics, Vol. III* (pp. 1–136). London and New York: Routledge.

Coats, A.W. (1992). Changing Attitudes to Labour in the Mid-Eighteenth Century. In A.W. Coats (ed.), *On the History of Economic Thought. British and American Economic Essays, Vol. I* (pp. 63–84). London and New York: Routledge.

Coke, R. ([1670] 1995). A Discourse of Trade in Two Parts. In L. Magnusson (ed.), *Mercantilism. Critical Concepts in the History of Economics, Vol. I* (pp. 300–369). London and New York: Routledge.

Davenant, C. (1995). An Essay Upon the Probable Methods of Making a People Gainers in the Balance of Trade. In L. Magnusson (ed.), *Mercantilism. Critical Concepts in the History of Economics, Vol. III* (pp. 207–365). London: Routledge.

Fortrey, S. ([1673] 1995). Englands Interest and Improvements. In L. Magnusson (ed.), *Mercantilism. Critical Concepts in the History of Economics, Vol. I* (pp. 276–299). London and New York: Routledge.

Furniss, E. ([1920] 1965). *The Position of the Laborer in a System of Nationalism*. New York: Augustus M. Kelley.

Gee, J. ([1729] 1969). *The Trade and Navigation of Great-Britain Considered*. New York: Augustus M. Kelley.

Hay, J. (2008). Remarks on the Laws Relation to the Poor. In L. Magnusson (ed.), *Mercantilist Theory and Practice, Vol. IV* (pp. 335–384). London: Pickering & Chatto.

Heckscher, E.H. (1995). *Mercantilism, Vol. II*. London: Routledge.

Hont, I. (2005). *Jealousy of Trade, International Competition and the Nation-State in Historical Perspective*. Cambridge, MA: Belknap.

Johnson, E.A. (1937). *Predecessors to Adam Smith*. New York: Prentice-Hall.

Lipson, E. (1943). *The Economic History of England, Vol. III. The Age of Mercantilism*. London: Adam and Charles Black.

Magnusson, L. (2015). *The Political Economy of Mercantilism*. London and New York: Routledge.

Magnusson, L. (2020). On Happiness: Welfare in Cameralist Discourse in the Seventeenth and Eighteenth Centuries. In E. Nokkala & N. Miller (ed.), *Cameralism and the Enlightenment* (pp. 23–46). London and New York: Routledge.

Mandeville, B. ([1714] 1988), *Fable of the Bees*. Indianapolis, IN: Liberty Fund.

Martyn, H. (1701). *Considerations upon the East India Trade*. London: A. and J. Churchill.

Mun, T. ([1621] 1995). A Discourse of Trade, From England unto the East Indies. In L. Magnusson (ed.), *Mercantilism. Critical Concepts in the History of Economics, Vol. I* (pp. 1–48). London and New York: Routledge.

Petty, W. ([1899] 1986). A Treatise of Taxes and Contributions. In C.H. Hull (ed.), *The Economic Writings of Sir William Petty* (pp. 1–97). Fairfield, NJ: Augustus M. Kelley.

Petyt, W. (Philanglus). (1995). Britannia Languens, or A Discourse of Trade. In J.R. McCulloch (ed.), *Classical Writings on Economics, Vol I* (pp. 275–504). London: William Pickering.

Pocock, J.G. (1985). *The Machiavellian Moment*. Princeton, NJ: Princeton University Press.

Postlethwayt, M. ([1757] 1968). *Britain's Commercial Interest Explained and Improved,* *vol. I*. New York: Augustus M. Kelley.

Roberts, L. ([1641] 1995). The Treasure of Traffike. In L. Magnusson (ed.), *Mercantilism. Critical Concepts in the History of Economics, Vol. I* (pp. 231–275). London and New York: Routledge.

Robinson, H. ([1650] 2008). The Office of Addresses and Encounters. In L. Magnusson (ed.), *Mercantilist Theory and Practice, Vol. IV* (pp. 63–72). London: Pickering & Chatto.

Thomas, P.J. (1926). *Mercantilism and the East India Trade*. London: P.S. King.

Thompson. E.P. (1991). Time, Work-Discipline and Industrial Capitalism. In E.P. Thompson (ed.), *Customs in Common* (pp. 352–403). London: The Merlin Press.

Vanderlint, J. (1954). *The System or Theory of the Trade of the World*. Baltimore, MD: Johns Hopkins University Press

Viner, J. (1954). Foreword. In *The System or Theory of the Trade of the World*. Baltimore, MD: Johns Hopkins University Press.

Wadell, D.A.G. (1958–1959). Charles Davenant (1656–1714) – a Biographical Sketch. *Economic History Review*, *11*(2), 279–288.

2 Adam Smith—a champion for the poor!

Daniel Rauhut

Mark Blaug notes that Adam Smith is an economist that everybody knows, but he questions how many did, in fact, read him: 'Once upon a time there was a man who actually read *The Wealth of Nations*; not a summary, nor a volume of selected passages, but the Wealth of Nations itself'. Then he gives a brief summary on half a page of what this man would have read in *The Wealth of Nations*, chapter by chapter. 'Now, of course, I may have exaggerated somewhat', Blaug confesses, 'There probably never was any such a man' (Blaug 1978, p. 36). Since he wrote this about 40 years ago, at least some scholars have read the works of Adam Smith thoroughly. Among these, Amartya Sen and Emma Rothschild are the most notable.

Social considerations, social relations and ethics are not among the first things one thinks of when hearing the name Adam Smith. One reason for that is that Adam Smith has become known as an advocate of 'self-interest', 'the invisible hand' and a 'laissez-faire market'. He is considered a representative of the class of capitalists, favoring the market and non-government intervention (Roll 1992). Alas, myths and stereotypes, claims Thomas Sowell (1974), bias the view of Adam Smith and his economic thought. 'Everyone has heard of the classical economists' social conservatism, blind faith in the market, denials of depression, and dismal prognoses of subsistence wages. These have become as axiomatic in the literature as they are grossly inaccurate in fact' (Sowell 1974, p. 3). Completely unfounded, Smith is still today considered as an advocate of self-interest, pro-rich, anti-government economics. It is, however, improper to consider him as just an economist, as he contributed to many other disciplines as well (Norman 2018, pp. 181–182).

Without doubt, Smith is the father of modern economics (Barber 1971, Backhouse 1991). He was one of the first to argue that the motivation behind economic activity was self-interest and the desire to maximize production. He also saw this as a collective goal. It was Adam Smith who formulated the system of competitive markets, and he was one of the first economists to produce an economic theory, covering most aspects of economic activity including utility, moral and political aspects, the fundamental problems of distribution and allocation (Whitehead 1991).

Many ethical aspects of distribution, including poverty, and allocation are discussed thoroughly by Smith in his *Theory of Moral Sentiments* (1759). Roger Backhouse (1991) points out that the *Theory of Moral Sentiments* constituted a theory of natural justice, from which Smith later on could develop the concept of self-interest (see also Dwyer 1992, Plank 1992, Rothschild 1995, 2001). Smith's *Wealth of Nations* (1776) dealt mainly with economic growth, invisible hands and economic liberty (Blaug 1978).

Smith's view on poverty has been revisited by the numerous studies of Amartya Sen (e.g. 1982, 1983, 1999a, 1999b), showing that Smith actually had a great knowledge on the causes of, for example, poverty and famines. Sen has also shown that Smith explicitly presented suggestions of how to deal with poverty. This essay discusses Adam Smith's view on poverty. Three main problems are dealt with: (1) How does Smith define poverty? (2) Why does poverty occur according to Smith? (3) Which measures, both short-term and long-term, does Smith suggest for dealing with poverty?

The individual, admiration and sympathy

Most people feel sympathy, pity and compassion for other persons, for their joys in life as well for their sorrow. However, Smith (2000a) argues, our feelings are rotten to some extent since we seem to sympathize more with our joy than sorrow, and we tend to admire and worship the rich and despise and neglect the poor. We observe and parade the riches, admire their success and try to imitate the way they live and the way they act. Everybody feels sympathy and share a fellow feeling with the rich and important persons (Smith 2000a, p. 71):

> The poor man, on the contrary, is ashamed of his poverty. He feels that it either places him out of the sight of mankind, or, that if they take any no-tice of him, they have, however, scarce any fellow-feeling with the mis-ery and distress which he suffers [...] The poor man goes out and comes in unheeded, and when in the midst of a crowd is in the same obscurity as if shut up in his own hovel [...] They turn away their eyes from him, or if the extremety of his distress forces them to look at him, it is only to spurn so disagreeable an object from them.

What Smith (2000a) did 1759 in *The Theory of Moral Sentiments* was to cor-rectly notice that poverty is more than hunger and starvation. Poverty has also a social aspect, which makes it relative.[1] A person is relatively poor if he or she cannot appear in public without feeling shame or cannot take part in the social life of a community. The social aspects of poverty stem from our admiration and respect for wealth and greatness and our contempt and scorn for weakness and poverty (Smith 2000a, p. 84):

> This disposition to admire, and almost worship, the rich and the pow-erful, and to despise, or, at least, to neglect, persons of poor and mean

conditions, though necessary both to establish and maintain the distinction of ranks and the order of society, is, at the same time, the great and most universal cause of the corruption of our moral sentiments.

According to Smith (2000a), our corrupted moral sentiments do not only cause relative poverty but also social stratification. If we want to show noble moral sentiments, we should not despise the poor and person of mean or simple conditions.

The social interests of each individual, that is, becoming an admired and powerful person and avoid becoming poor and despised, play an important role in forming the self-interest of each and every person. The underlying idea is that under a specific set of institutional arrangements, social and private interests harmonize with each other. Competition and the 'invisible hand' constitute parts of the specific set of institutional (social) arrangements to promote the social interest of the individual, that is, the self-interest (Blaug 1978).

Starvation and the surplus of labor

Food, clothing and lodging are the basic needs of mankind, according to Smith (2000b, p. 77).

> A man must always live by his work, and his wages must at least be sufficient to maintain him. They must even upon most occasions be somewhat more; otherwise it would be impossible for him to bring up a family, and the race of such workmen could not last beyond the first generation.

If the wages do not suffice to reach the subsistence level, people will be absolutely poor,[2] and as a result there will be a shortage of workers. Improving the conditions of living for the poor would lead to an increased supply of workers, since fertility will rise with increasing incomes. An increased supply of workers will facilitate progress and economic growth. Smith also provides an ethical argument for improving the conditions of the poor. The improvement for the poor living under simple conditions is not a burden to a society, nor is it to be regarded as an inconvenience, because (Smith 2000b, p. 90):

> [n]o society can surely be flourishing and happy, of which the far greater part of the members are poor and miserable. It is but equity, besides, that they who feed, cloath and lodge the whole body of the people, should have such a share of the produce of their own labour as to be themselves tolerably well fed, cloathed and lodged.

Morris Altman (2000) argues that Smith implicitly agrees to some sort of redistribution of real income, and he does so using an ethical argument. It is possible to improve the total welfare in a society by an income redistribution from well-off persons to persons who are less well off. Smith is 'assuming that the marginal utility of real income of the latter exceeds that of the former. Smith, however, never specifies the extent to which real income should be distributed from the well to do to the less well off' (Altman 2000, p. 1105). In accordance with the previous remarks on the need for workers, income redistribution would also be a guarantee that there will be no shortage in the supply of labor.[3] In addition, Sowell (1974) stresses that Smith wanted the shipment of necessities to the poor to be financed by tolls and taxes on the rich. Furthermore, he favored a tax system which 'would be somewhat progressive and redistributive, based on the ability-to-pay principle' (Sowell 1974, p. 22, cf. Hollander 1973).

Personally, however, I doubt that Smith favored any kind of redistribution of real income unless it was to ensure a stock of labor. This redistribution took the form of poor relief. Smith (2000b) gives no clear evidence of anything else. Sowell (1974, p. 11) notes that Smith 'stressed the creation of wealth, rather than its transfer'. Contrary to Malthus, Smith was a supporter of the Poor Laws, which was a kind of redistribution of income. Smith emphatically opposed the stipulation in the Poor Laws denying the poor any form of support if they were permanent residents of other parishes. This obstructed the freedom of movement of labor, which was essential to economic growth, according to Smith (Barber 1971). The Poor Laws also obstructed the poor from escaping the hardships of poverty, which prevents society from being 'flourishing and happy'.

Food, clothing and lodging constitute the basic needs of a person. Without them, a person will die. Smith concluded that society has an obligation to ensure the poor this basic right. As Sen (1997, p. 27) puts it,

> while Smith was often cited by imperial administrators for justification of refusing to intervene in famines in such diverse places as Ireland, India and China, there is nothing to indicate that Smith's ethical approach to public policy would have precluded intervention in support of the entitlements of the poor.

Sen is indeed right in his conclusion.

Famines, hunger and the government

The government could mitigate starvation through public poor relief, but apart from that, it ought to do as little as possible concerning poverty. According to Smith (2000b), the actions of government are the actual cause of not only hunger and poverty but also famines due to its intervention in matters that the government should not interfere with.

As mentioned above, Smith opposed the statutes in the Poor Laws which prevented recipients of poor relief from moving to another parish. They were not allowed to move, even if they could obtain a job elsewhere. The government intervention prolonged the suffering and the misery of these people, and it denied the recipients the right to self-command over their lives (Smith 2000b).

Government intervention in the form of the statutes of apprenticeship also caused hunger and poverty, according to Emma Rothschild (2001), since these statutes prevented the free movement of labor. This obstruction of the free movement of workers causes an unproductive use of labor, especially if the statutes of apprenticeship forces them to stay in decaying manufactures. As a result, the country (Smith 200b, p. 255f.),

> can afford no general resource to the workmen of other decaying manu-factures, who, wherever the statute of apprenticeship takes place, have no other choice but either to come upon the parish or to work as common labourers, for which, by their habits, they are much worse qualified than for any sort of manufacture that bears any resemblance to their own. They generally, therefore, chuse to come upon the parish.

The only option for workers remaining in decaying sectors of the economy are to claim poor relief from the parish, which, indeed, is a very unproductive use of skilled labor.

Smith (2000b) claims that famines are rarely caused by the scarcity of food but because there are agents who profit from the situation (cf. Sen 1982, Rothschild 2001). According to him, famines can be, but are seldom, caused by wars and drought or by farmers cutting off the supply of corn (Smith 2000b, p. 563):

> Whoever examines, with attention, the history of dearths and famines [...] will find, I believe, that a dearth never has arisen from any combi-nation among the inland dealers in corn, nor from any other cause but a real scarcity, occasioned sometimes, perhaps, and in some particular places, by the waste of war, but in by the far greatest number of cases, by the fault of the seasons; and that famine has never arisen from any other cause but the violence of government attempting, by improper means, to remedy the inconveniencies of a dearth.

Smith argued that the government should not intervene directly against pov-erty, hunger and famines in any other form than poor relief. Due to improper regulations and statutes, direct government intervention in other fields actu-ally caused poverty, hunger and famines. Free trade in corn was the best way to prevent famines, according to Smith (Rothschild 2001).

Smith was concerned with social security, and that this should be extended to the poor and landless. In times of economic and social transformation social security was needed. Rothschild (1995, p. 732) argues,

> There is very little support in his early political economy [...] for the view of modern proponents of free market economics that social security is inimical to economic development. [...] Smith thought that the wellbeing of the poor was both an end in itself and a means to the end of public prosperity.

The government could be used as an instrument to improve social security for the poor and landless.

The role of the government and the market

Government intervention is, in general, harmful and ineffective. These are the reasons why Smith has been considered to try to limit the size of government. This view is, however, only true to a certain extent. It is true that Smith (2000b) did not want the government to deal with commerce, business and management. When it started to do business, this usually meant monopolies and privileges for a chosen few. Politicians should not do business because they are 'not only careless of the public's long-run interests but extravagant with its tax money' (Sowell 1974, p. 15, cf. Hollander 1973, Rothschild 2001). But does this automatically mean that Smith desired a minimal state? On the contrary, he favored certain government intervention, and the scope of this intervention is far wider than usually assumed (Sowell 1974). Smith advocated progressive taxation so that the rich also could contribute to the public expense in a proportional way. He also welcomed government intervention to support social equality (Rothschild 2001). To make the market work, government intervention was desirable: 'The classical economists not only accepted *certain* intervention in the market, *they suggested some themselves*' (Sowell 1974, p. 21f., italics added).

Smith 'presents a "Marxist" theory of the state' (Blaug 1978, p. 61). Blaug lists some of the inspirational sources of Smith, arguing that it is no exaggeration to describe these men as forerunners of 'the materialist conception of history' (Blaug 1978, p. 61). These are not exactly the kind of comments one would expect to hear regarding the 'father' of self-interest, the invisible hand and the market economy! According to Smith (2000b), the government should deal with three things. The first task is to protect society from aggression, violence and invasion, performed by military force, from other countries. The second task is to establish a judicial administration with the aim of protecting the members of society from injustice and oppression. The third task is that of (Smith 200b, p. 779):

erecting and maintaining those public institutions and those public works [...] that the profit could never repay the expence to any individual or small number of individuals, and which it therefore cannot be expected that any individual or small number of individuals should erect or maintain.

This includes education for children, moral instruction for people of all ages and infrastructure (good roads, canals, bridges, ports, etc.). Poor relief also falls into this category. Eric Roll (1992) adds health care[4] and monetary policy to the list of duties falling into the third category of government tasks. However, there is one more: legislation. This is not explicitly mentioned when Smith discusses the public institutions needed for commerce, but without legislation and clear rules the market will not work efficiently.

Smith has for long been regarded as a spokesman of a minimal state, providing only a minimum of services. However, private agents can provide several of the things Smith lists as government duties. Education, health care and infrastructure are good examples of this. Moreover, poor relief can be provided, in the form of charity and altruism, from private agents.

Although Smith advocated education provided by the government, he did not justify them economically, argues Rothschild (1998, p. 212).

> Smith at no point argues that universal education will lead to an increase in national wealth. His concern is rather that the very change—in the division of labour—which has brought an increase in prosperity is itself a source of social impoverishment. Education is needed as a consequence of economic development, and not as a cause of future development.

Instead, education and instruction are seen as a preparation for one's public life, 'in the sense of judging the projects of government, for one's private life with one's friends and one's family, and for one's public life in private enterprise, or in the economy' (Rothschild 1998, p. 220). If an individual is not educated or instructed properly, he or she will not be able to take part in the life of the community or appear in public without feeling inferior. Government education can be seen as a way to prepare persons for this and to mitigate subjectively perceived social inferiority, as well as to integrate the poor socially into the community (Rothschild 1995).

After Smith (2000b) spends most of his book arguing that the government should not intervene in most areas, the first chapter of the fifth book in *The Wealth of Nations* is devoted to what activities the government actually should undertake. On these 132 pages, Smith tries to convince the reader that government activity is needed in the provision of public goods, such as infrastructure, education, health care and poor relief, and that the government is needed to supplement the market (see also Hollander 1973, Sowell 1974, Rothschild 2001). Without these government activities, the free market *cannot* function. This is everything but the rhetoric of an advocate of a laissez-faire liberalism! On the contrary, Smith tried to establish under what conditions the market would operate most efficiently, specifying an institutional structure (Rosenberg 1960). To enable the free market to work the way Smith wants it to work, the government is needed to uphold the rules of the market system so nobody increase their personal liberty on the expense on others. 'The market is like a game in which all can freely participate, but government is needed to set up and enforce fair rules of play' (Whitehead 1991, p. 62).

What Smith says is that the government is needed in selective and well-defined areas, that is, producing public goods. Hereby, the government supplements the market in the pursuit of the common good; government action in other areas will actually cause poverty, hunger and famines due to improper regulations and statutes (Hollander 1973, Rothschild 2001).

The importance of economic growth

Smith (2000b, p. 771) states that in every society the institutions and laws favor the rich (cf. Marx 1983). 'Civil government, so far as it is instituted for the security of property, is in reality instituted for the defence of the rich against the poor, or of those who have some property against those who have none at all.'

By removing the institutional obstacles for ordinary people to improve their economic situation, the market and the liberal reward of labor could improve the conditions of living for the broad majority of the population (Smith 200b, p. 93):

> The liberal reward of labour, as it encourages the propagation, so it increases the industry of the common people. The wages of labour are the encouragement of industry, which, like every other human quality, improves in proportion to the encouragement it receives.

The wealth of a nation is nothing but the aggregate wealth of its members (Rosenberg 1960, Hollander 1973).

Due to our admiration of the rich, a free market would offer the possibility to climb socially for the lower classes, and the possibility to fall for others. A free market economy would enable social mobility. Since wealth means authority and admiration, the laws and institutions will protect persons who have become wealthy. At the same time, persons who lose their wealth will face the conditions of ordinary people (Smith 2000b. See also Smith 2000a).

According to Smith, introducing a system of a free market economy makes it possible to improve the conditions of living for the majority of the population. The material aspirations of the workers will encourage them to work harder, which in turn will improve their wages. This will, in turn, encourage them to work even harder, and so on. The result will be a prosperous society. After all, since the wealth of a nation depends on the aggregate wealth of its members, '[n]o society can surely be flourishing and happy, of which the far greater part of the members are poor and miserable' (Smith 2000b, p. 90).

In a free market economy, where the government produces public goods, the social aspirations of the individuals together with economic freedom (i.e. the absence of 'improper' regulations and statutes by the government) will lead to an economic growth, which, in turn, will lead to prosperity. Smith (2000b) stresses the importance of promoting economic growth, since growth leads to higher wages and higher profits. It is not in the wealthiest countries that the highest wages are found, but in the countries with the fastest growing economies. If the wages are rising above the subsistence level, fewer people will face poverty (cf. Sowell 1974). Joseph Schumpeter (1954) adds that Smith believes that economic progress means new technology, which will increase employment and raise the wages. Smith (2000b) argues that in progressive countries with a high economic growth (e.g. Britain and the United States), the wages are way above the subsistence level, while countries with traditional economies (e.g. China), wages are still at the subsistence level and declining.

In sum, according to Smith, economic growth is the key to the wealth of nations (Hollander 1973). Since '[n]o society can surely be flourishing and happy, of which the far greater part of the members are poor and miserable' (Smith 2000b, p. 90), economic growth will also be an important means to fight poverty.

A dual definition of poverty

It must be stressed that his view on poverty differs somewhat from what most people think Smith stands for. According to Sowell (1974), myths and prejudices have biased our perception of Smith. Emma Rotschild (1992, p. 85) agrees:

> Smith was considered [...] as a friend of the poor. [...] Malthus, in his 1798 *Essay*, reproves Smith for the "error" of mixing two distinct inquiries: into "the wealth of nations" and into "the happiness and comfort of the lowest orders in society".

Rothschild (1995) argues that Smith considered social security and the integration of the poor to be preconditions for development and economic prosperity. That Smith's view on poverty is still valid today is clearly shown in the writings of Amartya Sen (1983, 1999b).

Smith does not define poverty as absolute or relative. Instead, he sees poverty as both absolute and relative. Food, clothing and lodging constitute the basic needs of man. If a person lacks the means to meet these basic needs, he or she is poor. This definition of poverty includes the constituents of a definition of absolute poverty. Smith also stresses the social consequences of poverty, arguing that the poor man will be ashamed of his poverty and that non-poor persons, in their admiration of wealth and success, will look down on the poor person. Poverty is in this case based on a perceived social inferiority. The latter is a significant trait of relative poverty. When Smith argues that 'nobody' takes any notice of a poor person, this can be interpreted to mean either that 'nobody', *in fact*, takes notice of that person or that the poor person *subjectively* feels that 'nobody' takes any notice of him or her. In either case, the fact that the poor person feels that 'nobody' takes any notice of him, true or not, causes the subjective feeling of social inferiority. As a result, a person who feels socially inferior relative to others does not necessarily have to be absolutely poor. Defining poverty in this way, as Smith does, also include the constituents of relative poverty.

The causes of poverty

Subjectively perceived social inferiority occurs as a result of our admiration and worship of riches and success. At the same time, we despise weakness and poverty. According to Smith, this has to do with our corrupted moral sentiments. Social stratification and social rank play an important role as well when it comes to relative poverty, and it must be stressed that Smith was probably one of the first economists—if not the very first—to identify this issue when dealing with social welfare. Absolute poverty is caused by insufficient food, clothing and lodging. Improper regulations and statutes of the government, in turn, usually cause this insufficiency. At times, Smith adds, wars and years of bad harvests can also cause hunger, starvation and poverty.

Just as Smith shows great knowledge and insight into humankind in his analysis of socially perceived poverty, his lack of insight is striking when it comes to why absolute poverty exists. It is nothing but a simplified political rhetoric to argue that 'improper'—whatever that means—government regulations and statutes have caused more hunger, starvation and poverty through history than wars and failure of the harvest. Nevertheless, while the government may not have been infallible policy-wise, to blame it for being the major cause of poverty and starvation is unfair.

The cures of poverty

Smith explicitly mentions public poor relief as a measure against poverty, which is one of the morally good activities that the government should be involved in. Public poor relief is necessary to ensure a minimum supply of workers during, for example, a famine or drought. He does not explicitly argue that a public poor relief system is a short-term measure against poverty, but it can implicitly be assumed to be so, for public poor relief can offer no long-term solution to the scourge of poverty. It can offer only a short-term mitigation of *absolute* poverty.

The subjectively perceived social inferiority, that is, relative poverty, can neither be mitigated nor erased by short-term measures. Nor will public poor relief help. Smith assumes that one of the individual's social interests is to become an admired and powerful person and avoid becoming a poor and despised person. To fight this subjectively perceived social inferiority, social ambitions, based on self-interest, are needed, and public poor relief does not help to achieve social ambitions.

Although there was no contemporary empirical evidence, Adam Smith considered migration as a short-term solution to poverty and unemployment. He saw poverty and unemployment as push factors causing migration and wages high enough to provide for a worker and his family as a pull factor. Free mobility of labor would allow an optimal allocation of the factor commodity labor. Moreover, employment changes necessary to equalize wages between different regions would occur. Hence, migration would not only promote economic growth and prosperity but also reduce poverty (Rauhut 2010).

According to Smith, the long-term measures against poverty rest on economic growth. Only economic growth can remove the obstacles to improvements of the economic situation and the living conditions for the broad majority of the population. In a nation with high economic growth, wages will increase and move upwards, away from the subsistence level. Smith (2000b) compares the development in Britain and the United States, on the one hand, and China, on the other. Wages are high in countries with high rates of economic growth. Higher profits and wages follow economic growth. Higher wages will lead to higher consumption, which, in turn, will lead to a higher demand for workers. This will promote a continuous higher economic growth, as in Britain and the United States.

Since '[n]o society can surely be flourishing and happy, of which the far greater part of the members are poor and miserable' (Smith 2000b, p. 90), actions to reduce poverty are needed to improve the wealth of the nation. Smith was more concerned with the creation of wealth than the transfer of it (Sowell 1974). He thought that wealth and economic growth could be created when three parts were in harmony with each other: (1) The government should only produce public goods to supplement the market. (2) The free market creates wealth through economic growth and technological change. (3) The individuals are given economic and social freedom to achieve their own personal goals. Since Smith considers freedom to be a 'positive-sum' game and not a 'zero-sum' game, this does, however, not mean that individuals are allowed to do so at the expense of other individuals' freedom. When these three conditions are met, the market, the government and the individuals will, through the 'invisible' hand and the self-interest, create a wealthy and prosperous nation.

As described above, absolute poverty can be fought, but not the feeling of social inferiority. The feeling of social inferiority is caused by our corrupted moral sentiments: we love to admire the rich, the successful and the fortunate persons, and we love to look down on the poor, the miserable and unfortunate persons. The question is if Smith really sees the feeling of subjectively perceived social inferiority as something negative. On the one hand, it will not be possible for an individual to take part in the life of the community or appear in public without feeling inferior if he or she is not properly educated or instructed. Preparation of the individuals for the public life through government education also serves to mitigate subjectively perceived social inferiority and to integrate the poor socially into the community in the long run. On the other hand, feeling socially inferior is not seen as something entirely negative by Smith: it will make us work harder to achieve our material and social aspirations, which will both make us more productive as workers and consume more goods. Increased consumption will in turn promote economic growth. Smith's economic system will, at least according to himself, enable social mobility for those who manage to create a fortune, thus being a person that other persons actually admire. The subjectively perceived feeling of social inferiority plays a central role in the creation of wealth, almost like an invisible hand: the reward for working hard is a higher income and a fulfilment of one's material and social aspirations, which will, in turn, encourage the individual to work hard also in the future. If the individuals are given economic and social freedom to achieve their own personal goals, they will try to overcome their feeling of subjectively perceived social inferiority. In this reasoning, the feeling of subjectively perceived social inferiority is in itself an important tool for mitigating poverty.

Concluding remarks

Only the person who reads more than excerpts and selected passages from *The Wealth of Nations* will realize that Adam Smith has quite a lot of interesting thoughts and ideas regarding ethics, social considerations, social inequality, social injustice and poverty. Those who read *The Theory of Moral Sentiments* realize that the idea of social conservatism in Smith is indeed inaccurate and biased by myths and stereotypes. In his numerous studies, Amartya Sen has showed that Adam Smith is very much alive and kicking, and that he was very knowledgeable regarding poverty.

Smith's views on poverty are not those of a laissez-faire liberal. He is aware that poverty can be both absolute and relative. The absolute poverty is a scourge, which, if necessary, should lead to government intervention in the form of poor relief. While poor relief is a short-term measure against absolute poverty, economic growth is a long-term measure. By promoting economic growth, more people will be better off.

The feeling of subjectively perceived social inferiority is related to relative poverty, which Smith considers to be caused by our corrupted moral sentiments. Implicitly, Smith seems to regard social inequalities as something positive. Feeling socially inferior will make us work harder to improve our material and social aspirations and to create a fortune, thus being a person that other persons admire. The feeling of subjectively perceived social inferiority is an important institution in itself to mitigate poverty.

Smith also opposed *social injustice*, which is not to be confused with *social inequality*. While social inequality served as an incentive to improve one's situation relative to others, social injustice prevents one from doing so. Just like Marx (1983), Smith (2000b) argued that in every society the institutions and laws favored the rich; many government statutes and regulations also caused poverty, especially the obstruction of the free movement of labor. By removing the institutional obstacles, the economic situation of ordinary people could be improved and the labor could be used in a more productive way.

A personal reflection on Smith's view of poverty is that it contains a contextual approach to poverty, that is, poverty can only be understood when the socio-economic context is taken into account. A person can take part of the public life in one community, as well as appear in public without feeling shame in that community, but not in another community. A person can be considered wise and intelligent, and thereon looked up to by the other members of the community. The same person can be regarded as an illiterate, stupid and poor person, and will be looked down on, in another community. The socio-economic context will decide who are the poor and the stupid, as well as who are the admirable.

Adam Smith was a theoretical economist. He did not study the empirical world, but he drew examples from other books (Kindleberger 1976). While earlier economists tried to explain how things were, Smith simply explained how things ought to be. Drawing examples from books to make abstract systems and theories makes Smith unique (Backhouse 1991, Blaug 1994). This is how he revolutionized economic thinking (Roll 1992). It was, however, not only economic thinking that he revolutionized. His ideas on the causes and cures to poverty were ahead of his time. The view that the government was the only actor with a genuine interest in a well-educated and healthy workforce, which would reduce the exposure to poverty, did not mature until the twentieth century. That migration can mitigate poverty and unemployment was a radical thought in Smith's own time. When it comes to poverty and social injustice, he is not the brutal laissez-faire liberal that he is usually accused of being. The numerous studies of Amartya Sen (e.g. 1982, 1983, 1999a, 1999b) show that Smith actually had great knowledge of the causes and cures to poverty. Alas, myths and stereotypes still bias his views and his ideas. It is a pity.

Notes

1 Andreβ (1998) provides a general overview of relative poverty. For a more thoroughly discussion on the definition of relative poverty, see Runciman (1966), Tawney (1931), Townsend (1979, 1987) and Rowntree (1902), and the latter's discussion on what he calls 'secondary' poverty.

2 See Andreβ (1998) for a general overview on absolute poverty. For a more detailed discussion on absolute poverty, see Malthus (1992), Joseph and Sumption (1979) and Rowntree (1902), and the latter's discussion of what he calls 'primary' poverty.

3 Fertility can remain at the same level, which will ensure a new generation of workers. This, in turn, will promote progress and economic growth.
4 Smith (2000b) does not mention health care explicitly. Roll (1992) does not discuss why he has included health care. However, it can be supposed that it will benefit not only the individual workers if these are fit and healthy, but also the capitalists and employers. Since everybody will benefit from a public health care, it can be assumed that Smith would have supported a production of these kind of public goods. In any case, there is nothing in Smith (2000b) rejecting this view.

References

Altman, M. (2000). A Behavioral Theory of Economic Welfare and Economic Justice: A Smithian Alternative to Pareto Optimality. *International Journal of Social Economics, 27*(11), 1098–1131.

Andreβ, H.-J. (1998). Empirical Poverty Research in a Comparative Perspective: Basic Orientations and Outline of the Book. In H.-J. Andreβ (ed.), *Empirical Poverty Research in a Comparative Perspective* (pp. 1–26). Aldershot: Ashgate.

Backhouse, R. (1991). *A History of Modern Economic Analysis*. Oxford: Blackwell.

Barber, W.J. (1971). *De ekonomiska idéernas historia*. Stockholm: Bokförlaget Aldus.

Blaug, M. (1978). *Economic Theory in Retrospect*. Oxford, London and Northampton: Cambridge University Press.

Blaug, M. (1994). *The Methodology of Economics*. Cambridge: Cambridge University Press.

Dwyer, J. (1992). Virtue and Improvement: The Civic World of Adam Smith. In P. Jones and A. Skinner (eds), *Adam Smith Reviewed* (pp. 190–216). Edinburgh: Edinburgh University Press.

Hollander, S. (1973). *The Economics of Adam Smith*. London: Heinemann Educational Books.

Joseph, K. and Sumption, K. (1979). *Equality*. London: John Murray.

Kindleberger, C.P. (1976). The Historical Background: Adam Smith and the Industrial Revolution. In T. Wilson and A. Skinner (eds), *The Market and the State. Essays in Honour of Adam Smith*. Oxford: Oxford University Press.

Malthus, T. (1992). *An Essay on the Principle of Population*. Oxford: Oxford University Press.

Marx, K. (1983). *Capital, Vol. I*. London: Lawrence & Wishart.

Norman, J. (2018). *Adam Smith: The Father of Economics*. New York: Basic Books

Plank, F. (1992). Adam Smith: Grammatical Economist. In P. Jones and A. Skinner (eds), *Adam Smith Reviewed* (pp. 21–55). Edinburgh: Edinburgh University Press.

Rauhut, D. (2010). Adam Smith on Migration. *Migration Letters, 7*(1), 105–113.

Roll, E. (1992). *A History of Economic Thought*. London: Faber & Faber.

Rosenberg, N. (1960) Some Institutional Aspects of the Wealth of Nations. *Journal of Political Economy, 68*(6), 557–570.

Rothschild, E. (1992). Adam Smith and Conservative Economics. *Economic History Review, 45*(1), 74–96.

Rothschild, E. (1995). Social Security and Laissez Faire in Eighteenth-Century Political Economy. *Population and Development Review, 21*(4), 711–744.

Rothschild, E. (1998). Condorcet and Adam Smith on Education and Instruction. In A. Oksenberg Rorty (ed.), *Philosophers on Education* (pp. 209–226). London and New York: Routledge.

Rothschild, E. (2001). *Economic Sentiments – Adam Smith, Condorcet, and the Enlightenment.* Cambridge, MA: Harvard University Press.

Rowntree, B.S. (1902). *Poverty – A Study of Town Life.* London: Macmillan & Co Ltd.

Runciman, W.E. (1966). *Relative Deprivation and Social Justice: A Study of Attitudes to Social Inequality in Twentieth-Century England.* Berkeley: University of California Press.

Schumpeter, J.A. (1954). *History of Economic Analysis.* New York: Oxford University Press.

Sen, A. (1982). *Poverty and Famines – An Essay on Entitlement Deprivation.* Oxford: Clarendon Press.

Sen, A. (1983), Poor, Relatively Speaking. *Oxford Economic Papers, 35*(1), 153–169.

Sen, A. (1997). *On Ethics and Economics.* Oxford: Blackwell.

Sen, A. (1999a). *Commodities and Capabilities.* New Delhi: Oxford University Press.

Sen, A. (1999b). *Development as Freedom.* Oxford: Oxford University Press.

Smith, A. (2000a). *The Theory of Moral Sentiments.* Amherst, NY: Prometheus Books.

Smith, A. (2000b). *The Wealth of Nations.* New York: The Modern Library Classics.

Sowell, T. (1974). *Classical Economics Reconsidered.* Princeton, NJ: Princeton University Press.

Tawney, R. H. (1931). *Equality.* London: George Allen & Unwin.

Townsend, P. (1979). *Poverty in the United Kingdom.* London: Penguin Books.

Townsend, P. (1987). Deprivation. *Journal of Social Policy, 16*(2), 125–146.

Whitehead, J.W. (1991). The Forgotten Limits: Reason and Regulation in Economic Theory. In K. Renwick Monroe (ed.), *The Economic Approach to Politics: A Critical Reassessment of the Theory of Rational Action* (pp. 53–73). New York: Harper Collins Publishers.

3   Malthus and the poor

Martin Dribe

> However powerful may be the impulses of passion, they are generally in some degree modified by reason. And it does not seem entirely visionary to suppose that, if the true and permanent cause of poverty were explained, and forcibly brought home to each man's bosom, it would have some, and perhaps not an inconsiderable, influence on his conduct; at least the experiment has never yet been tried. Almost everything that has been hitherto done for the poor has tended, as if with solicitors care, to throw a veil of obscurity over this subject, and to hide from them the true cause of their poverty.
>
> Malthus 1826, p. 286

Thomas Robert Malthus (1766–1834) is best known for his *Essay on the Principle of Population*, which appeared for the first time in 1798, followed by a number of subsequent, enlarged editions.[1] In this book, Malthus, for the first time in a systematic way, presented a theory of the relationship between the economy and population, a theory which came to be extremely influential in its time; it retains considerable influence, even in contemporary discussion on population and economy. Besides presenting his Principle of Population, Malthus, especially in later editions (from 1803 and onwards), paid considerable attention to the conditions of the poor and the way in which English society tried to deal with the problem of poverty, most notably through the Poor Laws.

The principle of population

In the *First Essay* of 1798, Malthus began with two basic postulates: 'Food is necessary to the existence of man', and 'the passion between the sexes is necessary and will remain nearly in its present state' (Malthus 1959, p. 4). According to Malthus, human populations, as well as the populations of most other species, had a tendency to grow geometrically (1, 2, 4, 8, etc.) since 'a thousand millions are as easily doubled every twenty-five years by the power of population as a thousand' (Malthus 1992, p. 17). In effect, what Malthus observed was that in the absence of any checks to reproduction and assuming a constant rate of increase, the growth of population followed an exponential growth model:

$$K_t = K_0 e^{rt}$$

where K_t is the population at time t, K_0 is the starting population, and r the rate of increase.

Turning to food production, Malthus, as the other classical economists, believed that diminishing returns to labor in agriculture with a fixed supply of land implied that the increase in yields as more land was brought under the plow got lower and lower because the new land most likely was of inferior quality, except under very special circumstances, such as the clearing of totally virgin areas. When all land was cleared increased production could only be obtained by ever increasing inputs of labor and capital. According to Malthus, technical change could perhaps in the short run have increased returns, but in the long run, agricultural production always faced the problem of diminishing returns. Under the most favorable conditions imaginable, food production could perhaps increase linearly, or in arithmetic progression (1, 2, 3, 4, etc.) (Malthus 1992, p. 19).

These two different trends in growth—geometrical for population and arithmetical for food production—imply that population growth always had a tendency to outgrow food and other resources. As long as resources were available, the population tended to grow geometrically and in the absence of other checks on population growth it was ultimately stopped by the availability of food. In reality, however, it was only under special circumstances that population had increased geometrically for longer periods of time, such as the colonization by Europeans of the New World, but, of course, also in this case it was just a matter of time before all this land also had been used up, and diminishing returns set in to limit the growth of the population.

Malthus identified two main checks to population growth: positive checks and preventive checks. The former stopped a growth already under way and took the form of increased mortality through diseases, epidemics, war, plague, famine, and so on—what Malthus labeled misery. The preventive checks instead stopped population from outgrowing resources by people foreseeing the difficulties that would arise from a rapidly growing population, and acting actively to limit the growth. According to Malthus, this could happen if people showed moral restraint and did not marry unless they possessed the resources to provide for a family. Other means of limiting the number of children born without abstaining from sexual intercourse, Malthus referred to as vice, which should be condemned (Malthus 1992, p. 22f.). He was also clearly against deliberate fertility control within marriage. In the appendix of the 1817 edition of the *Essay*, he wrote (Malthus 1992, p. 369),

If it were possible for each married couple to limit by a wish the number of their children, there is certainly reason to fear that the indolence of the human race would be very greatly increased; and that neither the population of individual countries, nor the whole earth, would ever reach its natural and proper extent.

In the first edition of the *Essay*, there was a clear focus on the positive checks, while in subsequent editions Malthus put more and more trust in the preventive checks, at least when it came to Europe (England), while positive checks still were the most important in the 'uncivilized parts of the world', such as in Asia (Malthus 1992, p. 43).

Thus, in the long and medium term, the availability of food determined the level and growth of the population in the Malthusian model. The population could not grow geometrically but was forced to grow pari passu with the availability of food by the operation of either preventive or, ultimately, positive checks. Malthus saw this relationship between population and economy as a kind of natural law applicable to both humans and animals. If the population increased faster than the production of food, it eventually led to lack of food, which, in turn, caused food prices to increase and real wages to decline. This led people to postpone marriage because of difficulties providing for a family, or if the preventive check was not effective enough, to increased mortality due to lack of food. This, in turn, led to lower population growth or even population decline, which tended to lower food prices and raise real wages, providing the preconditions for a new expansion of the population. Hence, the population size oscillated around the means of subsistence. Any improvement in the standard of living led the population to increase through lower mortality and increasing fertility following easier access to marriage, which, in turn, increased food prices and pressed wages towards subsistence level. This so-called Malthusian trap made increases in the productive potential of the economy, following, for example, technical change, meaningless as long as the preventive check was not in full operation. The effect of such an exogenous productivity increases only had one long-term effect. It raised the sustainable level of population without improving the conditions of the population (see, e.g., Lee 1980, Clark 2007).

Historical confirmations

In their monumental reconstruction of English population history, E.A. Wrigley and Roger Schofield (1981) set out to test the Malthusian theory on historical England. Using series of various demographic indices as well as grain prices and real wages, they studied the relationship between economic and demographic change in both the short and the medium term. Their main conclusion was that there was, indeed, a relationship between medium-term cycles in population size and prices, so periods of increasing population were followed by increasing prices of grain, which seems to be in accordance with a basic Malthusian formulation. This relationship appears to have been present until about 1800, but not thereafter, indicating that the

Principle of Population was in operation until about the time it was laid out by Malthus.

Gregory Clark (2007) gave a similar account, arguing that real income per person in England did not change over the long term before 1800, leaving eighteenth-century laborers no better off than their counterparts a 1,000 years (or even 100,000 years) before (Clark 2007, Chapter 1).[2] This argument was based on a wide range of indicators of living standards, from real wages of laborers, to food consumption and stature. The short- to medium-term increases in income per person following exogenous demographic events, such as the Black Death, or technological innovations were pushed back by an increasing population, as postulated by Malthus. This situation changed with the Industrial Revolution around 1800, which set England, and ultimately the entire Western world, on the path to modern economic growth with sustained increase in both income per person and population (Kuznets 1966).

Turning to the checks to population growth, Wrigley and Schofield (1981) argue that mortality fluctuated more or less independently of the economy in the medium term, indicating that positive checks were not the main regulator of the population system in early modern England. Instead there appears to have been a clearer connection between fertility and the economy in the medium term.[3] Periods of increasing prices, and thus lowering of real wages, led to lower fertility. This was, however, not accomplished through deliberate fertility control within marriage but through postponement of marriage. When real wages declined in times of high prices, marriages were postponed which led to lower fertility and lower population growth. This pattern also fits quite well with the particular marriage and household formation pattern of pre-industrial Western Europe, in which people married rather late (25–30 years), many never married at all (up to 25 percent) and where marriage was intimately connected to the setting up of an independent household (Hajnal 1965, 1983). Under these circumstances, declining real wages made it more difficult for people in pre-industrial Western Europe to marry and form a household, which had important effects on the growth of the population.

Other studies have reached somewhat different conclusions about the workings of the Malthusian checks in pre-industrial England. In a time-series analysis of the period 1541–1840, Esteban Nicolini (2007) found support for positive checks only up to the mid-seventeenth century, and preventive checks only up to the mid-eighteenth century, and hence that the Malthusian system started to dissolve well before the Industrial Revolution. Using different wage data and various estimation techniques, Nicholas Crafts and Terence Mills (2009) found that both the preventive and positive checks ceased to be in operation by the mid-seventeenth century, that is, long before the industrial revolution. Clark approached the issue by looking at differences in completed fertility by wealth, as indicated in wills for men dying in the first half of the seventeenth century. He found more surviving children for wealthier men than for poorer men, which he interpreted as support for the Malthusian preventive check being in operation in this period (Clark 2007,

Chapter 4). Using data for longer time periods, subsequent research showed that these fertility differences between rich and poor declined over time but were present in England for men dying up to the late the eighteenth century (Clark and Cummins 2009, 2015). Based on family reconstitution data, Nina Boberg-Fazlic et al. (2011) found similar fertility differentials, in both gross and net fertility, for marriage cohorts up to the late seventeenth century, but not thereafter.

While Malthus viewed England as the prime example of a society in which preventive checks had the greatest possibilities of successful operation, China, in many ways, acted as the model of the Asian population system, where positive checks dominated and where overpopulation forced people to live in misery. This view, however, has been called into question by historical demographers of China (Lee and Wang 1999). The Chinese demographic system was characterized by early and, at least for women, universal marriage, but also by comparatively low marital fertility. Life expectancy at birth does not seem to have deviated a great deal from what was found in pre-industrial Europe. A distinctive feature of Chinese demography was the importance of sex-selective infanticide, mainly of females. This demographic system resulted in a quite modest population growth: only 0.5 per 1,000 before 1750. Thus, despite pronounced differences in family systems the demographic outcome in terms of fertility, mortality and population growth was quite similar to most of Europe, which refutes the view held by Malthus and many others concerning the Asian population system.

Malthus and the English Poor Laws

As the previous discussion has shown, the root of low living standards and poverty in a Malthusian world is the fact that the population always tends to grow faster than the means of subsistence. In Book III of the *Essay*, Malthus stated that 'the tendency in population fully to keep pace with the means of subsistence must in general prevent the increase of these means from having a great and permanent effect in improving the condition of the poor' (Malthus 1992, p. 185). Technological advances creating productivity increases on the fixed supply of land only raised the standard of living for the common man temporarily since, in the absence of an effective restraint on marriage and fertility, higher wages lowered death rates and increased birth rates, leading to faster population growth, which, eventually, pressed wages back to subsistence level. In other words, all efforts to increase the level of well-being without the presence of marriage restraint meant only that more people could live in the same area on the same subsistence level.

Basing himself on this analysis, Malthus spent large parts of his *Essay* (especially in the editions from 1803 onwards) to argue against the English Poor Laws.[4] In the 1817 edition of the *Essay*, he defined the problem. 'The problem is, How to provide for those who are in want, in such a manner as to prevent a continual increase of their numbers, and of the proportion which they bear to the whole society' (Malthus 1992, p. 302). He also gave the solution (Malthus 1992, p. 308):

> It may indeed be affirmed with the most perfect confidence that there is only one class of causes from which any approaches towards a remedy can be rationally expected; and that consists of whatever has a tendency to increase the prudence and foresight of the labouring classes. This is the touchstone to which every plan proposed for the poor should be applied.

Malthus identified a number of drawbacks of the English Poor Law system, especially the allowance system, which provided assistance to families with children whose income was below a certain level.[5] According to Malthus, such a system first tended to increase population without increasing the means of subsistence, by removing the checks on family formation and childbearing (Malthus 1992, pp. 100, 103f., 120, 289). In the longer run, it led to increased supply of labor which put downward pressure on wages. In the short run, however, the mechanisms were likely different. The relief paid in addition to wages could be expected to reduce the supply of labor and thus put an upward pressure on wages in the short run (see, e.g., Blaug 1963). According to Malthus, however, the Poor Laws forced wages down also in the short run, since there was a fixed amount of money available that could be used to pay either wages or relief (Boyer 1990, p. 56).

The Poor Laws, according to Malthus, also endangered the independence of the English peasantry by encouraging people to marry without having the necessary means to support a family, which made them totally dependent on parish assistance. In addition, they lowered both the wish and the ability to save among common people, who instead lived from hand to mouth with little thought of the future. Without the Poor Laws, according to Malthus, people would have been more prudent, since the risk of economic distress and death would deter them from lavish behavior (Malthus 1992, p. 101). Thus, the Poor Laws removed one of the strongest checks to idleness and wasteful behavior and allowed poor people to 'marry with little or no prospect of being able to support a family without parish assistance' (Malthus 1992, p. 100).

The part of the poor relief that provided food to the poor working in public workhouses also had negative effects, according to Malthus, since it had to be taken from more productive and deserving segments of society (Malthus 1992, p. 100). This also had the effect of driving up prices for provisions, which 'spread the evil over a much larger surface' (Malthus 1992, p. 89).

The analysis of the Poor Laws presented by Malthus became very influential on his contemporaries (see, e.g., Smith 1951, Huzel 1969, Digby 1986, p. 164f., Boyer 1990, Chapter 2). In his book on the work of Malthus, James Bonar (1885) states that Malthus's view on the Poor Laws 'have influenced public opinion and legislation about the destitute poor almost as powerfully as the Wealth of Nations has influenced commercial policy' (Bonar 1885, p. 304f.).

One of the clearest examples of this was the 1834 Poor Law Report, which, by and large, presented a picture closely resembling that given by Malthus on the effects of the Poor Law system, that is, it was more a cause than a cure of poverty (e.g., Huzel 1969, Boyer 1990). The Poor Law Report also proposed an abolition of the assistance to able-bodied workers outside of workhouses and believed that this would solve the problem of unemployment (Boyer 1990, pp. 60–64).

Most of the discussion in the *Essay* conveys a picture of the poor as healthy adults in prime working ages who got payment in addition to the wages, or who preferred to rely on poor relief without working at all. Much less attention is, however, paid to the groups of sick, handicapped, or elderly who were unable to work, and who could not be expected to contribute much to population growth. In fact, as has been pointed out for instance by Barry Stapleton (1986), the *Essay* lacks a deeper analysis of the structure of poverty in nineteenth-century England. Instead, Malthus focused his attention on the moral status of the lower classes of society, and the way the Poor Laws may have affected them.[6]

As we have just seen, one of the main drawbacks of the Poor Laws and similar systems, according to Malthus, was their alleged tendency to make people marry and have children without having the necessary means to provide for their families. This followed directly from the Principle of Population, as was discussed above. Several authors have tried to empirically test this relationship for nineteenth century England. Huzel (1969, 1986), for example, used different kinds of parish and census data to compare the demographic development in areas characterized by considerable poor relief with areas where this relief was of much less significance. These comparisons do not support Malthus's view that the poor relief system promoted early marriages, high fertility and thus high rates of population growth. Instead, Huzel maintains that the direction of causality probably ran the other way, that is, the Poor Laws were an effect of high rates of population growth and low wages, rather than the other way around. A similar conclusion was reached by Blaug (1963, 1964) in two studies of the English Poor Laws using mainly nineteenth-century survey data. He viewed the Poor Laws in an almost Keynesian way as basically a way of dealing with structural unemployment, or underemployment, in a lagging rural sector with wages below subsistence level. The aid in addition to wages provided by the Poor Laws gave increasing purchasing power to a very weak consumer group, which most likely had an expansionary effect on the economy (Blaug 1963).

Moreover, according to Blaug, the levels of payments in the poor relief system were not so high as to promote early marriages or excessive childbearing, although it was difficult for many people to maintain a family without assistance. To the extent that the poor relief system had any effects on the demographic development, it was probably to lower infant and child mortality, but this effect did not have a large impact on overall growth rates of the population (Blaug 1963, 1964; see also Huzel 1969).

William Petersen, however, has questioned the validity of the empirical analyzes of both Mark Blaug and James Huzel, arguing that the data they used were far too crude to actually test the hypotheses put forward by Malthus (Petersen 1979, p. 121f.). In a somewhat similar vein, George Boyer (1990) also questioned Huzel's method of simply looking at the association between parish-level indicators of poor relief on the one hand and birth and marriage rates on the other, without controlling for other important fertility determinants, most notably socioeconomic factors. In a re-analysis of Huzel's data, including controls for, for example, population density, income, infant mortality, and housing, he found strong support for Malthus's claim that child allowances promoted higher fertility at the parish level (Boyer 1990, pp. 155–164). He also found that the increased generosity of the poor relief leading up to 1834 was an important explanation for the increasing fertility in England at that time, and that the later abolishment of the system could help to explain stagnating birth rates in the period after the 1830s (Boyer 1990, pp. 168–171).

Thus, Malthus held a very negative view of the Poor Laws and proposed their abolition, although he realized that this could not be accomplished at once but had to be done very gradually so that it was barely noticed by the people; or as Malthus himself put it, 'so gradual as not to affect any individuals at present alive, or who will be born within the next two years' (Malthus 1992, p. 118). As has been pointed out by several authors, Malthus's views on poverty and the Poor Laws were quite complex: a mixture between theoretical and empirical analyzes as well as policy recommendations (e.g., Digby 1986). He also seems to have changed his opinion somewhat in later editions of the *Essay*, acknowledging that the Poor Laws probably did not promote population growth. This he attributed to the independence of the English lower classes and their ability to foresee the negative consequences of such a development (Malthus 1992, p. 101; see also Winch 1987, p. 45).

Nonetheless, the general solution to the problem of poverty, at least among the healthy, able-bodied parts of the population, was not found in welfare systems, such as the Poor Laws, but in a higher moral standard of the poor, which would lead to greater sense of independence and self-reliance and ultimately to moral restraint, that is, control of marriage and childbearing by the possession of resources to provide for a family (Malthus 1992, p. 308). Only then could poverty be alleviated among the less fortunate groups of society. What was unthinkable to Malthus, however, was that this restraint could be achieved within marriage, by poor families deliberately limiting the number of children within marriage. Not until the neo-Malthusian movement in the late nineteenth century did these ideas receive increasing support.[7]

Malthus today

Is Malthus still relevant today? In one sense, the answer to this question is yes, definitely. The view that population growth is a major obstacle to economic growth and development has survived from Malthus into the twenty-first century, although the interest in global population growth has diminished somewhat in recent years due to widespread fertility decline in most parts of the world. As we have seen, Malthus believed that there was an intrinsic tendency of the population to outgrow the means of subsistence, leading to misery for the majority of the population. In the post-World War II period, the Malthusian perspective has been highly influential and has dominated the debate on population and economy, although the focus of interest has shifted over time.[8] In the 1950s, there was concern about the negative effects of rapid population growth on savings and investments, and thus ultimately on economic growth (Coale and Hoover 1958), while the 1960s and early 1970s saw a renewed focus on food shortage and overuse of non-renewable resources as the main effects of population growth. In his book *The Population Bomb*, American biologist Paul Ehrlich (1971) argued that it was already too late, and that millions of people would starve to death during the 1970s and 1980s.

Similar fears also characterized the report of the Club of Rome called *The Limits to Growth* in 1972 (Meadows et al. 1972). According to this report, the reserves of oil and gas would not last beyond 2030, and even though a revised, and less pessimistic, report was published two years later, the main concerns of rapid population growth was still the same (Mesarovic and Pestel 1974). In the 1980s and 1990s, the focus shifted towards environmental degradation, such as air pollution and deforestation leading to climate changes with potentially enormous effects on living conditions in many parts of the world (see, e.g., Ehrlich and Holdren 1971, UNFPA 1991, Bongaarts 1992, Harrison 1992, Kelley 2001).

Although this basically Malthusian view has been highly influential, there have been others, mostly economists, who have stressed the positive effects of a growing population, and the great potential of the economy to adapt to changing circumstances, making it less likely that we will ever reach a point where resources are totally used up (e.g., Simon 1981, see also Kelley 2001 for a review). Instead, the price mechanism will ensure that substitutions and technical change provide the solution to the challenges of population growth. In between the worst pessimists and the rosiest optimists, there is of course also a middle ground of scientists who worry about the consequences of population growth, but see solutions, even though these solutions often will require difficult policy measures and tough adjustments to many people's way of life (e.g., Cohen 1995).

While Malthus's basic analysis of the relationship between population and economy has survived, the same cannot be said about his views on poverty, as expressed in his analysis of the Poor Laws. The idea that improvements in the living conditions of the poorer segments of the population would only lead to increased procreation and population growth, while leaving the long-term standard of living unchanged, is not shared by many economists today. Quite the contrary: poverty is most often seen as the cause of high fertility and high rates of population growth because families living under uncertain circumstances need children both as labor and as insurance against sickness, unemployment, or old age (e.g., Lee 2000). Thus, relieving poverty in developing countries and introducing other measures of insurance against risk are now viewed as crucial parts of a strategy for bringing about a transition from high to low fertility.

Notes

1 Especially the 1803 edition was greatly enlarged with empirical sections describing the Principle of Population in different parts of the world. In 1990, Cambridge University Press published a two-volume version of the *Essay*, edited by Patricia James. It takes the 1803 edition as its base and includes changes made in subsequent editions, and also includes the material remaining from the *First Essay* of 1798. Here, the short version of this edition, Malthus (1992), has been used.

2 There are also other studies confirming the basic Malthusian character of pre-industrial England, in the sense that wages were stationary in the long term and that there was a relationship between medium-term changes in population and wages; see, e.g., Lee and Anderson (2002), Crafts and Mills (2009).

3 In the short run, however, there was a clear relationship between year-to-year changes in grain prices and both mortality and fertility; see Lee (1981), Galloway (1988); Lee and Anderson (2002).

4 Malthus's analysis of poverty and his views on the English Poor Laws has been dealt with in several surveys of Malthus's work, for example Bonar (1885), Smith (1951), Winch (1987), Petersen (1979), and has also been critically examined in empirical analyzes, for instance, by Blaug (1963, 1964), Huzel (1969, 1986), Krause (1958), and Boyer (1990).

5 The relief system discussed by Malthus was the Old Poor Laws, as opposed to the New Poor Laws of 1834. The Old Poor Laws was a collection of various assistance forms, and since it was mainly implemented at a local level, there were also large regional variations. Until the late eighteenth century, assistance was mainly given to those unable to work because of age or sickness, but later acts also contained increasing assistance to able-bodied workers whose incomes were not enough to support their families. In some areas levels of minimum standards were set up and assistance were given to those whose income fell below these standards (see, e.g., Blaug 1963). This allowance system often included special assistance for families with more children and it was this aspect of the Poor Laws that drew most of Malthus's attention. See also Boyer (1990) for an economic analysis of the Old Poor Law system.

6 Stapleton, however, also cited an unpublished work by Malthus (The Crisis, A View of the Present Interesting State of Great Britain, by a Friend to the Constitution) which contains more recognition of this problem and where Malthus maintains that society has an obligation to provide for those who are unable to provide for themselves (Stapleton 1986, p. 33).

7 The proponents of this movement agreed with the basic Malthusian analysis of poverty but argued strongly for deliberate family planning within marriage as a way to relieve poverty. One of the pioneers of this neo-Malthusian movement in Sweden was the economist Knut Wicksell, who in a number of lectures around the country argued that poverty, which was aggravated by population growth, was the root of excessive drinking and other miseries (see, e.g., Wicksell 1880). He saw the use of contraceptives to limit the sizes of the poor families as an important instrument in relieving poverty.

8 See for example Wilmoth and Ball (1992) for an analysis of the population debate in American popular magazines. See also the review of the population debate in Kelley (2001).

References

Blaug, M. (1963). The Myth of the Old Poor Law and the Making of the New. *Journal of Economic History*, *23*(2), 151–184.

Blaug, M. (1964). The Poor Law Report Reexamined. *Journal of Economic History*, *24*(2), 229–245.

Boberg-Fazlic, N., Sharp, P., and Weisdorf, J. (2011). Survival of the Richest? Social Status, Fertility and Social Mobility in England 1541–1824. *European Review of Economic History*, 15(3), 365–392.

Bonar, J. (1885). *Malthus and His Work*. London: Macmillan.

Bongaarts, J. (1992). Population Growth and Global Warming. *Population and Development Review*, *18*(2), 299–319.

Boyer, G.R. (1990). *An Economic History of the English Poor Law, 1750–1850*. Cambridge: Cambridge University Press.

Clark, G. (2007). *A Farewell to Alms. A Brief Economic History of the World*. Princeton, NJ: Princeton University Press.

Clark, G. and Cummins, N. (2009). Urbanization, Mortality, and Fertility in Malthusian England. *American Economic Review: Papers and Proceedings*, *99*(2), 242–247.

Clark, G. and Cummins, N. (2015). Malthus to Modernity: Wealth, Status, and Fertility in England, 1500–1879. *Journal of Population Economics*, *28*(1), 3–29.

Coale, A.J. and Hoover, E.M. (1958). *Population Growth and Economic Development in Low-Income Countries*. Princeton, NJ: Princeton University Press.

Cohen, J. (1995). *How Many People Can the Earth Support?* New York: W. W. Norton & Company.

Crafts, N. and Mills, T.C. (2009). From Malthus to Solow: How Did the Malthusian Economy Really Evolve? *Journal of Macroeconomics*, *31*(1), 68–93.

Digby, A. (1986). Malthus and Reform of the English Poor Law. In M. Turner (ed.), *Malthus and his Time* (pp. 157–169). London: Macmillan.

Ehrlich, P.R. (1971). *The Population Bomb*, second edition. New York: Ballantine Books Inc.

Ehrlich, P.R. and Holdren, J.P. (1971). Impact of Population Growth. *Science, 171*, 1212–1217.

Galloway, P.R. (1988). Basic Patterns in Annual Variations in Fertility, Nuptiality, Mortality and Prices in Preindustrial Europe. *Population Studies*, *42*(2), 275–303.

Hajnal, J. (1965). European Marriage Patterns in Perspective. In D.V. Glass and D.E.C. Eversley (eds), *Population in History. Essays in Historical Demography* (pp. 101–144). London: Edward Arnold.

Hajnal, J. (1983). Two Kinds of Preindustrial Household Formation System. In R. Wall, J. Robin, and P. Laslett (eds), *Family Forms in Historic Europe* (pp. 65–104). Cambridge: Cambridge University Press.

Harrison, P. (1992). *The Third Revolution. Environment, Population and a Sustainable World*. London: I.B. Tauris.

Huzel, J.P. (1969). Malthus, the Poor Law, and Population in Early Nineteenth-Century England. *Economic History Review*, *22*(3), 430–452.

Huzel, J.P. (1986). The Demographic Impact of the Old Poor Laws: More Reflections on Malthus. In M. Turner (ed.), *Malthus and his Time* (pp. 40–59). London: Macmillan.

Kelley, A.C. (2001). The Population Debate in Historical Perspective: Revisionism Revised. In N.A. Birdsall, A.C. Kelley, and S. Sinding (eds), *Population Matters: Demographic Change, Economic Growth, and Poverty in the Developing World* (pp. 24–54). Oxford: Oxford University Press.

Krause, J.T. (1958). Changes in English Fertility and Mortality, 1781–1850. *Economic History Review, 11*(1), 52–70.

Kuznets, S. (1966). *Modern Economic Growth: Rate, Structure, and Spread*. New Haven, CT: Yale University Press.

Lee, R.D. (1980). A Historical Perspective on Economic Aspects of the Population Explosion: The Case of Preindustrial England. In R.A. Easterlin (ed.), *Population and Economic Change in Developing Countries*. Chicago, IL: University of Chicago Press, pp. 517–566.

Lee, R.D. (1981). Short-Term Variation: Vital Rates, Prices and Weather. In E.A. Wrigley and R.S. Schofield, *The Population History of England. A Reconstruction* (pp. 356–401). London: Edward Arnold.

Lee, R.D. (2000). A Cross Cultural Perspective on International Transfers and the Economic Life Cycle. In A. Mason and G. Tapinos (eds), *Sharing the Wealth: Demographic Change and Economic Transfers Between Generations* (pp. 17–56). Oxford: Oxford University Press.

Lee, R.D. and Anderson, M. (2002). Malthus in State Space: Macro Economic-Demographic Relations in English History, 1540 to 1870. *Journal of Population Economics, 15*(2), 195–220.

Lee, J.Z. and Feng, W. (1999). *One Quarter of Humanity. Malthusian Mythology and Chinese Realities*. Cambridge, MA: Harvard University Press.

Malthus, T.R. (1826). *An Essay on the Principle of Population*. 2 Vols., 6th edition. London: John Murray.

Malthus, T.R. (1959). *Population: The First Essay*. Ann Arbor: University of Michigan Press.

Malthus, T.R. (1992). *An Essay on the Principle of Population*. Cambridge: Cambridge University Press.

Meadows, D.H., Meadows, D.L., Randers, J. and Behrens, W.W. (1972). *The Limits to Growth. A Report for the Club of Rome's Project on the Predicament of Mankind*. London: Earth Island.

Mesarovic, M. and Pestel, E. (1974). *Mankind at the Turning Point. The Second Report to the Club of Rome*. New York: E. P. Dutton & Co.

Nicolini, E.A. (2007). Was Malthus Right? A VAR Analysis of Economic and Demographic Interactions in Pre-Industrial England. *European Review of Economic History, 11*(1), 99–121.

Petersen, W. (1979). *Malthus*. London: Heinemann.

Simon, J.L. (1981). *The Ultimate Resource*. Princeton, NJ: Princeton University Press.

Smith, K. (1951). *The Malthusian Controversy*. London: Routledge and Kegan Paul.

Stapleton, B. (1986). Malthus: The Origin of the Principle of Population. In M. Turner (ed.), *Malthus and His Time* (pp. 19–39). London: Macmillan.

United Nations Population Fund. (1991). *Population and the Environment: The Challenges Ahead*. New York: UNFPA.

Wicksell, K. (1880). *Några ord om samhällsolyckornas viktigaste orsak och botemedel med särskilt afseende på dryckenskapen*. Upsala: På författarens förlag.

Wilmoth, J.R. and Ball, P. (1992). The Population Debate in American Popular Magazines 1946–1990. *Population and Development Review, 18*(4), 631–668.

Winch, D. (1987). *Malthus*. Oxford: Oxford University Press.

Wrigley, E.A. and Schofield, R.S. (1981). *The Population History of England. A Reconstruction*. London: Edward Arnold.

4   David Ricardo on poverty

Christian Gehrke

David Ricardo's views on the causes and cures of poverty can be inferred from his statements and activities in three different but interrelated roles: from his writings as an economic theorist, from his speeches and activities as a member of parliament and parliamentary commissions, and from his engagements in charitable institutions as a wealthy stock-jobber-turned-landowner and British citizen.

As an economic theorist, Ricardo envisaged poverty as being closely related to the determinants of the long-term trend of real wages. He argued that a sustained reduction of poverty is conditional on a lowering of the population growth rate and a high rate of capital accumulation under free international trade. Provided that the rate of population growth is not exceeding the rate of capital accumulation, and food prices are not raised artificially by restrictions on corn imports, economic growth and productivity-enhancing technical progress could permanently keep the level of real wages above subsistence. While he focused his attention mainly on the long-run growth trend of the economic system, Ricardo acknowledged the existence of short-run fluctuations of output and employment. Because of his adherence to Say's law of markets, however, he denied the possibility of a 'general glut' of commodities. Phases of economic depression or 'national distress', characterized by mass unemployment, depressed real wages, and starvation, he attributed to sectoral imbalances arising from 'sudden changes in the channels of trade', to bad harvests in combination with corn import restrictions, or to monetary disturbances. Accordingly, the remedies he proposed for overcoming such crises consisted of a return to a sound monetary system, the removal of restrictions on inter-sectoral capital mobility and international trade, and policy measures that helped to restore favorable conditions for capital accumulation and economic growth. Ricardo's views of the effects of the introduction of machinery on the working class underwent a dramatic change, but this did not shake his faith in the belief that permanently higher living standards for the working poor could be achieved only in a growing economy, characterized by a high rate of accumulation and continuous labor-saving technological change.

Ricardo's general stance on issues of social policy can be explained by the underlying theoretical principles of his political economy noted above and by his partial adherence to the Malthusian population principle. He was strongly opposed to all forms of government intervention that might encourage population increase and thus destroy the prospects of improved living standards for the working classes. This is reflected in Ricardo's attitude to poor relief and Poor Law reform, and in his activities as a member of parliament and various parliamentary committees. He vigorously advocated the repeal of the old English Poor Laws, rejected all labor market regulations that impeded competitive wage-setting or conferred privileges to particular groups of workers, and was decidedly opposed to public works programs, even if funded by charitable contributions. He also rejected public expenditures in support of Robert Owen's initiatives for generating employment and raising wages, because he considered them to be incompatible with the principles of political economy. As a private citizen and propertied landowner, however, Ricardo actively supported a number of voluntary programs for poverty reduction, including one of Owen's relief schemes. Moreover, he engaged in the establishment and management of three savings banks for workers, served on the board of a society for the promotion of elementary education for children of the lower classes, and maintained from his own pocket two schools for children of the poor.

In this essay, Ricardo's views on the causes of poverty and its remedies will be organized along the lines of the aforementioned tripartite structure. It will be shown that his theoretical views differed in some important respects from those of Malthus, and that his statements and activities in those three roles, in spite of the existence of some seemingly incongruous elements, are mutually compatible.

The essay is organized as follows. The next section is devoted to a discussion of the theoretical background of Ricardo's views on the causes of poverty. We will take a closer look at his theory of the long-term trend of wages, his explanation of economic crises, and his analysis of the machinery problem. The section 'Ricardo on the Poor Laws and various social policy measures' deals with Ricardo's attitude, as a member of parliament and parliamentary commissions, to poor relief and Poor Law reform and to other social policy measures. The following section discusses Ricardo's private initiatives and engagement in charitable institutions for improving the living conditions of the working poor, and the final section offers some concluding remarks.

The theoretical background to Ricardo's attitude to poverty and poor relief

Determinants of the long-term trend of real wages

For Ricardo, the causes and remedies of poverty are closely related to the determinants of the long-term trend of real wages, and of short-term fluctuations around this trend. The former is determined by the level of the 'natural wage', and the latter are reflected in movements of the 'market wage' around this trend. In his *On the Principles of Political Economy, and Taxation*,[1] Ricardo defined the natural wage as 'that price which is necessary to enable the laborers, one with another, to subsist and to perpetuate their race, without either increase or diminution' (*Works* I, p. 93). Its level must enable the workers to purchase the set of commodities, consisting of 'food, necessaries, and conveniences', which have become 'essential from habit' for the worker and his family (*Works* I, p. 93). Ricardo stressed that 'subsistence requirements' should not be seen as strict physiological necessities (*Works* I, p. 100).

When the prices of necessaries change, money wages will have to change as well in order to keep the natural wage constant in real terms. Because of the cultural and conventional elements in the determination of 'subsistence wages', Ricardo argued that increases of the latter were both possible and desirable (*Works* I, p. 100). After thus defining the 'natural price of labor', Ricardo introduced the concept of the 'market price of labor' (*Works* I, p. 94; emphasis added):

> The market price of labour is the price which is really paid for it, from the natural operation of *the proportion of the supply to the demand*; labour is dear when it is scarce, and cheap when it is plentiful. However much the market price of labour may deviate from its natural price, it has, like commodities, a tendency to conform to it.

This 'tendency' Ricardo, like Malthus, attributed to population adjustments induced by wage variations (*Works* I, p. 94).

Market wages, then, are supposed to be governed by 'the proportion of the supply to the demand', and the statements quoted above would seem to suggest that wages can be raised above (or fall below) the subsistence level only temporarily. However, while drawing a close analogy between the tendency of market wages to fluctuate around the natural wage and that of market prices around natural prices, Ricardo emphasized the slowness of the adjustment processes in the former case, due to the time required for changes in population growth to make themselves felt in the labor market (*Works* I, p. 165; see also *Works* I, p. 220). Therefore, (market) wages might be kept permanently above subsistence in an 'improving society', where the rate of capital accumulation is constantly ahead of the rate of population growth (*Works* I, pp. 94–95).

Which, then, is the trend of real wages in the 'natural course of economic development', where capital accumulates and the population grows, but there is no technical progress? In the *Essay on Profits* (1815), Ricardo assumed that 'capital and population advance in the proper proportion, so that the real wages of labor continue uniformly the same' (*Works* IV, p. 12). He emphasized that this was a simplifying assumption, introduced only in order that 'we may know what peculiar effects are to be ascribed to the growth of capital, the increase of population and the extension of cultivation to the more remote and less fertile land' (*Works* IV, p. 12). Ricardo's aim was to bring out the effect of diminishing returns in agriculture on the profit rate; for this purpose, it was convenient to assume a constant real wage. However, Ricardo stressed that real wages were influenced by, and bound to change with, fluctuations in 'the proportion of the supply to the demand' for labor (*Works* IV, p. 23).

In the *On the Principles of Political Economy, and Taxation*, Ricardo likewise argued that in the 'natural course of economic development' the rate of capital accumulation, and thus the demand for labor, must slow down because of diminishing returns in agriculture (*Works* I, p. 101). Because of rising food prices money wages must rise in order to keep real wages at the subsistence level. Ricardo therefore stated a tendency of wages to conform to the subsistence level. However, he did not favor low real wages and a high rate of profit. He made this clear in his *Notes on Malthus*: '[F]or great as I estimate the benefits resulting from high profits I never wish to see those profits increased at the expense of the labouring class' (*Works* II, p. 373). In another note, Ricardo observed that he fully agreed with Malthus's statement that 'if a country can only be rich by running a successful race for low wages, I should be disposed to say at once, perish such riches!' (*Works* II, p. 220). And he added, 'We want the labourer to be abundantly provided, and maintain that the way to effect it is, by making the labour price of the chief commodity he consumes cheap' (*Works* II, p. 220). The import of cheap corn could keep down money wages and raise the rate of profits, which, in turn, would increase the rate of capital accumulation, and thus the demand for labor. Ricardo therefore relentlessly urged for the repeal of the Corn Laws, both in print and as a member of parliament.

In order for the laborers to be 'abundantly provided', it was also necessary, apart from a low corn price and a high rate of capital accumulation, that the workers participate in the sharing out of productivity gains from the introduction of technological improvements. Ricardo believed that those gains would be partly enjoyed by the workers in the form of rising real wages.[2] When Malthus criticized him for neglecting the fact that improvements must lower prices and raise 'the price of labour, estimated in necessaries' so that after a productivity increase 'the same number of commodities could not employ the same number of men' as before, Ricardo commented, 'I know it, and am rejoiced at it. If they could, all the advantage would go to profits. It is highly desirable that a part should go to increase the enjoyments of the labourer' (*Works* II, p. 373).[3]

Because he (partly) adopted Malthus's population theory, Ricardo is often supposed to have concurred also with the latter's position on the causes of poverty and distress. It is important to note therefore that Ricardo explicitly rejected Malthus's view that population increases must invariably be *preceded* by increases in food production (*Works* I, pp. 406–407). Moreover, Ricardo dismissed Malthus's 'wages fund reasoning' not only with regard to the latter's argument on the food supply-population nexus but also with regard to the alleged trade-off between the levels of wages and employment. Commenting on a passage in the fifth edition of the *Essay on Population* (1817), in which Malthus had asserted that 'Dr. Smith has clearly shown that the natural ten-dency of a year of scarcity is either to throw a number of labourers out of employment, or to oblige them to work for less than before', Ricardo drily noted (*Works* VII, pp. 202–203):

> I can neither agree with Adam Smith nor with you ... You do not always appear to me to admit that the tendency of the poor laws is to increase the quantity of food to be divided, but assume in some places that the same quantity is to be divided among a larger number.

Ricardo took exception also to Malthus's assertion that the two proposals, to fix a maximum price of provisions, and to proportion the price of labor to the price of provisions, 'are very nearly of the same nature ... both tend directly to famine' (*Works* VII, note, p. 203). On this he commented, 'A maximum tends to discourage future production, an undue increase of wages, or poor laws, tend to promote it' (*Works* VII, p. 203). He thus considered the supply of food to be governed by, and to adapt to, the effective demand for it: If the workers received higher money wages, and thus could increase their demand for food, its production would be expanded accordingly.

On causes and remedies of 'national distress'

In his *On the Principles of Political Economy, and Taxation*, Ricardo treated the depression after the Napoleonic wars as an example of those 'temporary reverses and contingencies' to which a great manufacturing country is par-ticularly exposed when capital has to be removed from one employment to another due to 'sudden changes in the channels of trade' (*Works* I, p. 263). The severe depression, which lasted roughly from fall 1815 to spring 1817 (Davis 2005, pp. 51–52), Ricardo attributed to a mismatch in the supply and demand structure, with excess supply of some and excess demand for other commodities. During the necessary adjustment processes, 'considerable dis-tress ... will be experienced by those who are engaged in the manufacture of such commodities', but this 'is an evil to which a rich nation must submit' (*Works* I, pp. 263, 266). Thus (*Works* I, p. 266),

> In rich and powerful countries, where large capitals are invested in machinery, more distress will be experienced from a revulsion in trade, than in poorer countries where there is proportionally a much smaller amount of fixed, and a much larger amount of circulating capital, and where consequently more work is done by the labour of man.

Ricardo stressed that such revulsions should not be confused with a dim-inution of the national capital in a retrograding society, even though the two states appear to be characterized by similar external signs, such as high unemployment and low wages. Depressions were not seen as an unavoidable cyclical concomitant of economic development that arose out of the inherent nature of the economic system, but rather as the result of 'shocks' or external disturbances that led to temporary adjustment problems, such as a war (or its termination), a bad harvest, or a change in technology. Because he regarded the problem to be caused by structural imbalances rather than by an insufficient aggregate demand, Ricardo maintained that the adjustment was best left to market processes, 'with low and high wage and profit levels playing their normal role in reallocating capital and labour from less to more rewarding outlets' (Winch 1996, p. 361). Ricardo's policy recommendations for dealing with the post-war distress therefore were to reintroduce a proper metallic base for the currency and to restore favorable conditions for capital accumulation and economic growth, primarily through reducing taxes and the burden of the national debt, the removal of restrictions on inter-sectoral capital mobility, and in particular the repeal of the Corn Laws, which exerted a downward pressure on profits (Winch 1996, pp. 360–361).

Implications of Ricardo's new view on machinery

When, during the post-war depression of 1815–1817, several groups of workers petitioned against the introduction of machinery in their industries, Ricardo was not yet in Parliament, but the views on machinery he had expounded in the first edition of his *On the Principles of Political Economy, and Taxation* provided support for those who opposed those petitions. Ricardo had maintained that the introduction of machinery in wage goods industries was advantageous not only to capitalists and landlords but also to the working class, because it checked the tendency of the rate of profits to fall and lowered the prices of necessaries (*Works* I, p. 120). In a parliamentary speech in December 1819, he claimed that 'it could not be denied, on the whole view of the subject, that machinery did not lessen the demand for labour' (*Works* V, p. 30). But when in April 1823 the cotton weavers of Stockport petitioned against the introduction of machinery in their industry, Ricardo (*Works* V, p. 303), to the surprise of many members of Parliament, announced that

> it was evident that the extensive use of machinery, by throwing a large portion of labour into the market, while, on the other hand, there might not be a corresponding increase of demand for it, must, in some degree, operate prejudicially to the working classes.

Ricardo had first expounded his new view in 1821, when, in the newly added chapter 'On Machinery', he had declared, 'I am convinced that the substitution of machinery for human labour is often very injurious to the interests of the class of labourers' (*Works* I, p. 388). When confronted in Parliament with the argument that the wages of artisans were more liberal where machinery was used than where it was not, Ricardo replied that his point was (Gordon 1976, p. 167),

> not that the use of machinery was prejudicial to persons employed in one particular manufacture, but to the working classes generally. It was the means of throwing additional labour on the market, and thus the demand for labour, generally, was diminished.

Moreover, Ricardo had argued that rising food prices due to diminishing agricultural returns must lead to rising money wages, which, in turn, provided incentives for substituting machinery for human labor: 'Machinery and labour are in constant competition, and the former can frequently not be employed until labour rises' (*Works* I, p. 395). This implied that with rising money wages newly accumulated capital would not be spent on additional wage advances, but rather on purchasing machinery. This seriously undermined the proportionality that Ricardo had presumed to exist between capital accumulation and the demand for labor (*Works* I, p. 395). And since the level of real wages was supposed to depend crucially on the demand for labor, in proportion to its supply, this meant that the prospects for improving permanently the living conditions of the workers through a high rate of capital accumulation were less favorable than he had so far presumed. Ricardo's crusade against the Corn Laws, which kept money wages high by prohibiting the importation of cheap corn, thus became even more important for preventing real wages from deteriorating. Ricardo frankly admitted that his former views had been erroneous, and that 'the opinion entertained by the labouring class, that the employment of machinery is frequently detrimental to their interests, is not founded on prejudice and error, but is conformable to the correct principles of political economy' (*Works* I, p. 392). Nevertheless, he opposed all measures for prohibiting the introduction of machinery. His argument was that if employers were forced to abstain from introducing cost-reducing machinery they could no longer compete in international markets (*Works* I, pp. 396–397; see also *Works* V, p. 303).

Ricardo on the poor laws and on various social policy measures

The poor laws and poor law reform[4]

The old English Poor Law was introduced in the late sixteenth century in order to replace the very basic system of social welfare that before the Reformation had been provided by the monasteries to those in extreme poverty due to illness, infirmity, family breakdown, or temporary unemployment. It was administered by the local parish authorities and financed by a local tax (the 'poor rates') levied on landed property, extended later also to manufacturing structures. The Poor Law underwent a first major change with the passage of Gilbert's Act of 1782, which introduced the principle of 'outdoor' relief (outside of the workhouse) for able-bodied paupers. A yet more drastic modification was introduced in 1795, when a number of agricultural districts in southeast England, after a meeting of the magistrates at Speenhamland, Berkshire, started to use the poor rates as a subsidy to wages of farm workers in full-time (if only seasonal) employment in order to ensure a minimum level of subsistence (Blaug 1958, pp. 196–198). The money subsidy, which was indexed to the price of bread (the 'bread scale'), included also child allowances. The 'Speenhamland system' was a reaction by the authorities to unusually high food prices; it was aimed initially at preventing food riots and social unrest. This allowance system was supplemented by the 'Roundsman system', by which the farmers could buy the labor of the unemployed poor at a very low wage from the parish authorities, who supplemented the difference up to the minimum subsistence wage. This 'outdoor relief' system provided incentives to farmers for paying less than the minimum subsistence wages and making up the balance in the form of parish relief. The sentiments that dominated the public discourse among the upper classes on the existing Poor Laws in England in the early nineteenth century were that the child allowances 'encourage[d] calculated childbearing as a more expedient means of survival than disciplined productive labour' (Block and Somers 2003, p. 28). The Speenhamland system was widely supposed to produce, through its guaranteed subsistence income, significant work disincentive effects.

Ricardo's first appointment upon entering Parliament was to the Poor Law Committee of 1819. However, his interest in social policy and in England's welfare system began long before he entered Parliament. His first statements on the Poor Laws are found in his correspondence from 1816–1817, when he was engaged in composing the passages relating to those laws for his *On the Principles of Political Economy, and Taxation* (*Works* I, pp. 105–108). 'Is it not desirable that the poor laws should be done away [with], and the laboring classes should receive the recompense for their labour rather in the shape of wages than in that of bounty?' (*Works* VII, p. 124). His opposition to the Poor Laws was based on the belief that the system was unsustainable in the long run because it provided strong incentives for reduced work effort and increased child-bearing (*Works* I, pp. 107–108).

Ricardo stressed, in particular, the long-term effects of guaranteed relief, which he considered to lead to the moral, physical, and intellectual degradation of the laboring poor (*Works* I, p. 108). He was seriously concerned about the increasing tax burden from the poor rates, which (especially in conjunction with the taxes raised for repaying the national debt) would drastically reduce the funds available for capital accumulation (*Works* I, pp. 105–106). That this had not yet happened Ricardo explained by 'the present mode of its collection and application', which had (*Works* I, p. 108),

> served to mitigate its pernicious effects. Each parish raises a separate fund for the support of its own poor. Hence it becomes an object of more

interest and more practicability to keep the rates low, than if one general fund were raised for the relief of the poor of the whole kingdom.

Ricardo was not only concerned about the general increase of the tax burden from the poor rates but also about their distributional effects. He therefore provided a detailed analysis of the incidence of the poor rates. Since in the case of agriculture the rates were levied in proportion to the actual value of the land (and not according to its rent value) and in the case of manufacturing in proportion to the value of the buildings (but not of the tools, machines, etc.), the tax burden had to be borne partly by the farmers and manufacturers, who, depending on the circumstances, would either have to make do with reduced profits or could shift the burden partly onto the consumers. 'Under some circumstances', Ricardo argued, the effects of the poor rates could 'be even advantageous rather than injurious to landlords' (*Works* I, p. 260).

Ricardo is often depicted, like Malthus, as a strict abolitionist, though as one who advocated a gradualist approach. He, in fact, variously emphasized that because the laws had been in force for too long, *immediate* repeal was impossible (*Works* I, p. 107, and *Works* VII, pp. 124–125):

> The ill effects of the poor laws then I suppose to be admitted and their abolition to be desirable the question then is how is it to be effected? Can it be by any other means than by gradually limiting their application, by encouraging the poor man to depend on his own exertions only? Is not this to be done by refusing all relief in the first instance to any but those whose necessities absolutely require it—to administer it to them in the most sparing manner, and lastly to abolish the poor laws altogether?

While Ricardo advocated gradualism, there remains some ambiguity with regard to the question whether the ultimate goal for him must necessarily consist in the complete abolition of the Poor Laws. John McCulloch, his most ardent disciple, suggested in 1830 that Ricardo would have favored a return to the Elizabethan statute.[5] In January 1818, Ricardo, indeed, indicated that he could consent to Poor Law reform, provided it removed incentives for population increase (see *Works* VII, p. 248). Moreover, in *On the Principles of Political Economy, and Taxation* Ricardo spoke of the Speenhamland system as a 'misapplication of the poor laws' (*Works* I, p. 162). Confining the 'abolition' to the measures of the Speenhamland system and returning to the Elizabethan statute may therefore, indeed, have been a course Ricardo would have endorsed. It must also be stressed that when Ricardo lamented the work disincentives triggered by the existing Poor Laws, this was *not* because he condemned idleness as immoral, but rather because idleness was liable to give rise to 'profligate and mischievous pursuits' (*Works* VII, pp. 184–185).

Ricardo generally supported all measures that could help to reduce the long-term supply of labor. He believed that improved living standards from rising real wages, a better education, the financial security deriving from workers' savings, and the inculcation of 'prudential habits' among the working classes could eventually lead to a lowering of the rate of growth of the population and of the labor supply. Voluntary restraint was, indeed, the main long-term remedy he proposed in a parliamentary speech in May 1823 (*Works* V, p. 303). Whether this also included artificial birth control devices (such as the use of sea sponges) is not known. It is not clear therefore how far Ricardo's support for a rational population policy went beyond a concerted campaign advocating voluntary restraint. Unlike John Stuart Mill, some decades later, he carefully avoided any explicit proposal of contraceptive measures, even in his private correspondence. Although he thought it unwise 'even to mention it' in public discourse, he also 'does not seem to have taken exception to Francis Place's claim', when commenting on the latter's manuscript (*Works* IX, p. 62) 'that artificial preventatives were to be favored over moral restraint' (Milgate and Stimson 1991, note, p. 117).

In discussions about appropriate measures for poor relief with Hutches Trower in 1818, Ricardo also rejected relief schemes that relied on voluntary contributions: 'To relieve the poor by any *extended* exercise of private charity would hardly be less objectionable than the evil of which we now complain' (*Works* VII, p. 248). Ricardo agreed with Trower's view that in times of national distress relief could not be suddenly withheld, and added, 'Great evils however result from the idea which the Poor Laws inculcate that the poor have a *right* to relief' (*Works* VII, p. 248).

As a member of the Poor Law Committee of 1819, Ricardo put forward similar arguments. In a speech on the second reading of the Poor Rates Misapplication Bill, on 17 May 1819, he reportedly opposed the bill (*Works* V, pp. 6–7):

> principally on the ground that it tended to increase the population. If at present there existed a difficulty of supporting the poor, in what situation would the country be placed in twenty years hence, when these children so educated grew up to manhood?

Ricardo's analysis of the causes of the plight of the poor and the solutions he proposed were similar to the analysis and proposals advanced by the committee in 1819. According to the committee report, the current distress of the laboring class reflected an unusually low demand for labor at a time when the labor force was expanding. The rapid population growth was attributed to the operation of the Poor Laws, while the funds available for capital accumulation, and thus the demand for labor, were considered to be diminished by the burden of high poor rates. While suggesting extensive reductions in poor relief in the medium and long run, the committee proposed that because of the current distress no changes to the laws should be implemented in 1819. The immediate recommendations of the report were limited to the removal of impediments to 'the free circulation of labor' and emigration; it also recommended, however, that ultimately parishes should be freed from 'the impracticable obligation of finding employment' for all who needed it, and that relief should be strictly confined to those unable to work (*Works* V, p. xxiv).

In May 1821, Ricardo in a parliamentary speech endorsed the Poor Relief Bill that would have prohibited the Roundsmen system (*Works* V, pp. 113–114). The effect of the measure would be, he argued, 'to regulate the price of labour by the demand, and that was the end peculiarly desired' (*Works* V, p. 114). It is difficult to ascertain whether high poor rates, indeed, led to low wages and high unemployment rates by stimulating population increase, as Malthus and Ricardo feared, or vice versa. Starting with Blaug (1963), twentieth-century historiography has rejected a direct effect of the Poor Laws in depressing wages and fostering population growth[6]; 'rather, increasing poor relief, demoralization of the laboring poor and distress of farming were considered as different aspects of an overall milieu that characterized the English early phase of industrialization' (Opocher 2015, p. 408).

Ricardo on public works

The year 1816 had witnessed the first experiment of the century in a policy of works for the relief of unemployment. Relief works were 'carried on in London and various parts of the country since the autumn of 1816, with funds raised by private subscriptions; in Edinburgh 1600 men were employed in making and improving roads' (*Works* VII, note, p. 116). Ricardo considered such programs for generating employment ineffective. His argument was that, when funded by taxes or charitable contributions, they merely diverted capital from other uses, and thus could not generate any *additional* employment. Because he believed that hoarding only occurred during severe financial crises, the alternative to contributing to the funding of relief works was, for him, not hoarding, but investing or consuming (Davis 2005, p. 169). The funds raised for setting the poor to work merely reduced private expenditures that otherwise would have generated productive employments elsewhere, thus adding nothing to the numbers employed (*Works* VII, p. 116). In a letter to Malthus, who supported such programs,[7] Ricardo wrote in January 1817 (*Works* VII, p. 116),

> I am not one of those who think that the raising of funds for the purpose of employing the poor is a very efficacious mode of relief, as it diverts those funds from other employments which would be equally if not more productive to the community. That part of the capital which employs the poor on the roads for example cannot fail but employ men somewhere and I believe every interference is prejudicial.

Ricardo adopted the same stance when during the 1819 depression the question was put before Parliament whether to adopt a measure, such as the 1817 Employment of the Poor Bill, by which Exchequer bills would be loaned to municipalities in Scotland to finance public works. In a parliamentary speech in December 1819, he cautioned the House against 'employing capital in the formation of roads and canals', because 'the capital thus employed must be withdrawn from some other quarter' (*Works* V, p. 32).

Ricardo's attitude to Owen's initiatives for poor relief

In June 1819, Ricardo became a member of a (privately organized) committee for considering Robert Owen's plan for ameliorating the condition of the lower classes. The 'plan' was the one proposed earlier by Owen to the parliamentary Poor Law Committee of 1817, which involved 'the establishment of small, self-contained communities in which the members shared a moderately communalized life style. Productive activity was to be a blend of agricultural and industrial pursuits, but the use of machinery in the latter was carefully controlled' (Gordon 1976, p. 65). Ricardo was reluctant to enter this committee, as he dissented from all of Owen's conclusions (*Works* VIII, pp. 45–46).

In July 1819, Ricardo was appointed to the committee, which appealed for the subscription of £100,000 for the establishment of an agricultural and manufacturing community as an experiment on the lines of New Lanark. On 1 December 1819, as the subscriptions amounted to less than £8,000, the committee resigned and in a final resolution urged that the government should facilitate the experiment by granting a portion of the Crown lands and use the funds raised so far for the relief of the poor (*Works* V, p. 468). Soon afterwards, a motion was presented to the Lower House for appointing a Select Committee for inquiring into Owen's plan (*Works* V, p. 30). The motion was turned down by 141 to 16 votes. Ricardo voted for the motion (*Works* V, p. 218).

In June 1822, Ricardo spoke on the occasion of a petition from the miners, iron-makers, and coal-masters of Dudley, 'praying that the House would enjoin a more strict observance of the law, which directs that labourers should be paid only in money, and not in provisions or other commodities' (*Works* V, p. 217). Ricardo opposed this petition (*Works* V, p. 218). He thus lent his support to Owen's idea of a provision system, even though he may not have been fully convinced of its beneficial effects. His main reason for opposing the petition rather seems to have been his zeal for non-interference with markets.

In June 1823, Ricardo became a member of a Select Committee on the Labouring Poor in Ireland, 'with a view to facilitating the application of the Funds of Private Individuals and Associations for their Employment in Useful and Productive Labour'. The appointment of the committee was due to a petition from Ireland, asking the House to consider how far (*Works* V, p. xxvvii),[8]

> Owen's plan for the employment of the poor ... could be applied to the employment of the peasantry of Ireland. The report, while admitting that Owen's plan might be suitable for private experiment, regarded it as not a fit subject of legislative assistance.

Miscellaneous social policy issues

The Peterloo Massacre and the Six Acts

Throughout the special session called after the Peterloo Massacre in 1819,[9] Ricardo voted against the measures known as the 'Six Acts' (*Works* V, pp. xxii, 28–29). Ricardo approved of the workers' demands for political representation and electoral reform, which he regarded as a means for preventing a social revolution (Milgate and Stimson 1991, pp. 100–124). In August 1821, in the aftermath of further instances of social unrest and demands for political reform, he maintained, in a letter to James Mill, 'The only prospect we have of putting aside the struggle which ... has commenced between the rich and the other classes, is for the rich to yield what is justly due to the other classes' (*Works* IX, p. 45).

The combination laws and restrictions on emigration

Ricardo's zeal for unrestricted markets extended also to the labor market, where the Pitt government had deemed it necessary to interfere in the bargaining process between workers and masters by introducing the Combination Act, which effectively suppressed trade union activity. Ricardo never addressed the Combination Laws in Parliament, but to McCulloch he wrote in December 1820 that 'they appear to me to be unjust and oppressive to the working classes, and of little real use to masters' (*Works* VIII, p. 316). Interestingly, Ricardo's views on the Combination Laws differed from those of Malthus, who argued that combinations are 'not only illegal, but irrational and ineffectual' (Malthus [1798] 1992, p. 119). Ricardo disagreed, 'A combination among the workmen would increase the amount of money to be divided amongst the labouring class' (*Works* VII, p. 203). As opposed to Malthus, Ricardo denied that the increased demand for wage goods from higher money wages must necessarily raise the prices of necessaries, except temporarily. Therefore, if workers succeeded in raising the rate of money wages without increasing the prices of necessaries, real wages would rise (and the general rate of profits would fall). Further evidence for Ricardo's opposition to the Combination Laws comes from his support, in 1821, for Francis Place's proposal of the repeal of the Combination Laws and the laws restraining emigration (*Works* IX, p. 55). In January 1823, Ricardo in a letter to Wilmot Horton supported a government-financed emigration scheme, which (*Works* XI, p. xvi),

> would enable us to get rid of the most objectionable part of the poor laws, the relieving [of] able bodied men; and what is for me by far the most important consideration, it could not fail to make the wages of labour more adequate to the support of the labourer and his family, besides giving him that as wages which is now given to him as charity.

Moreover, in 1823, Ricardo had promised his friend Joseph Hume to assist him in Parliament in his proposed motion against the laws restricting the emigration of artisans and the combination of workmen, but his premature death prevented him from acting on this promise (*Works* V, p. xx).[10]

The merchant vessels apprenticeship bill

In March 1823, a committee was formed to consider a proposal by William Huskisson, according to which 'every merchant vessel should have a number of apprentices in proportion to her tonnage' (*Works* V, p. 273). Ricardo opposed this bill, because the employers 'would be enabled to lower the rate of wages by increasing the number of apprentices' (*Works* V, p. 273). In Ricardo's view, the bill was not likely to raise the number of skilled seamen, as its advocates supposed (*Works* V, p. 276). He opposed the measure 'as imposing injurious restrictions on a particular trade, and interfering with the private rights of individuals connected with the trade' (*Works* V, p. 282). Ricardo was unsuccessful, however, and the bill was passed.

The Spitalfields Act

In May 1823, a petition from the London silk manufacturers was presented to the Lower House requesting the repeal of the Spitalfields Act, introduced during the eighteenth century in order to encourage the growth of the silk industry in the Greater London district. It sanctioned collective bargaining, barred employers in the London area from investing their capital in similar enterprises elsewhere in Britain, and included regulations concerning entry of apprentices, wage rates for various qualities of work, manning scales for machine work, and protection of hand work against competition from machine production. Ricardo expressed his astonishment that such an 'archaic' legislation could still be in force and argued that he saw no good reason for delaying its repeal (*Works* V, pp. 292, 296). He was convinced that in the case of repeal (*Works* V, p. 307),

> no doubt the number of weavers employed in London would be greater than at present. They might not, indeed, receive such high wages; but it was improper that those wages should be artificially kept up by the interference of a magistrate.

A malt and beer tax

In 1823, a petition from the table beer and ale brewers of London was presented to the Lower House, suggesting to remove the tax from beer and place it on malt. The petitioners' argument was that 'this would place the poor man and the rich on an equality. At present, the poor man, who could not brew his beer, paid a tax from which the rich man was exempt' (*Works* V, p. 294). The report of Ricardo's speech on 28 May 1823 reads, 'If the duty paid ought to attach on all persons consuming beer, it ought to attach equally. The motion should have his hearty support, because it went to accomplish that object'. The motion was turned down by 119 votes to 27 (*Works* V, pp. 301–302).

Ricardo's engagements in charitable institutions for the poor

As we found above, in Parliament and in print, Ricardo was skeptical about projects for poor relief funded by voluntary contributions, such as public works programs, had serious doubts about Owen's initiatives, and also dismissed the idea of replacing the existing system by a charity-based system of poor relief. As a private citizen, however, he actively supported charitable institutions providing elementary education for children of the lower classes as well as the establishment of savings banks for workers (Henderson 1984, 1987, Watarai 2009).

Educational institutions

Ricardo's schools at Minchinhampton

Soon after he retired to Gatcombe Park in 1815, Ricardo established a school at the neighboring village of Minchinhampton, on the Lancasterian system,[11] in which about 250 boys and girls were admitted (*Works* VI, note, p. 45, *Works* X, p. 169). In a letter to James Mill in August 1823, Ricardo (*Works* IX, pp. 328–329) reported that the two schools (for boys and girls separately),

> are going well—Both of them are always full, and many boys and girls are waiting for vacancies to be admitted. ... Considering the little attention which I can pay to the school from my occasional absence from it, the master had done very well. I cannot help flattering myself that I am performing a real service to this place by supporting these institutions.

That Ricardo took a serious interest in educational matters is shown also by the fact that his library contained several pamphlets on the Lancaster system of education (*Works* X, p. 402) and that he participated actively in Bentham's initiative for the foundation of a Chrestomathic school.[12] Moreover, during his Continental tour in 1822, he reserved one day for visiting Mr. Fellenberg's school at Hofwyl (Switzerland), of which several enthusiastic accounts had been published in England (*Works* X, p. 262).

Brougham's infant school

It is noteworthy, however, that Ricardo was keen to ensure that his support was strictly confined to education only. When he was invited by

Henry Brougham—via James Mill—to support the establishment of an infant school for the children of the poor (*Works* VII, pp. 356–357), Ricardo responded that he could not possibly contribute 'if it is part of the plan ... to feed as well as to take care of and educate the children', but 'if it is proposed ... only to educate the children that are to be admitted into this institution, my objection is of no value, and in that case I will willingly contribute' (*Works* VII, pp. 359–360).

Savings banks

In the early nineteenth century, British banks generally did not accept small deposits, which created problems for the lower classes. In order to provide a remedy, the first savings banks were established and managed by people of higher social ranking as voluntary activities around 1810 in Scotland. The savings banks collected deposits from workers and either deposited the money with chartered banks at fixed interest rates or invested it in government bonds. The idea rapidly spread to England as well, where the first savings bank, the Bath Provident Institution, was established in 1815. Ricardo actively participated in the establishment and management of the Provident Institution for the Western Part of the Metropolis (also known as the Westminster Bank for Savings), which was instituted on 1 January 1816. In reply to the question of his friend Hutches Trower to what he thought of savings banks, Ricardo responded on 4 February 1816 (*Works* VII, p. 16),

> I think them excellent institutions and calculated to improve the condition and morals of the poor, provided they are properly managed. My fear is that though they will at first be established by gentlemen of great respectability and fortune,—as they spread, they will at last be undertaken by speculative tradesmen, as a business from which to derive profit. The poor should have some check on the employment of the funds, or the same evils will arise as from the indefinite multiplication of country Banks.

In a further letter to Trower, Ricardo argued that these banks could not possibly provide a remedy for poor relief in the short run, but their long-term effects could be beneficial (*Works* VII, p. 26). The Westminster Savings Bank was so successful that after a few months the managers and trustees decided to open two other banks in greater London, which soon prospered as well. In 1817, Ricardo was active also in the formation of a savings bank in Tetbury, Gloucestershire. This was less successful in raising deposits, because manufacturing workers typically were more skeptical of Provident Institutions (*Works* VII, p. 220). Ricardo's interest in savings banks never waned, but after 1817, he was no longer active in their operation (Henderson 1987, p. 397).

Finally, an interesting fact to note about Ricardo's attitude to the laboring poor as a private citizen is that his practice as an employer ran counter to his own 'dogma' of competitive wage setting (Poynter 1969, p. 245). In November 1820, when asked by Trower if money wages in Gloucestershire had been reduced, as they had in Surrey, with the fall in the price of provisions, Ricardo replied, 'I believe they have lowered the price of labour here, but I, as a gentleman, I suppose, always pay the same' (*Works* VIII, p. 307).

Concluding remarks

Ricardo was convinced that the main precondition for a permanent and not merely transient reduction of poverty was a sustained reduction of the growth of the labor supply. Therefore, he rejected all forms of government interventions and relief schemes that might encourage population increase, and thus destroy all prospects of improved living conditions for the poor. He advocated a gradual repeal of the Poor Laws, particularly of the measures introduced in the Speenhamland system because he believed that this system failed to provide any incentives for restricting population growth. In his view, the current system encouraged the poor to look for systematic relief rather than to their own actions and exertions as remedies.

Ricardo's views on proper measures for short- and long-term poverty reduction underwent no major change with his candid admission of his erroneous former views on the machinery question. In Parliament, he continued to oppose any petition from groups of workers for restricting the introduction of machinery in their industries, although he now admitted that technological unemployment and 'considerable distress' are the likely short- and medium-run effects when improved machinery is 'suddenly discovered, and extensively used' (*Works* I, p. 395). Moreover, he also stressed that rising food prices from diminishing agricultural returns must lead to rising money wages, which, in turn, induced the substitution of machinery for labor. He thus acknowledged that distributional changes that are *inherently* produced in the course of economic development will lead to a reduced demand for labor. This implied that because of the increasing ratio of fixed to circulating capital the demand for labor could not be expected to increase in proportion to the rate of capital accumulation, so the long-term prospects of poverty reduction were less favorable than he had previously presumed. He argued, however, that real wages could still expected to rise if the workers had a share in the productivity gains that were associated with improvements in the manufacturing sector (cf. Gehrke 2015).

While Ricardo endorsed some elements of the Malthusian population theory, and in particular the idea of the dependence of the population growth rate on the level of real wages, he explicitly rejected the wages fund reasoning of Malthus. According to Ricardo, the stimulus for increasing the supply of necessaries provided by an increased effective demand was sufficient to encourage the application of additional capital in the production of food. This had important implications, because it meant that if the workers succeeded in their demands for higher money wages, or if money wages were indexed to the 'bread scale', this could well be effective in raising real wages.

As a private citizen, Ricardo's main aim when promoting savings banks and elementary education was 'to improve the condition and morals of the poor', and to 'inculcate' virtues like 'prudence, economy, and forethought' in the laborers and their offspring. His private initiatives for poverty reduction were fully in line with his long-term vision and (apart from his deliberate disregard of his own policy recommendation of competitive wage setting) compatible with his general theoretical outlook on the causes and cures of poverty.

Notes

1 See Ricardo (*Works* I). In this chapter, all references to Ricardo's *Works and Correspondence* (1951–1973) are given as *Works*, followed by the volume and page numbers.

2 Ricardo's concept of 'proportional wages' implied that commodity wages could rise with constant (or even falling) proportional wages; see Milgate and Stimson (1991, pp. 114–116) and Gehrke (2013).

3 See also Ricardo's statement in the third edition of his *On the Principles of Political Economy, and Taxation*: 'More is generally allotted to the labourer under the name of wages, than the absolute necessary expenses of production' (*Works* I, note, p. 348).

4 On the history of the Poor Laws and on Ricardo's role in the debates on Poor Law reform, see King (2013, pp. 151–157), Poynter (1969, pp. 237–248), and Boyer (1990).

5 As Blaug (1958, pp. 199–200) has noted, McCulloch never adopted the Malthusian attitude to poor relief and later became an outspoken opponent of the Poor Law Amendment Act of 1834. He argued that prior to the adoption of the Speenhamland system the existence of the poor relief had, in fact, checked the growth of population, and he therefore advocated a return to the original provisions of the Elizabethan statute.

6 For a recent contribution to this literature, see Clark and Page (2018). A summary account of the empirical findings and a discussion of theoretical arguments for and against the causality suggested by Ricardo and Malthus is provided in Block and Somers (2003).

7 In his *Principles of Political Economy* ([1820] 1989, pp. 511–512), Malthus proposed public works programs as effective measures for generating employment. Curiously, however, he had earlier put forward exactly the opposite view in a letter to Ricardo of January 1817; see Sraffa (1955, p. 543).

8 See also Ricardo's explanation for the sufferings of the Irish peasants and his brief comments on Owen's plan in a letter to Trower of 24 July 1823 (*Works* IX, p. 313–314).

9 After the Yeomanry killing of unarmed men and women at a protest meeting against the Corn Laws and for political reform at St. Peter's Field (Peterloo) on 16 August 1819, a new legislation consisting of six 'Acts' was introduced by the government in order to prevent future unrest and to suppress further meetings for radical reform.

74   *Christian Gehrke*

10 For more information on Hume's motion and Ricardo's role in the repeal of Combination laws, see Grampp (1979, pp. 506–507 and 511–515).
11 The Lancasterian system of education, named after the Quaker and educationist Joseph Lancaster (1778–1838), is a variant of the monitorial system, in which the education method applied was based on the abler pupils being used as helpers to the teacher. Lancaster's motto for his cost-saving method was, '*Qui docet, discit—* He who teaches, learns'.
12 From 1816 to 1821, Ricardo actively supported Bentham's plan of a Chrestomathic school, which 'was to apply Lancaster's system of education "to the higher branches of learning, for the use of the middling and higher ranks in life"' (*Works* VI, note, p. 112). For further details on Ricardo's engagement in Bentham's project, see *Works* (VI, pp. xxviii–xxxi).

References

Blaug, M. (1958). *Ricardian Economics: A Historical Study*. New Haven, CT: Yale University Press.
Blaug, M. (1963). The Myth of the Old Poor Law and the Making of the New. *Journal of Economic History, 23*(2), 151–184.
Block, F. and Somers, M. (2003). In the Shadow of Speenhamland: Social Policy and The Old Poor Law. *Politics and Society, 31*(2), 283–323.
Boyer, G.R. (1990). *An Economic History of the English Poor Law 1750–1850*. Cambridge: Cambridge University Press.
Clark, G. and Page, M.E. (2018). Welfare Reform, 1834: Did the New Poor Law in England Produce Significant Economic Gains? *Cliometrica*, doi:10.1007/s11698-018-017.4-4.
Davis, T. (2005). *Ricardo's Macroeconomics: Money, Trade Cycles and Growth*. Cambridge: Cambridge University Press.
Gehrke, C. (2015). Improvements in Production. In H.D. Kurz and N. Salvadori (eds), *The Elgar Companion to David Ricardo* (pp. 200–205). Cheltenham: Edward Elgar.
Gordon, B. (1976). *Political Economy in Parliament 1819–1823*. London: Macmillan.
Grampp, W.D. (1979). The Economists and the Combination Laws. *Quarterly Journal of Economics, 93*(4), 501–522.
Henderson, J.P. (1984). Ricardo and the Provident Institutions. *Research in the History of Economic Thought and Methodology, 2*, 65–76.
Henderson, J.P. (1987). *The Life and Economics of David Ricardo*. Boston, MA: Kluwer Academic Publishers.
King, J.E. (2013). *David Ricardo*. London: Palgrave Macmillan.
Malthus, T.R. ([1798] 1992), Malthus: *An Essay on the Principle of Population*, edited by D. Winch using the text of the 1803 edition as prepared by Patricia James for the Royal Economic Society, 1990, showing the additions and corrections made in the 1806, 1807, 1817, and 1826 editions, Cambridge: Cambridge University Press.
Malthus, T.R. ([1820] 1989). *Principles of Political Economy*, Variorum Edition, 2 vols, edited by J. Pullen. Cambridge: Cambridge University Press.
Milgate, M. and Stimson, S.C. (1991). *Ricardian Politics*. Princeton, NJ: Princeton University Press.
Opocher, A. (2015). Poor Laws. In H.D. Kurz and N. Salvadori (eds), *The Elgar Companion to David Ricardo* (pp. 404–409). Cheltenham: Edward Elgar.
Poynter, J.R. (1969). *Society and Pauperism: English Ideas on Poor Relief, 1795–1834*. London: Routledge and Kegan Paul.

Ricardo, D. (1951–1973). *The Works and Correspondence of David Ricardo*, 11 vols, edited by P. Sraffa with the collaboration of M.H. Dobb. Cambridge: Cambridge University Press.

Sraffa, P. (1955). Malthus on Public Works. *The Economic Journal, 65*(259), 543–544.

Watarai, K. (2009). Ricardo on Poverty: His Vision of a Market Society. *The History of Economic Thought, 50*(2), 1–20.

Winch, D. (1996). *Riches and Poverty. An Intellectual History of Political Economy in Britain 1750–1834*. Cambridge: Cambridge University Press.

5   Saving the poor

John Stuart Mill on poverty and the poor

Daniel Rauhut

John Stuart Mill is generally considered to be the last of the great classical economists. Ricardianism was long believed to have reached its most complete elaboration in Mill. According to Eric Roll, a more modern interpretation of Mill suggests that he 'stand[s] half-way in the evolution of economic analysis away from Ricardo's doctrines' (Roll 1992, p. 322). Joseph Schumpeter (1994), in turn, argues that the economics in Mill's *Principles of Political Economy* can no longer be considered purely Ricardian. He describes Mill's position as a half-way house between Ricardo and Marshall (Schumpeter 1994).

Mill was, as the other classical economists, more interested in the production, rather than the transfer, of wealth. Thomas Sowell points out that 'the classical economists are often depicted as defenders of the status quo, apologists for socio-economic powers (and practices) that be' and as believers in a 'natural harmony' which makes deliberate intervention in the economy unnecessary and detrimental' (Sowell 1974, p. 8). In some areas, Mill shares the opinions of the classical economists, for example the theory of wages (Backhouse 1991), but he reformulated the economic theory of value (Barber 1971, Syll 1999) as well as the theories of production and distribution (Barber 1971, Backhouse 1991). Mill (2001a) sets out the abstraction of the rational behavior of the economic man. In this work, Mill states that the method of the economic science was based on hypotheses (Roll 1992). This is a view which places Mill closer to Marshall than to Ricardo.

The question is if the reformulation of parts of the classical economics had any impact of Mill's social philosophy. His passionate advocacy for liberty (Mill 2001b), universal suffrage (Mill 2001c), and of the rights of women (Mill 1993, 2001c) indicates that Mill, at least in some issues, did not favor the social conservatism, something that, according to Sowell (1974), the classical economists did.

This essay discusses John Stuart Mill's views on poverty, and it proposes to give an answer to how Mill defined poverty, what he thought caused poverty and how the poverty problem could be solved. The essay will start with a discussion on Mill's relation to Malthusianism, followed by a discussion on how Mill defined poverty and its causes. The section 'Instincts, moral, intelligence and the 'system'' discusses Mill's view on the causes of poverty and the section 'Mill and the Ricardian theory of value and wages' contains Mill's questioning of the Ricardian theory of value. In the two following sections, 'The role of the government' and 'Democracy and the poor', the role of the government and democracy are discussed. The section 'An English version of Kathedersozialismus and Sozialpolitik?' discusses the originality in Mill's stance on poverty. The essay ends with some concluding remarks.

In the wake of Malthus

In his *Principles of Political Economy*, Mill uses the Malthusian theory of population as an axiomatic truth (Blaug 1978). Historically, wars, diseases and starvation have constituted the positive checks on the growth of the population. Preventive population checks control and limit the number of births. Mill (1862, p. 195) complains about the poorer classes habits to have many children. By reproducing themselves prolifically, the laboring classes create a numerous workforce, which, by its number, depresses wages (Mill 1862, p. 454):

> The dependence of wages on the number of the competitors for employment, is so far from comprehension, or unintelligible to the labouring classes, that by great bodies of them it is already recognised and habitual acted upon. It is familiar to all Trade Unions: every successful combination to keep up the wages, owes its success to contrivances for restricting the number of competitors; all skilled trades are so anxious to keep down their numbers, and many impose, or endeavour to impose, as a condition upon employers, that they shall not take more than a prescripted number of apprentices.

If the workforce is significantly reduced, the wages of the laboring classes will rise, and so will their standard of living. According to the Malthusian theory of population, the workforce can be reduced by preventive and positive population checks. However, says Mill, 'it cannot now be said that in any part of Europe, population is principally kept down by disease, still less by starvation, either in a direct or indirect form' (Mill 1862, p. 420).

If the population is to be kept down, the number of births must be limited. Mill hopes that the most effective way of family limitation is the emancipation of females (Blaug 1978). The uncontrolled population growth is also a problem related to the position of the women. By giving women the same rights as men, the size of families would decrease (Mill 1862).[1] In the hands of Mill, the Malthusian theory of population becomes an argument favoring family limitation and birth control (Blaug 1978). Already at the age

of 16, Mill was brought into court for distributing literature on birth control
(Winch 1985). Mill explained his relation to the Malthusian theory of population in the following way (Mill 1924, p. 74):

> This great doctrine, originally brought forward as an argument against
> the indefinite improvability of human affairs, we took up with ardent
> zeal in the contrary sense, as indicating the sole means of realizing that
> improvability by securing full employment at high wages to the whole
> labouring population through a voluntary restriction of the increase of
> their numbers.

Donald Winch (1985) stresses that Mill held on to this belief throughout his
life. According to Lars Pålsson Syll (1999), the neo-Malthusians of Mill's lifetime thought of him as the leading economist.

One definition of poverty?

Mill never provided an explicit definition of poverty, but implicitly he considered a person as poor if he or she could not afford the necessities of life.
The necessities of life are food, clothing and some sort of housing. In his
Principles of Political Economy, Mill discusses the different restrictions on early
marriage in the German states, France, Switzerland, Norway and England.
These restrictions were imposed to prevent people from having large families, which they could not provide for, families which the poor relief then
would have to handle. Mill gives numerous examples of how a man who
wants to marry must be able to show that he can provide for his family. If he
cannot demonstrate that he will be able to feed his family and afford clothing
and housing, he will not be allowed to marry. In this way, unrestricted population growth is successfully limited as is the number of dependants on poor
relief (Mill 1862).[2] A few years later, Mill advocated the same policy for the
government: to prohibit people who could not provide for themselves to be
married in England (Winch 1985, p. 35).

Mill provides a second piece of evidence of his view on poverty when he
says, 'since the state must necessarily provide subsistence for the criminal
poor while undergoing punishment, not to do the same for the poor who
have not offended is to give premium on crime' (Mill 1985, p. 335). The
prisons in nineteenth-century England were hardly any luxurious recreation
resorts. Giving subsistence to the prisoners simply meant giving them food
enough to keep them alive and the most elementary clothing and shelter.

These two examples indicate that Mill had an absolute view of poverty;
poverty is about meeting biological needs. This is, however, an incomplete
description of Mill's view. He states that 'poverty, like most *social evils*, exists
because men follow their brute instincts without due consideration' (Mill
1862, p. 446f.; emphasis added). This indicates that Mill also considered poverty as relative: poverty was a social problem, a social evil.

The conclusion is that Mill defined poverty in a dual way. On the one hand, poverty is about the inability to provide the necessities of life, that is, food, clothing and housing. On the other hand, considered poverty to be a social problem. Defining poverty as absolute *and* relative is not unique for Mill; several well-known liberals have defined it the same way.[3]

Instincts, moral, intelligence and the 'system'

According to the Malthusian theory of population, mankind is driven by its lusts and instincts. In the end, the overpopulation resulting from man's primitive lusts causes starvation and poverty. Mill supports this view (Mill 1862, p. 192f.). The scourge of poverty 'exist[s] because men follow their brute instincts without due consideration' (Mill 1862, p. 446). The reason why the poor, that is, the laboring classes, follow their instincts is that they lack intelligence and moral culture (Mill 1862, p. 198). According to Mill, poor people do not understand what is good for them (Mill 1862, p. 455). Since the laboring classes are reproducing themselves, and thereby become too numerous, the competition for vacancies in the labor market is very hard. This competition presses the wage rate down (Mill 1862, p. 454). At a certain point, the wage becomes too small to live on (Mill 1862, p. 439):

> There is a rate of wages, either the lowest on which the people can, or the lowest on which they will consent, to live. We will suppose this to be seven shillings a week. Shocked at the wretchedness of this pittance, the parish authorities humanely make it up to ten. But the labourers are accustomed to seven, and though they would gladly have more, will live on that (as the fact proves) rather than restrain the instincts of multiplication. Their habits will not be altered for the better by giving them parish pay. Receiving three shillings from the parish, they will be as well off as before though they should increase sufficiently to bring down wages to four shillings.

This indicates that Mill considered the poor relief system in itself as a cause of poverty for the unintelligent and morally uncultivated people of the laboring classes. In fact, the support given to families were based on two principles: 'that more should be given to the married than the single, and to those who had large families than to those who had not: in fact, an allowance was usually canted for every child' (Mill 1862, p. 438). Following the primitive instincts and multiplying in large numbers paid for the laboring classes, but it improved neither their standard of living nor their health. Mill concludes that 'Under the allowance system the people have increased so fast, and the wages sank so low, that with wages and allowance together, families were worse off than they had been before with wages alone' (Mill 1862, p. 440).

To sum up, Mill pointed to four causes of poverty: (1) the primitive instincts to reproduce in large numbers, (2) the inability of the poor to understand, due to lacking intelligence and a low moral standard—what is good for them at an aggregate level, (3) a too numerous labor force creating a hard competition for each vacancy, which, in turn, exerts strong downward pressure on wages, and, finally, (4) the mechanisms contained in the poor relief system itself that kept the poor in poverty.

Mill and the Ricardian theory of value and wages

In the previous section it was shown that Mill believed that a too numerous labor force lowers wages. If the working classes reduced their fertility, that is, reduced the size of the labor force, wages would rise and their standard of living would be improved. This puts the Ricardian theory of value and wages in doubt.

According to David Ricardo, labor has an absolute value, and this value does not change if the size of the labor force changes. 'Labor' is a factor of production, but its value is determined by the 'natural price', not by the market. Ricardo defines 'the natural price' as what is 'necessary to enable the laborers, one with another, to subsist and to perpetuate their race, without either increase or diminution' (McCulloch 1926, p. 52). A consequence of this is that the subsistence level determines the natural price of labor (e.g. Backhouse 1985, Roll 1992).

What Mill demonstrated was that the price of labor was not absolute, but changed with the size of the labor force. By reducing their numbers, the laboring classes could change their situation to the better and remove themselves from the subsistence level.

The role of the government

At first glance, Mill is very clear on what the government ought to do and not to do. The guiding principle is the following: '*Laisser-faire*, in short, should be the general practice: every departure from it, unless required by some great good, is a certain evil' (Mill 1985, p. 314). Besides performing the duties of a night-watch state, the government should control the educational system. According to Mill, 'the intervention of government is justifiable, because the case is not one which the interest and judgement of the consumer are sufficient security for the goodness of the commodity' (Mill 1985, p. 321).

The government should also impose labor market regulations to prevent the working classes from being exploited, and, especially, protect children and women. Furthermore, the government should own, but not necessarily run, social overhead capital, for example, roads, canals and railways (Mill 1985, pp. 321–322). The government should also promote geographical and scientific explorations around the world, as well as colonisation. Mill thought that subsidising emigration of the poor was a government task, and so was poor relief (Mill 1985, p. 333):

> Apart from any metaphysical considerations respecting the foundation of morals or of the social union, it will be admitted to be right that human

beings should help one another; and the more so, in proportion to the urgency of the need: and none needs help so urgently as one who is starving. The claim to help, therefore, created by destitution, is one of the strongest which can exist; and there is *prima facie* the amplest reason for making the relief of so extreme an exigency as certain to those who require it, and by any arrangements of society can be made.

However, Mill sees a danger in relying on the habitual aid of others to avoid starvation. To be on poor relief to stay alive does not solve the fundamental problems. Hence, he suggests that poor relief should be guided by the following principle: 'how to give the greatest amount of needful help, with the smallest encouragement to undue reliance on it' (Mill 1985, p. 334).

According to Mill, public poor relief cannot distinguish the deserving poor from the undeserving, but private charity can. However, private charity alone is inefficient when it comes to fighting poverty, because it either gives too much or too little help. Since the government must provide for the criminals in the prisons, it should do the same for the poor. The government should provide basic needs, such as basic food and elementary clothing and housing. Other needs should be provided by private charity (Mill 1985, p. 335):

> If the poor are left to individual charity, a vast amount of mendacity is inevitable. What the state may and should abandon to private charity, is the task of distinguishing between one case of real necessity and another. Private charity can give more to the more deserving.

According to Samuel Hollander, Mill took a somewhat different stance in the 1860s, claiming that a public poor relief system could improve utility. To rely on private charity was also a very uncertain way of staying alive. Mill's claims for educational programs to inform the poor of how to behave (reduce fertility) had fallen into deaf ears and Mill 'insisted upon general recognition that for the State to take on direct responsibility for living standards implied a corresponding necessity for direct control over population' (Hollander 1985, p. 741f.). Donald Winch (1985, p. 35) quotes Mill expressing it as legitimate for governments to 'forbid marriage unless the parties can show that they have the means of supporting a family'.[4]

The role of the government, as Mill saw it, is not that of a night-watchman state. On the contrary, he suggested a rather big government! Sowell points out that 'the classical economists were not rigidly opposed to all government intervention in the market [...] The classical economists not only accepted certain intervention in the market, they suggested some themselves' (Sowell 1974, p. 21f.). Mill was no exception to this rule. According to Schumpeter, he 'was not on principle averse to a large amount of government activity. He had no illusions about any philosophically determined "necessary minimum" of state functions' (Schumpeter 1994, p. 549).

Democracy and the poor

Like Alexis de Tocqueville, Mill held democracy to be the superior form of polity. He also shared de Tocqueville's fear that a mass democracy would lead to the tyranny of the majority (Gray 1986). John Gray (1986, p. 74) concludes that an,

> unlimited democratic government, from a liberal point of view, is rather a form of totalitarianism—the form predicted and criticised by J.S. Mill in *On Liberty*. No system of government in which property rights and basic liberties are open to revision by temporary political majorities can be regarded as satisfying liberal requirements.

Mill states that 'in all countries there is a majority of poor, a minority who, in contradistinction, may be called rich. Between these two classes, on many questions, there is a complete opposition of apparent interest' (Mill 2001c, p. 78). Since it cannot be taken for granted that the majority of the poor are aware of what is best for them, for the rich and for the country as a whole, the possibility of outvoting the persons with superior knowledge must be limited. However, this is not to say that the poor should not have the right to vote. By offering a plural voting system, Mill constructs a democratic system in which the threat of the unskilled mass is neutralized. All persons get one vote, but persons with education and intellect gets two votes. This ensures that everybody has a political voice (Mill 2001c, p. 84):

> The representative system ought to be so constituted as to maintain this state of things: it ought not to allow any of the various sectional interests to be so powerful as to be capable of prevailing against truth and justice and the other sectional interests combined.

Hence, he considered stable moral traditions and social conventions as necessary in a free society: a society without them would not survive for very long and 'the alternative to such norms is not individuality, but coercion and anomie' (Gray 1986, p. 60).

By receiving the right to vote, the poor will be able to make their voice heard politically. However, if the educated and the intelligent people with high moral standards are given a plural vote, the poor will not become a serious political threat to stability, existing social conventions and moral traditions. If a poor person becomes more intelligent, with a high moral cultivation and an education, that person will receive a plural vote. By changing the behavior, habits and moral standards of the poor, the latter can improve their own situation and become better off.

An English version of *Kathedersozialismus* and *Sozialpolitik*?

The brute instincts of reproduction, low intelligence, low cultivation and low moral standards caused a high fertility. In fact, the reproduction rate was too high, which produced a too numerous workforce. As a result, the competition for vacancies was so hard that the wages and the standard of living of the working classes fell. If the latter could be made to stop reproducing themselves, thereby increasing unemployment, all persons would (Mill 1862, p. 417 f.):

> find employment without overstocking the market: every laboring family enjoys in abundance the necessities, many of the comforts, and some of the luxuries of life; and, unless in case of individual misconduct, or actual inability to work, poverty does not, and dependence need not, exist.

Why does not the laboring classes understand that they should limit their numbers, and thereby press up the wages and their standard of living? Mill's answer is that the poor simply do not understand what is good for them (Mill 1862, p. 198). In his own words, 'they cannot be better taught than fed' (Mill 1862, p. 446). In Mill's eyes, the future of the laboring classes was neither bright nor promising. He also noticed that the middle classes possessed both higher intelligence and higher cultivation and moral standards, which led to a lower reproduction rate and a higher standard of living (Mill 1862, p. 195).

Mill believed that by improving the intelligence as well as the cultivation and moral habits of the laboring classes it would be possible to make them lower their reproduction rate voluntarily. A lower reproduction of the laboring classes would produce fewer workers and increase the competition for labor among the employers. A labor shortage would inevitably lead to higher wages and living standards among the laboring classes. How could improvements of the intelligence as well as the cultivation and the moral habits of the laboring classes—something that would reduce the brute instincts to reproduce—be realized?

Mill thought that primitive instincts (e.g. reproduction) could be fought successfully (Mill 1862, p. 447):

> Civilization in every one of its aspects is a struggle against the animal instincts. Over some even of the strongest of them, it has shown itself capable of acquiring abundant control [...] If it has not brought the instincts of population under as much restraint as is needful, we must remember that it has never seriously tried. What efforts it has made, have mostly been in the contrary direction.

Since Mill considered it possible to fight the instincts of reproduction and promote the standard of living of the laboring classes, how did he want to do this? He points to two different means: the improvement of the standard of general education of the masses, and the emigration of the poor (Mill 1985, pp. 124–125, 336–338). Winch (1985) points out that Mill believed that a higher educational standard for the masses would lead to the emancipation of women and birth (family) control.

For the character and educational level of the poor to be improved, it was necessary to make them behave better and to reduce their fertility. This view stands in bright contrast to the open and tolerant society which Mill usually advocates.[5] Nevertheless, he is very clear on this point, when he states that 'an education established and controlled by the State should only exist [...] carried on for the purpose of example and stimulus, to keep the others up to a certain standard of excellence' (Mill 2001b, p. 97).

If you want to change the existing society, and create a new and better one, the power of the government allows you to do so. Mill wanted to change the behavior of the poor, the laboring classes, and the uncultivated (Mill 1862, p. 456; 1985, p. 318):

> The uncultivated cannot be competent judges of cultivation. Those who most need to be wiser and better, usually desire it least, and if they desire it, would be incapable of finding the way to it by their own lights. [...] An education directed to diffuse good sense among the people, with such knowledge as would qualify them to judge of the tendencies of their actions, would be certain, even without any direct inculcation, to raise up a public opinion which intemperance and improvidence of every kind would be held discreditable, and the improvidence which overstocks the labour market would be severely condemned, as an offence against the common weal. But though the sufficiency of such a state of opinion, supposing it formed, to keep the increase of population within proper limits, cannot, I think, be doubted.

If the poor become educated and informed of how to behave to create a better and happier community, the efforts of the government will strengthen the mind and spirit of the laboring classes (Mill 1985, p. 320).

According to Hollander (1985), Mill's exhortations to educate and inform the poor how to behave, and to reduce the fertility, had been ignored in the 1860s. However, Mill insisted that the state should assume the responsibility for the standard of living of the population and, if necessary, take direct control of the population growth (Hollander 1985, p. 741f.).

Mill's second suggestion of how to deal with high fertility rates among the laboring classes was to let them emigrate, subsidized by the government, to the colonies. Young families who could not provide for themselves should be given priority. In the colonies, high fertility rates were highly desirable, because 'the colonies would be supplied with the greatest amount of what is there in deficiency and here in superfluity, present and prospective labor' (Mill 1862, p. 457). The result would be that there would be fewer workers in the English labor market, which, in turn, would make the wages and the standard of living increase for the laboring classes. At the same time, the latter would be more cultivated and intelligent through education, which would in turn make them lower their reproduction rate. In the colonies, wages were high due to the shortage of labor, which would enable young families to have both many children and a good standard of living. Although Mill does not say so explicitly, he gives a clear hint that the English taxpayers would not have to pay for the families with many children in the colonies if they could not provide for themselves. It might even be cheaper in the long run for the English taxpayers to pay poor people to emigrate than to feed them.

According to Mill, education can solve many of the problems concerning poverty, but not all. People who live from hand to mouth cannot be efficiently taught how to change their behavior (Mill 1862, p. 456). The poor relief system contained mechanisms for keeping the poor in poverty. It was also profitable for families to have many children, since the allowance was based on the number of children (Mill 1862, p. 438ff.). Mill wanted to change this. A new system for poor relief was needed to control the population growth (Mill 1862, p. 436):

> Leave the people in a situation in which their condition manifestly depends upon their numbers, and the greatest permanent benefit may be derived from any sacrifice made to improve the physical well-being of the present generation, and raise, by that means, the habits of their children. But remove the regulation of their wages from their own control; guarantee to them a certain payment, either by law, or by the feeling of the community; and no amount of comfort that you can give them will make either them or their descendants look to their own self-restraint as the proper means of preserving them in that state.

If the poor relief is given as a flat-rate support, independent of the size of the family, it would pay to have a small family. This would clearly send the message to the laboring classes: you can change your behavior and reduce the number of children the easy way, by education, or the hard way, by a flat-rate support independent of family size. Those who chose the hard way had either to starve, which meant that their numbers would eventually be reduced, or to emigrate.

Schumpeter points out that Mill's vision of changing the behavior of the poor and his advocacy for social reform, constitutes an attempt to change the existing social structure (Schumpeter 1994, p. 549):

> Before a new and more efficient structure could be erected, the old one had in any case—I mean, irrespective of what, if anything, one wished to put in its place—to be pulled down bit by bit in order to clear the ground. And until this had been done, the existing machinery of public administration was simply not up to any of those complicated tasks that modern regulation or *Sozialpolitik*, involves. It is to the credit of J.S. Mill's judgement that he was aware of this.

Roll argues that Mill was the first liberal who leaned towards 'Fabianism' and he considers him as an important factor in social reform (Roll 1992, p. 329):

> This movement of which Mill is the symbol began much earlier in England than elsewhere. Its equivalent in Germany for example, *Kathedersozialismus*, arose later; though when it arrived after the advance of German industrial capitalism it showed much resemblance to its English counterpart.

Saving the poor

This essay has demonstrated that Mill had a dual definition of poverty. He considered poverty both as absolute and relative. Four factors cause poverty, according to him: (1) the rate of reproduction of the humans was too high; (2) the poor did not have the capacity to understand what was best for them; (3) too many workers per vacancy pressed the wages downwards; and (4) the institutional setting, the poor laws, kept the poor in poverty.

For Mill, the government played a very important role in the fight against poverty. It should attempt to make the laboring classes change their fertility patterns through education. It was also the duty of the government to control population growth. Furthermore, it should subsidize emigration for those who did not want to change their morals and have fewer children. Finally, Mill considered it necessary to reform the English poor relief system. The destitute got a poor relief which depended on the number of children they had, that is, it paid to have many children. Instead, the poor families should be given a flat-rate support, which gave premium to small families.

Those persons from the laboring classes who were saved by education, and thereby attained a higher moral standard, cultivation and intelligence, would lower their fertility. They would then receive a plural vote in the general elections. The poor, on the other hand, that is, the persons whose moral standards, cultivation and intelligence remained low, would only have one vote.

That the laboring classes should reduce their fertility and thereby achieve a higher standard of living shows that Mill considered the value of labor as relative, determined by the simple law of demand and supply. This stance opposed the Ricardian theory of value and wages. Mill considered the Malthusian theory of population an axiomatic truth (Blaug 1978). Barry Stapleton (1986), however, stresses that Malthus (1992) lacked a deeper analysis concerning the causes of poverty in the nineteenth–century England. What Malthus presents is (Dribe 2005, p. 49),

> a picture of the poor as healthy adults in prime working ages who get payment in addition to the wages, or who prefer to rely on poor relief

without working at all. There is much less attention, however, on the groups of sick, handicapped and elderly who were unable to work, and who cannot be expected to have contributed much to population growth.

Finally, two personal reflections on Mill's view of poverty are presented. His view is that poverty depends on contextual factors. First, his dual definition of poverty suggests the importance of the context of the individual. The necessities of life as well as the different restrictions on early marriage differ across time and space. Poverty as a social problem is highly dependent on the social context in which poverty exists. Second, three of the four the causes of poverty listed by Mill—instincts, moral, intelligence and the 'system'—are contextual. These factors led to a too high fertility. The moral standard and intelligence will depend on the social context in the community in which the individual lives, and the societal 'system' is influenced by the structural context. In his own English·nineteenth-century world, Mill considered a high fertility as something negative, but in a different socioeconomic context a high fertility may be good: the colonies needed a large population and a large workforce. Third, Mill's advocacy of social reform represents an attempt to change the social structure. Again, a social reform aims at changing the context in which poverty exists.

Second, Mill relies on the Malthusian theory of population as an axiomatic truth. This means that if the axiom is false, Mills's ideas on what causes poverty and how it can be cured have no explanatory power. Notwithstanding this, the ideas he presents us with on how to fight poverty are radical: to reform the poor relief system, to subsidize the emigration of the poor, to raise the cultivation and morals among the laboring classes, and to make them lower their fertility by education are suggestions calling for far-reaching social reform. That it was John Stuart Mill who came up with these suggestions is not surprising at all: after all, he was a radical social reformer.

Notes

1 'It is seldom by the choice of the wife that families are too numerous; on her devolves (along with all the physical suffering and at least a full share of the privations) the whole of the intolerable domestic drudgery resulting from the excess. To be relieved from it would be hailed as a blessing by multitudes of women who now never venture to urge such a claim, but who would urge it, if supported by the moral feelings of the community' (Mill 1862, p. 452).
2 See Mill (1862), Book 2 Chapter 11, paragraph 3 and Chapter 12, paragraph 2, for a thorough discussion of this theme.
3 For example, Adam Smith defines poverty this way (Rauhut 2005), and so does Rowntree (Rowntree 1902, 1942) and Amartya Sen (Rauhut and Hatti 2005).
4 Mill expresses this in *On Liberty*, 1859 (Mill 2001b), but already in *Principles of Political Economy*, 1848 (Mill 1985), the same views were formulated.
5 See the discussion by Berlin (1984) of this issue.

References

Backhouse, R. (1991). *A History of Modern Economic Analysis.* Oxford: Blackwell.

Barber, W.J. (1971). *De ekonomiska idéernas historia.* Stockholm: Aldus.

Berlin, I. (1984). John Stuart Mill och människans livsmål. In I. Berlin (ed), *Fyra essäer om frihet* (pp. 185–218). Stockholm: Ratio.

Blaug, M. (1978). *Economic Theory in Retrospect.* London: Cambridge University Press.

Dribe, M. (2005). Malthus and the Poor. In D. Rauhut, N. Hatti, and C.-A. Olsson (eds), *Economists and Poverty* (pp. 41–55). New Delhi: Vedam Books.

Gray, J. (1986). *Liberalism.* Minneapolis: University of Minnesota Press.

Hollander, S. (1985). *The Economics of John Stuart Mill, Vols. I and II.* Oxford: Blackwell.

Malthus, T. (1992). *An Essay on the Principle of Population.* Oxford: Oxford University Press

McCulloch, J.R. ([1846] 1926). *The Works of David Ricardo, Esq, MP, with A Notice of the Life and Writings of the Author.* London: G. Bell and Sons.

Mill, J.S. ([1848] 1862). *Principles of Political Economy with Some of Their Implications to Social Philosophy Vol. 1.* London: Parker, Son and West Strand.

Mill, J.S. ([1873] 1924). *Autobiography.* New York: Columbia University Press.

Mill, J.S. ([1848] 1985). *Principles of Political Economy with Some of Their Implications to Social Philosophy. Book IV and V.* Reading, MA: Penguin Books.

Mill, J.S. ([1869] 1993). *On the Subjection of Women.* Internet Modern History Source-book. http://www.fordham.edu/halsall/mod/jsmill-women.html [Accessed on 30 June 2018].

Mill, J.S. ([1844] 2001a). *Essays on Some Unsettled Questions of Political Economy.* Kitchener: Batoche Books.

Mill, J.S. ([1859] 2001b). *On Liberty.* Kitchener: Batoche Books.

Mill, J.S. ([1861] 2001c). *Considerations on Representative Government.* Kitchener: Batoche Books.

Rauhut, D. (2005). Adam Smith – A Champion for the Poor! In: D. Rauhut, N. Hatti, and C.-A. Olsson (eds), *Economists and Poverty* (pp. 21–40). New Delhi: Vedam Books.

Rauhut, D. and Hatti, N. (2005). Amartya Sen, Capability Deprivation and Poverty. In: D. Rauhut, N. Hatti and C.-A. Olsson (eds), *Economists and Poverty* (pp. 275–296). New Delhi: Vedam Books.

Roll, E. (1992). *A History of Economic Thought.* London: Faber & Faber.

Rowntree, B.S. (1902). *Poverty – A Study of Town Life.* London: Macmillan & Co.

Rowntree, B.S. (1942). *Poverty and Progress.* Bristol: Longmans Green & Co.

Schumpeter, J.A. (1994). *History of Economic Analysis.* London and New York: Routledge.

Sowell, T. (1974). *Classical Economics Reconsidered.* Princeton, NJ: Princeton University Press.

Stapleton, B. (1986). Malthus: The Origin of the Principle of Population. In M. Turner (ed.), *Malthus and his Time* (pp. 19–39). London: Macmillan.

Syll, L.P. (1999). *De ekonomiska teoriernas historia.* Lund: Studentlitteratur.

Winch, D. (1985). Introduction. In J.S. Mill (1985) *Principles of Political Economy with Some of Their Implications to Social Philosophy. Book IV and V* (pp. vii–xxv). Oxford: Oxford University Press.

6 Marx and his followers on poverty

Johan Lönnroth

For Marx, poverty, like wealth, is an inevitable consequence of capitalist society. He makes a distinction between two poor groups: poor workers and the lumpenproletariat. Poverty in both groups is necessary for the capitalist class and its exploitation to function. Poor workers benefit the ruling capitalist class since they guarantee high profits and surplus value. The lumpenproletariat—consisting of the unemployed, the criminals and other extremely poor individuals—ensures that there is always a workforce willing to accept low wages. Unemployment and job insecurity mean that there is always a 'reserve army of labor' able and willing to take their place if workers insist on too high wages. Therefore, it is not simply that there are rich and poor; it is rather that some are rich because some are poor. For Marx, then, poverty is an integral feature of capitalist society, which is a direct consequence of the inequality inherent in the class system. He sometimes describes the horrible situation for the poor, but he seldom expresses that he feels sorry for them.

Marx meets Engels

Marx was born 1818 in Trier in Prussia, then belonging to the German Confederation. He studied law in Bonn, philosophy for Friedrich Hegel in Berlin and he took a doctor's degree in philosophy in Jena. The dissertation dealt with a comparison between Demokritos and Epikuros. Marx belonged to a group called 'left-wing Hegelians' with radical critics of religion and of the Prussian political system. He wrote for radical journals, which made a career in the Prussian state administration or in academia impossible. He married and in November 1843, he and his family moved to Paris. There he met a number of the leading left-wingers like the anarchists Pierre-Joseph Proudhon and Mikhail Bakunin. The most important figure he met, however, was the oldest son of a successful German textile industrialist, Friedrich Engels.

To understand Marx's opinion on poverty, it is necessary to begin with the influence from Engels. When the two met for the first time in Paris 1844, Engels showed him the manuscript in German to be published the next year as *Die Lage der arbeitenden Klasse in England* (Engels 1887). Karl Marx read it and was impressed. The book was written during Engels's 1842–1844 stay in

Manchester, the city at the heart of the Industrial Revolution. It was compiled from his own observations and from detailed contemporary reports.

Engels argues that the Industrial Revolution made workers, especially the agricultural workers, moving to the cities to work in the factories, worse off (Engels 1887 p. 175):

> We have seen [that] ... simultaneously with the small bourgeoisie and the modest independence of the former workers, the small peasantry also was ruined when the former union of industrial and agricultural work was dissolved, the abandoned fields thrown together into large farms, and the small peasants superseded by the overwhelming competition of the large farmers. Instead of being landowners or leaseholders, as they had been hitherto, they were now obliged to hire themselves as labourers to the large farmers or the landlords. For a time, this position was endurable, though a deterioration in comparison with their former one. The extension of industry kept pace with the increase of population until the progress of manufacture began to assume a slower pace, and the perpetual improvement of machinery made it impossible for manufacture to absorb the whole surplus of the agricultural population. From this time forward, the distress which had hitherto existed only in the manufacturing districts, and then only at times, appeared in the agricultural districts too.

Engels described the detrimental health effects of poverty among the industrial workers. He pointed out that in large industrial cities such as Manchester and Liverpool, mortality from diseases such as smallpox, measles, scarlet fever and whooping cough was four times that in the surrounding countryside. The overall death rate in Manchester and Liverpool was also significantly higher than the national average.

Engels also presented statistical examples from the older history of the industrial town of Carlisle. He showed a substantial increase in the overall mortality rate, especially among children, when the cotton mills were established there between 1779 and 1787. Engels also focused on the workers' wages and their living conditions. He argued that the industrial workers had lower incomes than their pre-industrial peers and that they lived in more unhealthy and unpleasant environments.

The *Manifesto*

Marx contributed to the only uncensored German-language left radical newspaper *Vorwärts!* (*Forward!*), which was based in Paris. After receiving a request from the Prussian king, the French government shut down the journal and Marx was deported from France. He moved to Brussels and Engels followed him. There the two produced a pamphlet commissioned by the

Communist League, established in London 1847, and written towards the end of the same year. A condition for staying in Brussels was a promise not to publish anything on the subject of contemporary politics. Thus, the pamphlet was published in more liberal England as the *Manifesto of the Communist Party* in February of the revolutionary year of 1848.

The first chapter of the *Manifesto*, 'Bourgeois and Proletarians', can be read as a tribute to the ability of capitalism to develop the productive forces: '[t]he bourgeoisie ... has accomplished wonders far surpassing Egyptian pyramids, Roman aqueducts and Gothic cathedrals' (Marx and Engels 1848, p. 16).

Capitalism has produced immense wealth, but it also fosters the new working class, the proletarians (Marx and Engels 1848, p. 18):

> In proportion as the bourgeoisie, i.e., capital, is developed, in the same proportion is the proletariat, the modern working class, developed – a class of labourers, who live only so long as they find work, and who find work only so long as their labour increases capital.

So, is this new class of proletarians poor? Yes, definitely in their spirits (Marx and Engels 1848, p. 18):

> These labourers, who must sell themselves piecemeal, are a commodity, like every other article of commerce, and are consequently exposed to all the vicissitudes of competition, to all the fluctuations of the market. Owing to the extensive use of machinery, and to the division of labour, the work of the proletarians has lost all individual character, and, consequently, all charm for the workman. He becomes an appendage of the machine, and it is only the simplest, most monotonous, and most easily acquired knack, that is required of him.

And the proletarian is poor also in the monetary sense (Marx and Engels 1848, p. 18):

> ... the cost of production of a workman is restricted, almost entirely, to the means of subsistence that he requires for maintenance, and for the propagation of his race. But the price of a commodity, and therefore also of labour, is equal to its cost of production. In proportion, therefore, as the repulsiveness of the work increases, the wage decreases.

What do Marx and Engels say? That the working class is bound to live in poverty? It is important to note that they write that the wage decreases 'in proportion'. Thus, the workers live in *relative* poverty as compared to capitalist wealth. To understand that the working class does not necessarily live in absolute poverty, we must also read the latter parts of the same chapter of the *Manifesto*, where Marx and Engels also introduce a class below the workers: the 'dangerous class', or 'lumpenproletariat' defined as (Marx and Engels 1848, p. 20):

> ... the social scum, that passively rotting mass thrown off by the lowest layers of the old society, may, here and there, be swept into the movement by a proletarian revolution; its conditions of life, however, prepare it far more for the part of a bribed tool of reactionary intrigue.

So here we meet the idea that this lowest class is an instrument used by the bourgeoisie to exhort the workers to go on working in order not to fall down into the lumpenproletariat.

In the first section, 'Reactionary Socialism', of the third chapter of the *Manifesto*, Marx and Engels also mention that the role of religion is to legitimize poverty and relieve the bad conscience of the upper classes (Marx and Engels 1848, p. 29):

> Nothing is easier than to give Christian asceticism a Socialist tinge. Has not Christianity declaimed against private property, against marriage, against the State? Has it not preached in the place of these, charity and poverty, celibacy and mortification of the flesh, monastic life and Mother Church? Christian Socialism is but the holy water with which the priest consecrates the heart-burnings of the aristocrat.

Marx on the class struggle in France

The Belgian Ministry of Justice accused Marx of breaking his promise not to publish anything on the subject of contemporary politics. He was arrested and he was forced to flee back to France, where with a new republican government in power he believed that he would be safe. But he was wrong. In June 1848, Marx moved to Cologne, where a Prussian parliament temporarily had installed a more liberal government. Together with Engels, he participated in the founding of the *Neue Rheinische Zeitung*, and took on the editorship.

In this journal, he published a set of articles later to become a booklet published by Engels in 1895 as *The Class Struggles in France 1848–1850* (Marx 1895). There Marx applied his ideas about poverty and lumpenproletariat as instruments of the ruling class to a real-life example. He goes back to the situation in France 1847, when the 'petty bourgeoisie' was 'offended and filled with moral indignation' over a growing lumpenproletariat. Marx writes that Paris was flooded with pamphlets blaming the luxury life of the capitalist establishment, named 'The Rothschild Dynasty'—antisemitism also played a role—or the 'Usurer Kings of the Epoch', for the moral dissolution.

Marx writes that in this situation the industrial bourgeoisie saw its interests endangered. For this purpose, the short-lived provisional government instituted in 1848 formed 24 battalions of Mobile Guards, each a 1,000 men strong, composed of young men from 15 to 20 years old. According to Marx, they belonged, for the most part, to the lumpenproletariat (Marx 1895, Part I, *The Defeat of June*, 1848):

> ... which in all big towns forms a mass sharply differentiated from the industrial proletariat, a recruiting ground for thieves and criminals of all kinds living on the crumbs of society, people without a definite trade, vagabonds, *gens sans feu et sans aveu* (men without hearth or home), varying according to the degree of civilization of the nation to which they belong.

Immediately after Louis Bonaparte's coup d'état of 2 December 1851, Marx dealt afresh with the history of France from February 1848 up to this event, which concluded the revolutionary period for the time being. In the pamphlet *The Eighteenth Brumaire of Louis Bonaparte*, published in New York 1852, Marx again describes the role of the very poor, again they are called the 'lumpenproletariat'. Bonaparte was constantly accompanied by persons affiliated with the so-called Society of 10 December. This society dates from the year 1849. On the pretext of founding a benevolent society, the lumpenproletariat of Paris had been organized into secret sections, each section led by Bonapartist agents, with a Bonapartist general at the head of the whole. Marx (1852, p. 38) writes,

> Alongside decayed roués with dubious means of subsistence and of dubious origin, alongside ruined and adventurous offshoots of the bourgeoisie, were vagabonds, discharged soldiers, discharged jailbirds, escaped galley slaves, swindlers, mountebanks, pickpockets, tricksters, gamblers, pimps, brothel keepers, porters, literati, organ grinders, ragpickers, knife grinders, tinkers, beggars. In short, the whole indefinite, disintegrated mass, thrown hither and thither, which the French call *la bohème*; from this kindred element Bonaparte formed the core of the Society of December 10. A 'benevolent society' – insofar as, like Bonaparte, all its members felt the need of benefiting themselves at the expense of the labouring nation.

According to Marx, Bonaparte, who in 1852 would become Emperor Napoleon III, constituted himself even as the 'chief of the lumpenproletariat'. He was himself an old, crafty 'roué', writes Marx, and he 'conceives the historical life of the nations and their performances of state as comedy in the most vulgar sense, as a masquerade in which the grand costumes, words, and postures merely serve to mask the pettiest knavery' (Marx 1852, p. 38). Thus, the new emperor was for Marx a clear example of the role of the very poor as an instrument for bourgeoise power.

Marx on English poverty

A reactionary government soon came to power in Prussia. It closed the *Neue Rheinische Zeitung* and Marx could not stay. He gave up his Prussian citizenship and moved to London in 1849. After they had settled there, Marx and his family spent the rest of their lives in England financially supported by Engels. Gradually, Marx engaged himself more and more in British political debate. He wrote about it in different European and American journals and spoke about it in meetings with the international workers' movement. The material is huge and I will here select just a few of his interventions in which he writes or speaks about living conditions for and poverty among the workers.

I will start with the text *Parliamentary Debates—The Clergy and the Struggle for the Ten-Hour Day—Starvation*, written on 25 February and published in the *New York Tribune* 15 March 1853.[1] First, let's look at some facts on the English factory laws. The key provisions of the 1850 act were as follows: women and young persons could only work from 6 a.m. to 6 p.m. or—in winter, and subject to approval by a factory inspector—7 a.m. to 7 p.m. Since they were to be allowed 90 minutes total breaks during the day, the maximum hours worked per day increased to 10.5. All work would end on Saturday at 2 p.m. The work week was thereby extended from 58 hours to 60 hours. Marx writes,

> The factory-law was so unblushingly violated that the Chief Inspector … had found himself necessitated to write to the Home Secretary, to say that he dared not, and would not send any of his Sub-Inspectors into certain districts until he had police protection…. And protection against whom? Against the factory-masters!

Marx asks if the masters suffered because of their violation of the law. The answer is no. The Chief Inspector reported that it was a settled custom of the male, and to a great extent of the female workers in factories, to be in bed until 9, 10 or 11 o'clock on Sunday, because they were worn out by the labor of the week:

> Sunday was the only day on which they could rest their wearied frames… It would generally be found that, the longer the time of work, the smaller the wages… The worker would rather be a slave in South Carolina, than a factory operative in England.

Poverty in the inaugural address

I continue with Marx's famous Inaugural Address to the International Workingmen's Association (commonly called The First International) meeting in London in September 1864.[2] He starts by saying that it is an important fact that the misery of the working masses has not diminished from 1848 to 1864, and yet this period is unrivaled for the development of its industry and the growth of its commerce. Marx refers to 'a moderate organ of the British middle class', predicting that if the exports and imports of England were to rise 50 percent, English pauperism would sink to zero. He quotes the liberal chancellor of the exchequer, William Gladstone (later to become prime minister):

> On April 7, 1864, the Chancellor of the Exchequer delighted his parliamentary audience by the statement that the total import and export of England had grown in 1863 ... about three times the trade of the comparatively recent epoch of 1843![3]

Despite this tremendous growth, Marx continues, in nine cases out of ten the humans had to struggle for their existence. And even the worst of the convicted criminals, the penal serfs of England and Scotland, toiled much less and fared far better than the workers.

However, this was not all. When the operatives of Lancashire and Cheshire were thrown into the streets, the House of Lords sent to the manufacturing districts a physician commissioned to find out the smallest possible amount of carbon and nitrogen to be administered in the cheapest and plainest form, which on average might just suffice to 'avert starvation diseases'. The medical deputy ascertained that 28,000 grains of carbon and 1,330 grains of nitrogen were the weekly allowance that would keep an average adult just above the level of starvation diseases,[4] and he found, furthermore, that quantity almost to agree with the scanty nourishment to which the pressure of extreme distress had actually reduced the cotton operatives. Marx continues,

> The same learned doctor was later on again deputed by the medical officer of the Privy Council to enquire into the nourishment of the poorer labouring classes. The results of his research are embodied in the 'Sixth Report on Public Health', published by order of Parliament in the course of the present year. What did the doctor discover? That the silk weavers, the needlewomen, the kid glovers, the stock weavers, and so forth, received on an average, not even the distress pittance of the cotton operatives, not even the amount of carbon and nitrogen 'just sufficient to avert starvation diseases'.

Marx also writes that, as a rule, great poorness of diet will only come when other privations have preceded it. Even cleanliness will have been found costly or difficult, and if there still be self-respectful endeavors to maintain it, every such endeavor will represent 'additional pangs of hunger'. And the human poverty is not the deserved poverty of idleness, it is the poverty of working populations. Indeed, the work which obtains the scanty pittance of food is for the most part excessively prolonged:

> Such are the official statements published by order of Parliament, during the millennium of free trade, at a time when the Chancellor of the

Exchequer told the House of Commons that 'the average condition of the British labourer has improved in a degree we know to be extraordinary and unexampled in the history of any country or any age'.

In the Inaugural Address, Marx also compares these official statements with the *Report of the Children's Employment Commission* of 1863, where it is stated, for instance, that

> the potters as a class, both men and women, represent a much degenerated population, both physically and mentally, that the unhealthy child is an unhealthy parent in his turn, that the future was fraught with the gradual extinction of the race, and that the degenerescence of the population of Staffordshire would be even greater were it not for the constant recruiting from the adjacent country, and the intermarriages with more healthy races.

Marx also 'reverses the medal':

> The income and property tax returns laid before the House of Commons on July 20, 1864, teach us that the persons with yearly incomes valued by the tax gatherer of 50 000 pounds and upwards had, from April 5, 1862, to April 5, 1863, been joined by a dozen and one, their number having increased in that single year from 67 to 80. The same returns disclose the fact that about 3,000 persons divide among themselves a yearly income of about 25,000,000 pounds sterling, rather more than the total revenue doled out annually to the whole mass of the agricultural labourers of England and Wales.

Marx notes that the number of male landed proprietors of England and Wales has decreased with 10 percent between 1851 and 1861. And he notes that if the concentration of the soil of the country in a few hands proceeds at the same rate, the land question will become singularly simplified, as it had become in the Roman Empire 'when Nero grinned at the discovery that half of the province of Africa was owned by six gentlemen'.

Marx concludes this section of the address on poverty and distribution:

> After the failure of the Revolution of 1848, all party organizations and party journals of the working classes were, on the Continent, crushed by the iron hand of force, the most advanced sons of labour fled in despair to the transatlantic republic, and the short-lived dreams of emancipation vanished before an epoch of industrial fever, moral marasm, and political reaction. The defeat of the continental working classes, partly owed to the diplomacy of the English government, acting then as now in fraternal solidarity with the Cabinet of St. Petersburg, soon spread its contagious effects to this side of the Channel.

Poverty in *Capital—A Critique of Political Economy*

Marx's magnum opus *Capital—A Critique of Political Economy* (Marx 1887) was published in German in 1867. There, in a section of Chapter 25, 'The General Law of Capitalist Accumulation', he follows up Engels's book from 1845, the journal articles on the subject and the Inaugural Address. He summarizes the situation for the English working class during the years 1846–1866. Marx starts by referring to the presentation of the budget by Gladstone in the House of Commons in April 1863. The chancellor of the exchequer had said that from 1842 to 1852 the taxable income of the country increased by 6 percent and in the eight years from 1853 to 1861 it had increased from the basis taken in 1853 by 20 percent! Then Gladstone says (Marx 1887, p. 455),

> The fact is so astonishing as to be almost incredible... this intoxicating augmentation of wealth and power... entirely confined to classes of property... must be of indirect benefit to the labouring population, because it cheapens the commodities of general consumption. While the rich have been growing richer, the poor have been growing less poor. At any rate, whether the extremes of poverty are less, I do not presume to say.

Marx comments on this old variant of the trickle-down effect (Marx 1887, p. 455):

> How lame an anti-climax! If the working class has remained 'poor,' only 'less poor' in proportion as it produces for the wealthy class "an intoxicating augmentation of wealth and power," then it has remained relatively just as poor. If the extremes of poverty have not lessened, they have increased, because the extremes of wealth have. As to the cheapening of the means of subsistence, the official statistics, *e.g.,* the accounts of the London Orphan Asylum, show an increase in price of 20% for the average of the three years 1860–1862, compared with 1851–1853. In the following three years, 1863–1865, there was a progressive rise in the price of meat, butter, milk, sugar, salt, coals, and a number of other necessary means of subsistence.

Just as in the Inaugural Address, Marx once again refers to Gladstone's Budget speech 7 April 1864. Marx now calls it 'a Pindaric dithyrambus on the advance of surplus-value-making and the happiness of the people tempered by poverty'. The masses are on the border of pauperism (Marx 1887, p. 455). Marx finally sums up the situation of the working class by means of a number of extremely exact statistical data—(perhaps because he wanted to give the text a scientific flavor) (Marx 1887, p. 456):

> The official list of paupers numbered in England 1844 was 851 369 persons; in 1856 it was 877 767 and in 1865 971 433 ... The crisis of 1866,

which fell most heavily on London, created in this centre of the world market, more populous than the kingdom of Scotland, an increase of pauperism for the year 1866 of 19.5% compared with 1865, and of 24.4% compared with 1864, and a still greater increase for the first months of 1867 as compared with 1866.

Marx also compares his statistics with those of Engels (Marx 1887, p. 456):

> F. Engels showed in 1844 exactly the same horrors, exactly the same transient canting outcries of 'sensational literature.' But frightful increase of 'deaths by starvation' in London during the last ten years proves beyond doubt the growing horror in which the working-people hold the slavery of the workhouse, that place of punishment for misery.

Irish poverty

In a report to the Communist Educational Association of German Workers in London dated 16 December 1867, Marx took up the special situation in Ireland during the last 20 years.[5] First, let's look at a short historical background: the Corn Laws—a protective legislation, combined with trade prohibitions—were repealed in 1846 after a campaign led by English industrialists. As a result, Irish corn lost its monopoly on the English market and the corn prices dropped. Because of an act of Parliament passed 1847–1848 Irish landowners had to support their own paupers. Hence, the landowners, most of them deep in debt, tried to get rid of the people and clear their estates.

Before 1846, Ireland had repeated cases of partial famine. Now famine became general. According to Marx, over one million died, partly from hunger, partly from diseases caused by hunger. In nine years, 1847–1855, more than one and a half million individuals left Ireland. Most of them fled to England, but many also fled to North America. Families clubbed together to send away the youngest and most enterprising. Marx wrote in the report, 'The despairing flight of starving Irish to England filled basements, hovels, workhouses in Liverpool, Manchester, Birmingham, Glasgow with men, women, children in a state almost of starvation'.[6] The effect of this starving mass of people selling their labor cheap was falling wages. And, of course, the English working class became as hostile to the Irish as the British working class today is towards immigrants from poorer parts of the European Union.

Critique of the Gotha Program

Marx had health problems and he was no longer so active in his last years of his life. He grappled with the law of value and all the equations and texts in what was to become parts II and III of *Capital—A Critique of Political Economy*, published after his death. I believe that he understood that the transformation of labor values to prices was impossible and that the so-called law of value—labor values as long-term equilibrium market prices under perfect competition—was wrong (Lönnroth 1977). I also believe that he understood that demand must be a part of the analysis of market prices.

His *Critique of the Gotha Program*, written in 1875 (Marx 1875), was his last contribution to have a major impact on the contemporary political debate. The text was an attack on the party platform adopted by the nascent Social Democratic Party of Germany at its initial party congress, held in the town of Gotha in 1875.

This text is famous for two reasons: first, for the sentence, 'From each according to his ability, to each according to his need', second, because of Marx's dismissal of the first part of the first paragraph of the program, 'Labour is the source of all wealth and all culture'. Marx wrote in part I,

> Labour is *not the source* of all wealth. *Nature* is just as much the source of use values (and it is surely of such that material wealth consists!) as labour, which itself is only the manifestation of a force of nature, human labour power.

Marx's *Critique of the Gotha Program* opposed the tendency of his German followers Wilhelm Liebknecht and August Bebel to make compromises with the reformist state socialism of Ferdinand Lassalle, who had close contacts with Otto von Bismarck with his combined policy of social policy and forbidding socialist organizations. He also wrote on the first paragraph: '[i]n fact, however, the whole paragraph, bungled in style and content, is only there in order to inscribe the Lassallean catchword of the "undiminished proceeds of labor" as a slogan at the top of the party banner'.[7] But there were also parts of the program that Marx called incontestable:

> In proportion as labour develops socially, and becomes thereby a source of wealth and culture, poverty and destitution develop among the workers, and wealth and culture among the nonworkers ... This is the law of all history hitherto. What, therefore, had to be done here, instead of setting down general phrases about 'labour' and 'society', was to prove concretely how in present capitalist society the material conditions have at last been created which enable and compel the workers to lift this social curse.

Thus, here is a clear contradiction, or a dialectical phenomenon to use a more popular concept used by the followers of Marx. First, 'poverty developed among the workers'. Second, material conditions have at last been created which enable and compel the workers to lift this 'social curse'. Liberation and prosperity grow in the womb of poverty to express the contradiction in the style of dialectics so often used by Marx. It means that the existence of poverty fosters capitalist development which in the long run leads to socialism and so liberty and prosperity.

After Marx: Lenin and Luxemburg

Marx died in 1883. The following three decades saw European capitalism develop in a rather stable manner and Marx's followers could not deny that the working class had a slow but rather stable increase in the living standard in the advanced capitalist states, especially so in the United States, Germany, France, Great Britain and Scandinavia. Slowly also social insurance systems were developed there. And revisionism and reformism gradually took over in the workers' movement.

But in underdeveloped Russia poverty among the working masses was a dominant problem and the majority of the social democratic party were revolutionaries, Bolsheviks. Their leader Vladimir Ilyich Lenin in a text from 1903 (Lenin 1903) wrote about poverty among the peasants in Russia. His purpose was to show why the poor peasants should unite with the urban workers rather than with the landlords living on the labor of others:

> What vast areas of land are concentrated in the hands of the big land owners is also to be seen in the fact that just under one thousand families (924) own more than ten thousand decitabines (ca 2.7 acres) each, and all together they own twenty-seven million dessiatines! One thousand families own as much land as is owned by two million peasant families.

For Lenin, to gradually reform Russia was impossible:

> Obviously, millions and tens of millions of people are *bound* to live in poverty and starvation and *will go on* living in poverty and starvation as long as such vast areas of land are owned by a few thousand of the rich. Obviously, the state authorities, the government itself (even the tsar's government) will always dance to the tune of these big land owners. Obviously, the rural poor can expect no help from anyone, or from any quarter, until they unite, combine in a single class to wage a stubborn, desperate struggle against the landlord class.

Another of the few working in the tradition of Marx who was interested in poverty was Rosa Luxemburg. She wrote a powerful article in *Die Gleichheit* (Equality), the socialist women's paper edited by Clara Zetkin, about the deaths of scores of homeless people in Berlin on New Year's Eve 1912.[8]

> ... a wall is coming up, and rarely one thinks of the misery in the mud on the other side. And suddenly there is an event that upsets everything. Suddenly, the terrible ghost of misery pulls from the face of our society the mask of dignity, and reveals this pseudo-harmony... Suddenly, beneath the pale and intoxicating pretensions of our civilization, we discover the abyss of barbarism and brutality. Human creatures in the dirt, suffocating from their pains, panting, falling away, leaving their last infected breath.

Today, we have to raise up these poisoned bodies of the Berlin home-less, who are the flesh of our flesh and the blood of our blood, borne aloft by thousands of proletarian hands, and we carry them into this new year of struggle by shouting: "Down with the obscene social system that creates such horror!"

Poverty goes South

Rosa Luxemburg was, however, not only interested in poverty in Europe but also in poverty as a phenomenon of the colonial South. This interest had to do with her critique of Marx in a small book written in 1912 and published in German 1913 as *Die Akkumulation des Kapitals: Ein Beitrag zur ökonomischen Erklärung des Imperialismus* (Luxemburg 1951). There she argued that Marx had made an error in *Capital—A Critique of Political Economy* where he treated capitalist states as closed systems. According to her, it was impossible for cap-italists in the long run to make large enough profits in a closed system since the demand for commodities would be too low. Therefore, capitalists sought to realize profits through investments and employing cheap labor in poor non-capitalist economies. This was the explanation of the phenomenon of imperialism as capitalist states sought to dominate countries like China and India. Luxemburg's conclusion was that socialism in one country was im-possible since capitalism could survive as long as it could expand in the non-capitalist surroundings. Therefore, capitalism could not break down until it had eaten up the whole world. Socialism in one country was impossible.

Also, Lenin tried to explain the survival of capitalism. In 'Imperialism and the Split in Socialism', published in December 1916, he tried to explain why the leading social democrats had lost their revolutionary faith (Lenin 1916):

> The *opportunists* (social-chauvinists) are working hand in glove with the imperialist bourgeoisie *precisely* towards creating an imperialist Europe on the backs of Asia and Africa, and objectively the *opportunists* are a section of the petty bourgeoisie and of a certain strata of the working class who *have been bribed* out of imperialist superprofits and converted to *watchdogs* of capitalism and *corruptors* of the labour movement.

Thus, for Lenin, poverty was mainly a problem in the countries dominated by European imperialism, and also in the weakest link of imperialism: Russia.

Marx today

With the Russian revolution and the development of Soviet Union and other communist party ruled dictatorships, Marx was reduced and distorted to a simple propagandist for the new system. His ideas of free worker's associa-tions, cooperatives and a dying state under socialism were forgotten and sub-stituted by Stalin's centrally planned economy. Poverty could simply not exist under the Soviet type of nationalist socialism. It was a phenomenon linked to capitalism, especially in what would be called the Third World.

In the Western world, we could see the growth of welfare institutions designed to assist the poor and eradicate poverty. After the new war came a period with stable capitalist growth and a more even income distribution. Marx more or less disappeared from libraries and university curricula, especially in countries like Sweden, where capital and labor cooperated under an agreement that gave capitalists the power over production and investment, the trade unions made collective agreements on wage setting and work conditions and the state built a strong public sector and social security arrangements.

With the crisis in the 1970s, the New Left tried to bring Marx back from the closet. It stated that the welfare state was only a palliative, or partial cure that it is there to ease the worst effects of capitalism, while ensuring that social harmony and status quo are maintained. Structural problems in capitalism were said to become individualized with attention shifted away from the real cause. In this sense, poverty was said to be maintained as poor people internalize their own failings. The poor were said to be partially soothed by the help being provided, and any revolutionary threat arising out of discontent was negated.

Then again, during the decades of 'moderation', Marx once more was more or less forgotten, but after the new financial crisis, he made a new comeback. Thomas Piketty's *Capital in the Twenty-First Century* is an example. Piketty writes that 'capitalism automatically generates arbitrary and unsustainable inequalities that radically undermine the meritocratic values on which democratic societies are based' (Piketty 2014, p. 1). But I fail to see that this very impressing book has much to do with Marx.

I hope that the reader will allow me to end with a personal declaration. In my opinion, only two of Marx's ideas have survived until today: worker alienation and historical materialism. His analysis of poverty is only remembered as an explanation of the reserve army. Marx has become a little like Jesus or Mohammed; a number of political sects claim that they represent the true interpretation of what the founding father really meant. Shortly before he died, he wrote a letter to Jules Guesde and Paul Lafargue, and accused them of 'revolutionary phrase-mongering' and denying the value of reformist struggles. Marx also made his famous remark that, if their politics represented Marxism, *'ce qu'il y a de certain c'est que moi, je ne suis pas Marxiste'* ('what is certain is that I myself am not a Marxist').[9] Myself, I like Marx. But I am not a Marxist.

Notes

1 In Marx-Engels Archive. https://www.marxists.org/archive/marx/works/1853/02/25.htm. Downloaded 5 November 2019.
2 In Marx-Engels Archive. https://www.marxists.org/archive/marx/iwma/archive/eichhoff/iwma-history/ch03.htm. Downloaded 8 November 2019.

3 Marx-Engels Archive. https://www.marxists.org/archive/marx/works/1864/10/27.htm. Downloaded 6 November 2019.
4 'Carbon compounds provide energy and cellular building blocks, while nitrogen is a crucial component of proteins, necessary for cell growth and function. It is nitrogen that builds tissue. Nitrogen is a component of amino acids which are the building blocks of protein' (Lauder 2017).
5 Marx-Engels Archive. https://www.marxists.org/archive/marx/works/1867/12/16.htm. Downloaded 10 November 2019.
6 Marx-Engels Archive. https://www.marxists.org/archive/marx/works/1867/12/16.htm. Downloaded 10 November 2019.
7 I have written about how this faulty sentence was imported into Sweden and how Knut Wicksell influenced Hjalmar Branting and other social democratic leaders to dismiss Marx on those grounds in Lönnroth (1991).
8 Published 5 February 1912. https://www.marxists.org/archive/luxemburg/1912/02/05.htm. Downloaded 15 November 2019.
9 Marx-Engels Archive. https://www.marxists.org/archive/marx/works/1880/05/parti-ouvrier.htm. Downloaded 13 November 2019.

References

Engels, F. (1887). *The Condition of the Working Class in England*. In Marx-Engels Archive, https://www.marxists.org/archive/marx/works/download/pdf/condition-working-class-england.pdf. Downloaded 10 November 2019.

Lauder, A. (2017). How Carbon and Nitrogen Work Together, *SoilsForLife*, 15 November. https://www.soilsforlife.org.au/why-carbon-flows-with-alan-lauder/how-carbon-and-nitrogen-work-together. Downloaded 11 December 2019.

Lenin, V.I. (1903). To the Rural Poor – An Explanation for the Peasants of What the Social-Democrats Want. In Lenin, *Collected Works*. https://www.marxists.org/archive/lenin/works/1903/rp/3.htm. Downloaded 14 November 2019.

Lenin, V.I. (1916). Imperialism and the Split in Socialism. *Sbornik Sotsial-Demokrata*, No. 2, 2 December. https://www.marxists.org/archive/lenin/works/1916/oct/x01.htm. Downloaded 14 November 2019.

Luxemburg, R. (1951). *The Accumulation of Capital: A Contribution to an Economic Explanation of Imperialism*, translated by Agnes Schwarzschild and with an introduction by J. Robinson (originally published in German 1913). https://www.marxists.org/archive/luxemburg/1913/accumulation-capital/accumulation.pdf. Downloaded 13 November 2019.

Lönnroth, J. (1977). *Marxism som matematisk ekonomi*. Göteborg: Nationalekonomiska Institutionen vid Göteborgs Universitet.

Lönnroth, J. (1991). Before Economics. In B. Sandelin (ed.), *The History of Swedish Economic Thought* (pp. 11–43). London and New York: Routledge.

Marx, K. (1852). The Eighteenth Brumaire of Louis Bonaparte. First published in the first issue of *Die Revolution* in New York. In Marx-Engels Archive. https://www.marxists.org/archive/marx/works/download/pdf/18th-Brumaire.pdf. Downloaded 4 November 2019.

Marx, K. (1875). Critique of the Gotha Programme. Written and circulated in German 1875, published in English by Progress Publishers Moscow 1970 with a foreword by Engels from 1891. In Marx-Engels Archive. https://www.marxists.org/archive/marx/works/1875/gotha/ch01.htm. Downloaded 9 November 2019.

Marx, K. (1887). *Capital – A Critique of Political Economy, Volume I*, first published. In German in 1867, first English edition edited by Engels and published in 1887. In Marx-Engels Archive. https://www.marxists.org/archive/marx/works/download/pdf/Capital-Volume-I.pdf. Downloaded 10 November 2019.

Marx, K. (1895). The Class Struggles in France 1848–1850 (originally a number of articles in Neue Rheinische Zeitung published in 1850) with an introduction by Engels. In Marx-Engels Archive. https://www.marxists.org/archive/marx/works/1850/class-struggles-france/. Downloaded 8 November 2019.

Marx, K. and Engels, F. (1848). *Manifesto of the Communist Party*. In Marx-Engels Archive. https://www.marxists.org/archive/marx/works/download/pdf/Manifesto.pdf. Downloaded 2 November 2019.

Piketty, T. (2014). *Capital in the Twenty-First Century* (original: *Le capital au XXI siècle*, 2013). Cambridge, MA: Harvard University Press.

7 Alfred Marshall, poverty and economic theory

A historical perspective

Carl-Axel Olsson[†]

> ... free human beings are not brought up to their work on the same princi-
> ples as a machine, or horse, or a slave. If they were, there would be very little
> difference between the distribution and the exchange side of value.
>
> Marshall 1898

That Alfred Marshall (1842–1924) chose to devote himself to the academic
discipline of political economy was very much due to a desire to understand
poverty as a social phenomenon and investigate how it could be combated.
This assertion may perhaps seem a trifle surprising. It is not altogether un-
common, in fact, for Marshall to be presented in the context of the history
of economic thought as the very prototype of the neoclassical economist; the
advocate of the hypothetical-deductive method; and the constructor of the
partial equilibrium analysis, with associated assumptions concerning atom-
ism, methodological individualism, reductionism and ceteris paribus. This
picture is not false, of course, but it is incomplete, and it fails to include
his interest and involvement in the social problems of the age, especially
those relating to poverty in society. Nor does it include—and it is important
to make this point—his view regarding the limitations of economic theory
when seeking insights into complex social problems. Thus, it was this interest
in the problem of poverty that formed the base from which Marshall selected
the scholarly route he was to follow, and this interest did not flag as his academic career proceeded. Inside Alfred Marshall the analyst, there was also
Alfred Marshall the preacher and an unresolved ambivalence between the
scientific and the ethical. John Maynard Keynes (1933, p. 169) writes in his
celebrated and now classic biography of Alfred Marshall that

> Alfred Marshall belonged to the tribe of sages and pastors; yet, like them,
> endowed with a double nature, he was a scientist too. As a preacher and
> pastor of men, he was not particularly superior to other similar natures.
> As a scientist he was, within his own field, the greatest in the world for
> a hundred years.

The present essay examines Alfred Marshall's vacillation between his roles as 'preacher' and 'scientist' from a standpoint rooted in the poverty problem.

Interest in poverty

When Marshall started his academic studies at Cambridge, he focused with success on the mathematical field (Corry 1968, Whitaker 1977, Rima 1990). However, mathematics did not challenge him sufficiently, for he cherished a hope that his academic studies would also lead to a fuller knowledge of the conditions then prevailing in society. Marshall wanted to use this knowledge as a weapon in the war against poverty—an ambition, it has to be said, which was not wholly original among the educated classes of the time.[1] The value judgments underpinning this social mission consisted of a complicated mixture of religious, ethical and philosophical (utilitarian) conceptions and ideas drawing their nourishment from the spirit of the Victorian age.[2]

Therefore, if an ecclesiastical career was uninteresting and mathematics showed itself to be an inadequate vehicle for the 'mission', the question that arises is why he chose economic science. Marshall himself has answered the question, and the answer is to be found in Keynes's biography (Keynes 1933, p. 166f.). It revolves around a note which Marshall wrote in 1917. He was 75 years of age and had retired from the Chair of Political Economy at the University of Cambridge nine years earlier. He had intended the note for the wastepaper basket, but for some reason his wife, Mary Paley, rescued it for posterity. The note reveals that when the young Marshall was in full swing with his mathematical studies he began to reflect on the question, 'How far do the conditions of life of the British ... working classes generally suffice for the fullness of life?' To find an answer to this question, he was urged by 'older and wiser men' to study political economy. The first consequence of this suggestion was that Marshall immersed himself in John Stuart Mill's *Principles of Political Economy*. One result of this reading was a continued interest in the inequalities between rich and poor which prevailed in society, and he concluded that these inequalities perhaps had some connection with the fact that the prerequisites for achieving a reasonable living standard were highly diverse. The difference between being poor and not being poor resulted from '*inequalities of opportunity* [emphasis added] rather than of material comfort'. However, Marshall was not satisfied with this supposition, or should we say hypothesis. In fact, what he did was to attack the problem by means of what we would today call field studies (Keynes 1933, p. 166):

> ... in my vacations I visited the poorest quarters of several cities and walked through one street after another, looking at the faces of the poorest people. Next, I resolved to make as thorough a study as I could of Political Economy.

And that was what he did, as we know. His interest in the social problem and the conviction that it ought to have a prominent place in economic science did not diminish with the years either. In the introductory chapter to *Principles of Economics* in 1890, he hopes that his fellow men may outgrow the belief that poverty is necessary, and claims that 'this is what gives to economics their chief and their highest interest' (Marshall 1920, p. 4),[3] after having stated that 'the study of causes of poverty is the study of a large part of mankind'[4] (Marshall 1920, p. 3). We will have reason to refer again to these views, and to *Principles of Economics*.[5]

Referring again to the note of 1917, this concludes with an admission which bears on the problem of the ability of economic science to solve social problems. Marshall confesses that in spite of having devoted 50 years of his life to the scholarly study of economics, his knowledge of the object of his studies was still defective. Perhaps it had not even improved. 'I am conscious of more ignorance of it than I was at the beginning of the study' (Keynes 1933, p. 167). In terms of knowledge of the causes of poverty and the question of how we are to regard the relation between rich and poor, Marshall already had a fairly resigned attitude ten years after the publication of *Principles of Economics*, despite the fact that he devoted much space to the distribution problem, both theoretically and historically.[6] In a reply by letter to a Bishop Wescott in 1900, Marshall writes with regard to the Christian exhortation to take from the rich and give to the poor: 'I would promote all such by every means in my power that were legitimate; and I would not be specially scrupulous in interpreting that word'. But this is no easy task, and the economic theory of distribution is manifestly unable to offer much guidance. 'I am not ashamed to confess that I know of no simple means by which a fair wage can be assured to all workers' (Pigou 1956, p. 386).

We will now leave the 'mature' Marshall for the moment and revert to his early career as a political economist and to the development of his interest in social problems, especially those associated with the economic situation of the working class.

Marshall's early career

In 1868, Marshall became an assistant lecturer in political economy at St John's College, Cambridge. He was to remain in that post for nearly ten years; yet he published very sparingly during that period. Two of his early articles appeared in *Bee-Hive*, a well-known workers' journal, in 1874. Their titles are 'The Laws of Political Economy. What They Can Teach, and What They Cannot Teach' and 'The Province of Political Economy' (Harrison 1963).[7] Around the same time, he also published a lecture on the topic of 'The Future of the Working Class'. We will have more to say about this.

The first two articles have virtually the character of debating contributions posing the key question of whether it is possible for economic science to distinguish between facts and value judgments. In brief, whether economic laws are always superior to social ideals and the moral code, which the practitioner of the science may be thought to uphold. In principle, it seems to be Marshall's opinion that the two aspects ought to be kept separate, but he realizes the difficulties (Harrison 1963, p. 425):

> But many of these cases which political economy presents to our moral judgement are not so clear. With regard to these it is absolutely necessary to keep entirely distinct two questions; that which must be decided according to the laws of political economy, viz., what consequences will follow from a postponed (sic) course of action, and that which must be decided by our moral judgements, viz., whether an action which produces these consequences is right.

In the second article, Marshall cites the authority of John Stuart Mill. 'There have always, indeed, been important controversies respecting the limits of political economy'. But many great economists have not hesitated to pronounce on great ethical and social problems. Mill's *Principles of Political Economy* is a good example, since it discusses 'principles of political economy with some of its applications to social philosophy'. Marshall continues—and these comments are perhaps not without a degree of topicality (Harrison 1963, p. 426),

> Those writers who have most furthered the science have not in general been those for whom its chief attractions were in the athletic exercise, which its reasonings offer to the vigorous intellect, or in the entertainment, which its results provide for the curious inquirer. Rather have they been men whose eager interest in the great problems of social life and well-being rendered it intolerable to them that one of the constituent elements of the solution of these problems should needlessly remain in a condition of vague uncertainty. They have seen that those portions of the problems of life to which political economy devotes herself are at once so complex that they cannot be treated at all without the aid of a special machinery, and so nearly homogeneous that they can well be treated by such machinery.

Perhaps what we have here is an indication of what Marshall would focus his attention on later on, that is, the designing of this 'special machinery', the engine of analysis which was to become the theoretical foundation of *Principles of Economics* and would contain what Joseph Schumpeter has called Marshall's set of 'handy tools' (Schumpeter 1941).[8] It is worth noticing that even at this early stage, Marshall clearly grasped the limitations of theoretical analysis when dealing with complex social problems. The pressing question in this perspective was what the future looked like for the working classes in England. Marshall tackled the question in a lecture in 1873. Again, he relied on Mill, or to be more accurate, on Mill and his wife.[9]

The topic had been discussed in one of the chapters of Mill's *Principles of Political Economy*. According to Mill, it was thanks to his wife that the topic was examined. Marshall is full of admiration for her contribution (Pigou 1956, p. 101):

> All the instances that he (Mill) gives of this tend to show how our progress would be accelerated if we would unwrap the swaddling clothes in which artificial customs have enfolded woman's mind and would give her free scope womanfully to discharge her duties to the world. But one instance strikingly illustrates the intimate connection, to which all history testifies, between the free play of the full and strong pulse of woman's thoughts and the amelioration of the working classes.

Who are the working classes? The answer is not clear, and Marshall gets himself involved in an attempt to solve the riddle. He considers that there is an important distinction between 'a gentleman' and 'a working man' but finds it difficult to establish criteria for this. He further observes that there is an elaborate social scale among workers. It is not enough to distinguish between 'skilled' and 'unskilled'. However, Marshall is hopeful of the prospects for future improvement of the conditions of workers generally and thus also of their opportunities of becoming 'gentlemen'.

But society has its darker side, and it is there that we find 'those vast masses of men who, after long hours of hard and unintellectual toil, are wont to return to their narrow homes with bodies exhausted and with minds dull and sluggish' (Pigou 1956, p. 105). To remedy the situation of these most lowly of classes is a considerably more difficult task, but not impossible. However, what it demands is neither more nor less than a new society. We cannot take the present for granted, and in this respect, history has something to teach us (Pigou 1956, p. 109):

> The ancients argued that Nature had ordained slavery: that without slaves the world could not progress; no one would have time for culture; no one could discharge the duties of a citizen. We have outgrown this belief. But have we outgrown the conception that many people have to live by the sweat of their brow so that others may live in luxury? May not the world outgrow this belief, as it has outgrown the other? [...] It may and it will.

The difficulties entailed in changing these unequal conditions have been exaggerated. Various proposed solutions have not infrequently been associated with one form or another of social change in a socialist direction. 'But such a subversion is not required for the country which we are to picture to ourselves'. What is needed is a society in which every employee is nothing less than a gentleman. What is the mark of such a society? Marshall's answer is both verbose and a little obscure, but the main points are as follows: Another form of division of labor is required, and a shortening of working hours.

Monotonous jobs offer no opportunities for mental and intellectual stimulation. Everyone in this 'fancied society' will have the same opportunities of participating in its prosperity. It requires a reasonable population level,[10] but above all equality of educational opportunity for children and young people. Education is assigned an important role in the proposed transformation of the society, as it emerges clearly when Marshall goes on to discuss what obstacles stand in the way of making this future society a reality.

One objection to the idea of cutting the working hours for the labor force is that it would reduce the potential for growth of industry and therefore of the economy as a whole. Marshall does not believe in this objection. With continued scientific progress and technical innovation, labor productivity will increase and ensure enhanced prosperity. There are productivity gains to be had in agriculture as well.

Will not a curtailment of working hours bring a threat to international competitiveness and stagnation of foreign trade? Marshall does not find this particularly convincing either. It is the high level of education that constitutes the most important element of competitiveness. Possibly, some capital will leave the country. On the other hand, shorter working hours for the labor force do not mean that real capital is lying idle: 'In our society the hours of labour are to be very short, but it does not follow that the hours of work of the machinery would be short too' (Pigou 1956, p. 113). Marshall puts his faith in the introduction of a system of shift working, each shift putting in six hours per day, for example. Such a system will facilitate the efficient use of machinery.

Nor does Marshall exclude the possibility of counteracting the capital flight outlined by the Mills. He proposes that the workers themselves can do this through 'associations' established for the purpose of owning and managing factories collectively. It is true that past experience of such 'associations' has not been particularly good, but Marshall believes that this is because their managements contained 'uneducated men, men who are unable to follow even the financial calculations that are required for an extensive and complicated business'. In other words, once more, education is the solution, which necessarily raises the question of how this high level of education can be achieved in the society of the future. Is there not a risk that some parents will fail to let their children benefit from the education on offer, thus creating a new class of uneducated? (Pigou 1956, p. 114):

> This is the danger most to be dreaded. But even this danger is not so great as it appears. An educated man would not only have a high conception of his duty to his children; he would be sensitive to the social degradation, which he and they would incur if he failed in it. Society would be keenly alive to the peril to itself of such a failure, and would punish it as a form of treason against the state.

There is a pedagogical duty here, and it rests on the state. It is a matter of bringing about a change of attitude among the citizenry. '... just as a man who has borrowed money is bound to pay it back with interest, so a man is bound to give to his children an education better and more thorough than he himself received' (Pigou 1956, p. 117).

However, it is not only a question of people being educated to think like gentlemen. A change of attitude can yield socioeconomic profits. Actually, the difference between the value which an educated individual can create for society and that which an uneducated individual generates is many times greater than the cost of the education itself. In modern terminology, what Marshall is asserting is the importance of 'human capital'.

Marshall on 'progress and poverty'

The American economist Henry George published his book *Progress and Poverty* in 1880, and a year later, it came out in England. The book attracted much attention in Britain and achieved a remarkable volume of sales. Because of its success, Henry George made an acclaimed lecture tour of Britain and Ireland in 1882. There were many, especially among intellectuals, who were impressed by George's ideas.[11] The majority of the British economists were, however, somewhat unresponsive to *Progress and Poverty* and failed to pay much attention to George's thinking—with one exception: Alfred Marshall. He seized the opportunity to deliver a number of lectures on the subject.[12]

A principal theme of Henry George's book is his criticism of the private ownership of land. With a growing population and speculation in land on the part of both private individuals and firms, the land rent tends to rise, which threatens the productive use of labor and capital. In this way, progress itself contains the cause of poverty. George's solution, besides various proposals for land reform (such as nationalization), was based on taxation of landownership and above all the taxing of the incremental value generated by landownership.[13]

For Marshall, Henry George's book was a reminder to us all that 'we ought not to be content with our progress as long as there is so much suffering in the world' (Marshall 1969, p. 184). His first lecture is entitled 'Wealth and Want: Do They Increase Together?' Thus, it discusses the connection between economic progress and the distributional consequences it entails. The question had formed a subject for discussion in Henry George's book. George had also supplied an answer. 'Mr. George says that progress drives a wedge into the middle of society, raising those that are above it but lowering those that are below' (Marshall 1969, p. 188).[14]

Marshall began his discourse with an economic historical review of the last 200 years, establishing that the pattern followed by productivity and prices had led to rising real wages. Technical developments, in the form of railways, the telegraph, gas lighting and medical care, for example, had brought about higher living standards even for the common man. Nevertheless, despite the rising prosperity, society had not enjoyed a corresponding reduction of poverty. 'The existence of a large pauper class is a disgrace to the age'. The conclusion arrived at in this introductory lecture is that increased prosperity does not necessarily mean that all classes of society will benefit from it. Marshall is optimistic about the future just the same. He places special trust in the capabilities of the laboring classes. 'I believe that the good will increase and evil diminish, that the working classes will now set themselves to abolish systematic want and pauperism, and that they will do it before very many years are over' (Stigler 1969, p. 190).

Poverty and the theory of distribution

The title of the second lecture is 'Causes of Poverty', and here Marshall becomes rather more analytical, discussing the question of distribution within a theoretical framework.[15] He begins by criticizing George for basing his conclusions on outdated doctrines of distribution such as the wage-fund theory and Ricardo's theory of rent.[16] In the modern interpretation of the distribution problem, the three production factors, land, capital and labor, are treated as equivalents. They all contribute to the production result and each is therefore entitled to a remuneration related to its contribution. As regards the labor factor, this, in turn, can be divided into 'different grades or classes of labour. Each of these classes of labour has its work in production; we may call it a factor in production'. Moreover, from these starting points it is possible to formulate a general theory of distribution (Stigler 1969, p. 193):

> ... the great law of distribution is that the more useful one factor of production is, and the scarcer it is, the higher will be the rate at which its services are paid. For instance, if two skilled laborers, after allowing for the expense of the machinery they use, can do as much work as five unskilled, they will get as much wages as the five unskilled can get, if they stay in the trade.

How the factors of production are deployed may vary from country to country, and this is reflected in the remuneration which each respective factor receives. The question that springs to mind at once is what this general principle of distribution has to do with poverty. Now Marshall comes back to the difference between skilled and unskilled labor. Supposing that the number of unskilled workers increases compared with the number of skilled workers, then the former will have difficulties finding jobs, thus depressing the wages for this category relatively to skilled workers and also to capital (Stigler 1969, p. 182):

> On the other hand—and this sentence is the kernel of all that I have to say about poverty—if the numbers of unskilled laborers were to diminish sufficiently, then those who did unskilled work would have to be paid good wages.

This requires commitments on the part of society. Marshall again emphasizes the importance of education, but other changes are needed as well.

'A first-rate education, general and technical, to be given to every child. Laziness and drunkenness should to be treated severely, the most abundant tenderness and charity to misfortune. There will then be no pauperism and even no poverty' (Marshall 1969, p. 195).

Historically, these tendencies have been counteracted by forces which, in essence, are those of class. Admittedly, it is true that during the last 100 years the middle class has become (Marshall 1969, p. 197),

> frugal and self-controlled, and in spite of their want in education, they grew in moral strength. But the working classes missed this great opportunity of rising. The new wealth was spent, not in keeping children in school, but bribing them in factories at too early age; not in enabling the industrious and upright to bring up their families to a higher and better life than their own, but in pampering the most worthless … A well fed and well educated population is in the long run the best investment for a nation's capital. But many of the English working classes have not been properly fed, and scarcely any of them have been properly educated. The result is that we English are not nearly as fine a set of people as we might have been; and we have still poverty and pauperism among us.

Is nationalization of land a solution?

Marshall's third lecture poses the question whether 'nationalisation of land is the remedy for poverty'. This question cannot be answered without some knowledge of economic history. But knowledge is not enough in itself. It must be subjected to economic analysis. Such an analysis must include a study of the connection between different forms of landownership and poverty. 'One of the favourite panaceas for poverty has always been a rearrangement of the rights to the land' (Marshall 1969, p. 200). However, the solution is not without problems. There is an obvious risk that historical experience(s) will obscure the theoretical treatment of the question of nationalization of the land as things are at present.

There is an abundance of historical examples, says Marshall, of unjust acquisition of land and of autocratic land ownership. Moreover, these have rightfully been the subject of criticism and moral censure. However, can today's landowners be held accountable? In addition, what is to be our stance with regard to the assertion that the land belongs to the nation? The question is which nation. Marshall resorts to rhetoric (Marshall 1969, p. 201):

> If the Normans took England by force from the Saxons, who had taken it by force from the Britons—and if we are to undo all original wrongs, ought we not to instate in possession the descendants of the Ancient Britons—at all events till historians are able to tell us who it was from whom the Ancient Britons stole the land?

The relevant question with regard to nationalization as a means for eliminating poverty is whether the present landownership affects national prosperity in a negative way, and Marshall distinguishes three such possible situations. First the landowner may, by virtue of his position, exercise political, social and religious power over his inferiors—this is the landowner as tyrant. Marshall had little time for this argument. Political and social developments in his England had reached a stage where there is little reason to fear this kind of situation even though there were historical examples of such exercise of power. The second reason for a change in landownership has to do with farming techniques. Large-scale landownership would have an inhibiting influence on the introduction of new and more efficient methods of cultivation. Marshall felt that there was not much to be said for this argument either. Economic history showed that England had long played a crucial role in agricultural progress. This applied not only to methods of cultivation but also to the development of machinery and efficient animal husbandry. It was these types of improvements which the English colonists took with them to North America and put into practice there.[17]

Third, had the English system of agriculture resulted in agricultural workers having less favorable conditions and therefore being at greater risk of falling into poverty than 'peasant proprietors in foreign countries'? This argument is associated with John Stuart Mill and certain other authors. Marshall found it less than completely convincing, however, and argues that 'they drew sweeping inferences from exceptional cases ...' having to do with 'Poor Laws, Corn Laws and other misfortunes', in other words with the policy in force. But 'since then the position of the peasant proprietors has in many cases deteriorated, while that of the English labourers has immensely improved' (Marshall 1969, p. 203). Mere landownership did not constitute either a guarantee of a decent living standard or a solution to the problem of poverty. On the other hand, Marshall did not exclude the possibility that the ownership of land may promote the emergence of new personal qualities in the individual: 'I think that the purchase of a small plot of land, not as commercial investment, but as one of affection, like the purchase of a dog, often has a healthy influence on character' (Stigler 1969, p. 183).

Perhaps this is a somewhat drastic—not to say ill considered—comparison. Nevertheless, the conclusion was that nationalization of the land cannot furnish a solution to the problem of poverty. Instead, it is a matter of bringing about a mental change among the lower classes while preventing the potential for development created by market competition from being lost. Marshall concluded his discourse with some expressions of hope with reference to the conduct and conditions of the working classes in the near future. 'My remedy for poverty ... is to increase the competition of capital and of upper classes of industry for the aid of the lower classes. What steps are to be taken to this end?' (Marshall 1969, p. 209).

Marshall identifies five such steps. The first one has to do with the demographic condition of the nation. The marriage age was too low among workers compared with the middle classes. Early marriage brings many children, which hinders the improvement of the lot of the most disadvantaged classes. Marrying later would not only reduce childbirths but also create better conditions for saving prior to marriage. The second step requires children not to be put out to waged labor at too early an age. However, this step presupposes assistance from the state, meaning that it must offer 'a good general and technical education to all, and a first-rate education to even the poorest child who shows a special fitness for it' (Stigler 1969, p. 209). However, the third step makes a demand on the workers. They have to take active part in the endeavor of getting the most morally depraved paupers to raise from the wretchedness of their plight. 'It cannot be done without their aid. And then public and private charity might be given to the upright, industrious, and thrifty working-men without fear of doing more harm than good' (Stigler 1969, p. 183).

Marshall thus comes back once again to the role of education. In the third stage, the emphasis is on what we would nowadays call on-the-job or in-service training, in the sense here of 'the education that the working classes are given themselves, both in the workshop and out of it'. It is not quite clear whether the initiative for these measures was up to the working class itself or whether the responsibility rested on the government.

In the fifth and final step towards the elimination of poverty, Marshall became both moral and sympathetic. But at the same time, it contained an appeal to every citizen in the nation, especially the women (Marshall 1969, p. 210):

> ... we should all get a higher sense of duty. This would save money and time spent in excessive drinking and crime. It would cause us all to be gentler and more helpful to our neighbours; it would strengthen the family bond, which is the basis for progress; and lastly it would make us spend our money more wisely. We should avoid silly show, and we should aim at beauty in dress, but not at rapid following of the fashions. And, thus at last I am getting to the end of all. Man is the perfection of nature, but woman is one step further still. Progress in general and the abolition of poverty depend above all things on the strength and gentleness and purity and earnestness of the women of England. It is they that form character when it is most plastic.

Joint mobilization on the part of the two sexes will bring it about that poverty—and this is Marshall's final word—'will vanish away' (Stigler 1969, p. 183).

Are there two Marshalls, and was 1885 the turning point?

Apart from a brief guest appearance at Oxford, the Marshalls stayed at Bristol until 1884 when Alfred Marshall was appointed to the chair at Cambridge, which he occupied until his retirement in 1908. Marshall's inaugural lecture in 1885 was entitled 'The Present Position of Economics' (Pigou 1956, p. 152ff.). However, it contains considerably more than a description of the subject's position. The lecture has virtually the character of a policy statement or manifesto. Primarily, Marshall argues the case for making 'economics' an independent subject at the university. In so doing, he discusses the problems of the present position of the economic science with reference to its classical representatives, most notably Ricardo. The scholarly contribution of the historical schools is also discussed, and so is the importance of Auguste Comte's positivism (Olsson 1994, p. 12ff.). We will leave these problems aside and instead pose the question whether Marshall in his manifesto was expressing a changed view of the problem of poverty and how to combat it. Or instead, perhaps, whether his 'social mission', which, of course, was the starting point of his study of political economy, was now being toned down in favor of a more analytical approach to economic conditions, especially the problem of distribution, and thus also to what five years later would feature as a part of *Principles of Economics*.[18]

Marshall opens his discourse with a criticism of the early nineteenth-century economists, especially Ricardo, although this is never explicitly stated. The thrust of the criticism is that these 'classical' economists ignored history and failed to notice some important actual circumstances. 'They regarded man as, so to speak, a constant quantity and gave themselves little trouble to study his variations' (Pigou 1956, p. 154f.). The omission was not very great as long as the economic analysis concerned itself with money or foreign trade, but it did 'great harm when … [it] treated … the relations between the different industrial classes'. Human labor was regarded as a mere commodity, which could be dealt with in a mechanical fashion within the framework of the forces of supply and demand (Pigou 1956, p. 155):

> In particular, they did not see that the poverty of the poor is the chief cause of that weakness and inefficiency which are the cause of their poverty: that they have not the faith that modern economists have in there possibility of vast improvement in the condition of the working classes.

What Marshall asserts is that modern economists no longer needed to assume a 'wage fund' or an 'iron law of wages'. The field was open for the pattern of distribution to differ from the one stipulated by the classical political economists (meaning Ricardo).

Marshall also refers to a methodological question, which has relevance for the poverty problem. He takes as his starting point Auguste Comte, who raised the question of whether it is possible to separate studies of economics from social and political conditions and phenomena, and also whether social problems such as poverty, for example, are not too complex and changeable to be capable of being understood from a purely economic perspective. Marshall does not reject this view, but he adds that a more comprehensive approach requires a science (and a theory?) embracing the whole society.

> No doubt if that existed Economics would gladly find shelter under its wing. But it does not exist; it shows no signs of coming into existence. There is no use in waiting idly for it; we must do what we can with our present resources.

What Comte had not noticed sufficiently was that the only method available to us in dealing with complex social problems is one based on breaking the problem down into its component parts. 'When it is broken up each separate part offers a foothold to treatment by a special scientific organon, if there be one ready' (Pigou 1956, p. 164). It is quite reasonable to hold that this is the task which Marshall set himself with regard to the analysis of the economic sphere of our society. In addition, with the introduction of the partial equilibrium analysis in *Principles of Economics*, he would restrict his task further still.

In the absence of an all-embracing theory of society, there remains the question of what contribution history can make to the understanding and combating of the social evils from which the nation suffers. The 'younger' German historical school economists had undoubtedly helped to trace 'the history of economic habits and institutions [...] But they did not throw light on the particular economic problems of our age'. Its representatives have emphasized the importance of facts and the assembling of facts along with consideration of the historical conditions before any theoretical conclusions can be drawn. Marshall does not consider this a fruitful approach for economic science (Pigou 1956, p. 166):

> The answer is that facts by themselves are silent. Observations discover nothing directly of the actions of causes ... The conditions of human life are so various: every event is the complex result of many causes, so closely interwoven that the past can never throw a simple and direct light on the future.

What, then, is the task of the political economist in society? Marshall comes back to his original 'mission' by way of conclusion. The primary task of economic science is 'to take part in the great work of inquiring how far it is possible to remedy the economic evils of the present day'. This task entails finding ways of increasing economic prosperity and ensuring that this prosperity is distributed fairly. It does not happen today and this is paradoxical. 'Never was there an age so full of great social problems as ours' (Pigou 1956, p. 172). This places heavy demands on the representatives of economic science (Pigou 1956, p. 173):

They might then take a wise and active part in relieving misery without making pauperism; in helping the people to educate themselves and rise to a higher level; to become not only more efficient producers but also wiser consumers, with greater knowledge of all that is beautiful, and more care for it.

The view that all individuals should have the possibility of a decent life is not the sole preserve of 'impetuous socialists and ignorant orators'. It is a view which would be a guiding principle for all economists learning their trade at Cambridge. It was true that the economic science was still 'in its infancy', but Marshall declares that it is his ambition (Pigou 1956, p. 174)

to increase the numbers of those, whom Cambridge, the mother of strong men, sends out in the world with cool heads and warm hearts, willing to give some at least of their best powers to grappling with the social suffering around them.

Does the inaugural lecture of 1885 mean that Marshall changed his social commitment in any vital respect vis-à-vis both the poverty question and his view of the working class—that in terms of pure methodology he was taking a more theoretical and analytical road, and that he had reached a 'turning point' signifying that the 'mission' has to make way for a purely theoretical approach? The question is controversial and subject to debate. I have difficulty finding evidence of a 'turning point', so I abstain from entering the debate.[19] The future will have to speak for itself.

The poverty question in *Principles of Economics*

When Marshall's *Principles of Economics* appeared in 1890, a good part of the contents was already familiar, at least to his early students. It has been said that by 1890 there were already 'Marshallians' everywhere. H.S. Foxwell stated as early as 1887 that Marshall's former students occupied around half of 'the economic chairs in the United Kingdom'.[20] Eight editions of the book would be published—the last one in 1920, and we will revert later to its concluding words. But let us first examine the question whether the existence of poverty is a topic covered in *Principles of Economics*. Marshall is very clear about this question. On the first few pages of the book, he is already emphasizing the importance of the task confronting economic science when grappling with the problem of poverty. The reason is simple. The task of political economy is to study people 'in the ordinary business of life'; it examines that part of individual and social action which is most closely connected with the attainment and with the use of the material requisites of wellbeing (Marshall 1920, p. 1).

The terms of existence of the extremely poor element in the big cities—'the Residuum'—are unacceptable, as is the poverty found both in town and country caused by inadequate wages. Poverty means that children, in particular, are forced to grow up with (Marshall 1920, p. 1 ff.)

> insufficient food, clothing, and house-room; whose education is broken off early in order that they may go to work for wages; who thenceforth are engaged during long hours in exhausting toil with imperfectly nourished bodies, and therefore have no chance of developing their higher mental faculties.

Poverty is not only degrading; it causes and aggravates poverty in the body of the nation. There is a vicious circle of poverty.

The important question at this point is whether economic progress can help to eliminate the problem so that 'all should start in the world with a fair chance of living a cultural life, free from the pains of poverty ...' This question is one which economic science cannot answer fully. For the answer lies in how human nature, both morally and politically, can be made to change. When facing this problem, economists have no special competence. Perhaps economic science can help by presenting facts and disclosing connections; 'and this it is which gives to economic studies their chief and their highest interest' (Marshall 1920, p. 4).

Limitations of the theory

Let me for a moment break the chronology of the present essay and cite some of the concluding sentences of the last edition of *Principles of Economics*. They almost have the character of a sum-up. Marshall was 78 years old and had four years left to live. This is how he concludes Chapter XIII of the sixth and last of the 'Books' of *Principles of Economics* (Marshall 1920, p. 722):

> And now we must conclude this part of our study. We have reached very few practical conclusions; because it is generally necessary to look at the whole of the economic, to say nothing of the moral and other aspects of a practical problem, before attempting to deal with it all: and in real life nearly every issue depends, more or less directly, on some complex actions and reactions of credit, of foreign trade and of modern developments of combination and monopoly. But the ground which we have traversed in Books V. and VI. is, in some respects, the most difficult of the whole province of economics; and it commands, and gives access to, the remainder.

The question is why Marshall refers just to Books V and VI, and why these are regarded as so central to an understanding of 'the whole province of economics'. Book V covers the entire 'the engine of analysis' and appurtenant 'handy tools' for the static partial equilibrium analysis and for understanding pricing in a market, and the title is 'General Relations of Demand and Supply, and Value'—in other words, the very foundation of the neoclassical theory of value and price. The next section, Book VI, deals with 'The Distribution of National Income'. In my view, one would have expected distribution to be discussed as a problem falling under the general theory of value and prices. However, it is with regard to this question that Marshall brings to the fore the limitations inherent in the theory of exchange, particularly when it is applied to the factor markets, not least the labor market. It has to be emphasized that this view of the matter is not new. Ingrid Rima has played a leading role in pointing out the problematical connection between the two parts and has pursued the thesis that there is an asymmetrical relationship between Books V and VI (Rima 1990, p. 415ff.). The thesis seems plausible. What has attracted less notice is that Alfred Marshall himself, as it appears to me, was aware at a relatively early stage of the tension existing between the two parts of *Principles of Economics*. As early as 1898, he published an article defending himself against critics who had objected to his treatment of the distribution problem. Despite his well-known reluctance to answer the criticisms, he chose, on this occasion, to offer some clarifications (Marshall 1898).[21] The question is whether the theory of exchange, more specifically 'the engine of analysis', in addition to covering the market in goods, can also be used as a theory of value and prices in the factor market and thus serve as an 'engine' in the case of distribution questions as well. Gradually, however, Marshall moves on to more fundamental methodological problems of economic science such as the relation between a static/mathematical analysis on the one hand, inspired by and analogous to physics and astronomy, and on the other a dynamic/evolutionary analysis based on a biological approach. In addition, in this discussion, Marshall makes no secret of the limitations entailed in the main theme of Book V: the treatment of 'General Relations of Demand, Supply, and Value'.

The theory confronted with new problems

The problem of classical political economy was how the needs of a growing population could be satisfied with the scarce resources furnished by nature (land). However, this problem, says Marshall, belongs to 'the earlier stages of economic reasoning'. The situation had changed (Marshall 1898, p. 42):

> The chief difficulties of economic science are now in another direction; they arise rather from the good than from the evil fortunes of mankind. The increasing command which progress is giving us over forces of nature is altering the conditions of work and life rapidly and in many various ways. It is altering the character as well as the magnitude of economical and social forces.

This does not mean that we have to condemn analogies with mechanics in such conceptions as equilibrium and the regular swing of a pendulum before it comes to rest. But (Marshall 1898, p. 43),

> the catastrophes of mechanics are caused by changes in the quantity and not in the character of the forces at work: whereas in life their character changes also. 'Progress' or 'evolution', industrial and social, is not mere increase and decrease. It is organic growth, chastened and confined and occasionally reversed by decay of innumerable factors, each of which influences and is influenced by those around it; and every such mutual influence varies with the stage, which the respective factors have already reached in their growth.

Analogies with physics are useful 'in the earlier stages of economic reasoning', but the question is whether they are equally useful 'in later stages'. Marshall is in doubt: 'Even though economic reality becomes increasingly complex, our ambition must be to abandon the analogies with physics and develop a method which will be "more biological in tone"' (Marshall 1898, p. 39). Economic progress makes quite different demands on the economic science, especially so where the distribution question is involved. It is in this set of problems and the change 'in tone' that the possible asymmetry between Book V and Book VI manifests itself, and Marshall makes no real secret of the methodological difference between them.

In both books, certainly, the main theme is,

> the broad causes that govern the relative prices of different kinds of effort and sacrifice, that is, of the factors of production of commodities; and thus the exchange side of *the general problem of value* is advanced together with the distribution side.

Nevertheless, there is a difference, and perhaps a crucial one. Marshall characterizes it as a change of tone—'there is a growing difference in tone (!)' (Marshall 1898, p. 54; emphasis added).

From abstraction to construction

In Marshall's view, the theory contained in Book V serves as 'the theoretical backbone of our knowledge of causes which govern value'. The theory is relevant to an understanding of 'exchange' and 'distribution'. However, he is careful to point out that the theory is an abstraction with but little connection with reality. In those instances where the theoretical analysis refers to actual conditions in a market, these are to be considered as illustrations whose purpose is to reinforce the theory, and not to increase the empirical content. The primary task of the theory is to give 'power to order and arrange knowledge' (Marshall 1898, p. 52). It is with this background in mind that we should consider the conception, or rather the assumption, of equilibrium as a natural starting point and a useful abstraction in the arranging and ordering of economic forces. This is a first and necessary step, but not a sufficient one. The function of abstraction is 'to give increased power to common sense, and common sense is the outcome of the experience of life, our own life and that of our ancestors; it is a biological rather than a dynamical instrument'. But the abstraction must be followed by 'construction', and it is this scientific phase that Marshall introduces and elaborates on in Book VI. The distribution question is brought to the foreground, and Marshall confronts it in these terms (Marshall 1898, p. 54):

> There we have very little to do with oscillations of a mechanical sort about a centre of equilibrium. We discuss demand and supply in their general relations, but even more and more from a biological point of view ... The keynote of the Book (VI) is in the fact that free human beings are not brought up to their work on the same principles as a machine, or horse, or a slave. If they were, there would be very little difference between the distribution and the exchange side of value.

What is it that makes the question of distribution require mechanism and equilibrium to be replaced by another approach? What is the reason why the factor markets, especially the market for labor, can no longer be understood within the framework of partial equilibrium analysis? What does Marshall mean by his examples of 'peculiarities of the labor markets' in Chapters IV and V of Book VI? Is the answer to unemployment and poverty to be found there?

For Marshall, going from 'abstraction' to 'construction' means that the mechanistic equilibrium approach must make room for the introduction of 'time', 'progress' and a dynamic or—as Marshall prefers to call it—'biological' perspective. It is with the transition from the abstract to the real economy that Marshall identifies 'the peculiarities of the labor market'. Particularly problematic is the supply of labor in the labor market. Markets for labor are unlike any other markets, and the 'peculiarities' which characterize them are, for the most part, to the detriment of the workers. Moreover, Marshall believes that these disadvantages lead to a cumulative worsening of the position of the workers and therefore to a tendency for the problems of unemployment and poverty to increase. It is primarily the workers' weak negotiating position that Marshall has in mind. That position is weakest among 'the lowest grades of labour' (Marshall 1920, p. 568).

These 'asymmetrical' conditions make it impossible, for example, for workers to 'invest' in their children's education, nor can a worker be bought and sold like a machine. 'The worker sells his work, but he himself remain his own property: those who bear the expenses of rearing and educating him receive but very little of the price that is paid for his services in later years' (Marshall 1920, p. 561).

In the real economy (construction), it is not possible to solve the distribution problem in the context of any theory. The class situation, legal rules and the distribution of power must be taken into account (Marshall 1920, p. 518):

> ... the wages of every class of labour tend to be equal to the net product due to the additional labour of the marginal labourer of the class. This doctrine has sometimes been put forward as a theory of wages, but there is no valid ground for any such pretensions. The doctrine that the earnings of a worker tend to be equal to the net product of his work has by itself no real meaning.

Such a theory of wages is particularly inappropriate if economic progress is a prevalent feature, and 'our growing power over nature yields an ever larger surplus above absolute necessities; and this is not absorbed by an unlimited increase in the population' (Marshall 1898, p. 53). The key question will therefore be how this 'surplus' is divided between the classes and individuals composing the society. It is apparent that Marshall has no answer to this question. It is too large to be handled within the framework of any economic theory, while at the same time it is vital to any understanding of poverty in the society and the existence of 'the Residuum'.

Economic progress, and with it a growing 'surplus', says Marshall (1907), has been distributed unequally in the society. Certain groups have been vouchsafed a higher standard of living, greater individual freedom, increased opportunities and, hopefully, a more elevated moral stature. However, the material, intellectual and moral advances that accompany economic progress ought to be shared by all. The position of the poor and the deprived in society is not a phenomenon that has individual or genetic causes. Social circumstances constitute the decisive factor for the private individual. Therefore, society has a massive responsibility. Adam Smith's view of the role of the state is partly overplayed, for the fact that 'the spread of education ... cooperated with technical progress ...' means that the state has more and more tasks to fulfil. The content of the laissez-faire concept needs to be redefined without recourse to collectivist measures. 'Let everyone work with all his might; and most of all let the Government arouse itself to do that work which is vital, and which none but Government can do efficiently' (Marshall, in Pigou 1956, p. 336).

Distribution in a society does not obey any cast-iron rules. In a progressive society, it is possible to take action against poverty and limited opportunities for weak groups. The social aim must be to make every man a 'gentleman' and every woman a 'lady'. The way to achieve this is not to be found in any economic theory. Ethical considerations are paramount in the matter. When young, Alfred Marshall was advised to study John Stuart Mill. His studies induced him to choose a career in political economy. Schumpeter believes that this choice had nothing to do with intellectual curiosity: 'He was driven to it from ethical speculations by a generous impulse to help in the great task of alleviating the misery and degradation he observed among the English poor'

(Schumpeter 1951, p. 95). As far as the distribution question was concerned, he undeniably made a good job of managing John Stuart Mill's legacy.

Notes

1 Alfred Coats (1967, pp. 706–709, see also Coats 1990) writes:

> Marshall shared the value assumptions commonly held by educated middle- and upperclass Victorians whose sons formed the bulk of his Cambridge audiences; and although his sociological assumptions, like his ethical precon- ceptions [...] may be irrelevant to his technical economics and could usually be taken or left according to the reader's individual taste ...

2 Sir Alexander Gray (1980, p. 347) expressed the matter thus in *The Development of Economic Doctrine. An Introductory Survey* (1931): 'He was pre-eminently Victorian in his encyclopaedic approach, both to learning and to life: a man could be competent at many things without risking the accusation of dilettante'.

3 The citation and the subsequent references made to *Principles of Economics* relate to the eighth edition published in 1920.

4 Joseph Schumpeter (1951, p. 93) explains the matter in this way in *Ten Great Economists*:

> ... it was not primarily intellectual curiosity that brought Marshall into the economist's camp. He was driven to it from ethical speculations and by a generous impulse to help in the great task of alleviating the misery and deg- radation he observed among the English poor. When talking about preoc- cupation with the subject, he was constantly rebuffed by a friend steeped in the economist's wisdom of the time, and that was why he turned to Mill's Principles for enlightenment. There are other indications from Marshall's work which suggest that he first learned his economics from that source.

5 Marshall refers back to Mill in *Principles of Economics* as well. He reminds us that Mill, from having supported Ricardo's implicit assumption that 'the desire for wealth' was the superior and general behavioral assumption about the individual, changed his opinion in *Principles of Political Economy* 1848. 'A change had come over his tone of thought and of feeling before he published in 1848 his great economic work'. Quite clearly, Marshall wanted to don Mill's mantle. In Mill's time, perhaps the time was not ripe for repudiating the view that (Marshall 1920, p. 765)

> man's sole attitude is the pursuit of wealth from those which do not. The change in his attitude was a part of the great changes that were going on in the world around him, though he was not fully aware of their influence on himself.

6 See *Principles of Economics*, Book VI, which has the title 'The Distribution of the National Income'.

7 'These articles have never been republished, and they are not included in Keynes' avowedly "complete" bibliographical list of Marshall's writings. They not only attest to the depth of his concern with "Labour" but also shed light on the re- lations between the scientific and evangelical spirits which warred within him' (Harrison 1963, p. 422).

8 The handy tools are to be found primarily in the theory of partial equilibrium, with concepts such as substitution, coefficients of elasticity, consumer surplus, quasi-rent, the representative firm and the long and short terms. Keynes also pre- sents similar views. He declares that Stanley Jevons, in fact, changed the classical

theory of value in dramatic fashion: 'Jevons saw the kettle boil and cried out with the delighted voice of a child; Marshall too had seen the kettle boil and sat down silently to build an engine' (Keynes 1956).

9 The lecture was delivered at a meeting of the Reform Club, a Cambridge debating society, in November 1873. It was subsequently disseminated in printed form. It can be read in Pigou (1925). In the rest of this essay, I will refer simply to *Memorials of Alfred Marshall*, an edition from 1956 printed in New York. It is interesting to observe that the publisher, Alfred Pigou, who became Marshall's successor at Cambridge, chose to include a somewhat apologetic commentary in a footnote on the published lecture written by the author himself: 'It is here reproduced without amendment or alteration of any kind; though it bears marks of the over-sanguine temperament of youth' (Pigou 1956, p. 100).

10 That is to say, a society which has left the 'Malthusian trap' behind.

11 It is said, for example, that this was how Bernard Shaw became a socialist.

12 See Stigler (1969). George Stigler published the lectures later with introductory comments. Marshall and Henry George met at a debate held in Oxford in connection with George's guest appearance in England. With hindsight, Paul Samuelson (1962, cited from Staley 1991) thought that this debate constituted 'an historical moment in economics' and an occasion which he regretted having missed!

> Marshall said that George had not in any single case understood the authors he criticized, that he had not proved that the way to remedy poverty was not to divide up land, that there was no doctrine in George's book which was both new and true. The report makes hilarious reading and gives a picture of Marshall which does not come out in his writings.

13 Of course, there was nothing new about pointing out the illegitimacy of the existence of land rent. As early as in David Ricardo, we can find an analysis of the redistribution in favor of landowners, which takes place as capitalism develops. In this model, the losers are the capitalists, whose profits fall. Ricardo does not exclude the possibility of capitalism stagnating in consequence of such redistribution. John Stuart Mill too has his doubts about land rents and, above all, about rises in them; as late as 1873, he proposed 'a confiscatory tax on future increments of land values' (Stigler 1969, p. 181).

14 It is interesting that although Marshall devoted three lectures to Henry George's book, he had no high opinion of George as an economist. Marshall acknowledges that some socialists are good scholars and scientists, but George is not of that category. 'He is by nature a poet, not a scientific writer' (Marshall 1969, p. 186).

15 Marshall does not provide any definition of poverty at all. That it is related to other social groups and thus a relative concept is more or less given. Whether this 'relative' poverty increases as prosperity rises in a society is an implicit hypothesis, which Marshall developed later. Reflections on the topic of 'absolute' poverty are not found in Marshall.

16 Addressing himself directly to David Ricardo and perhaps Henry George, Marshall says, 'Happily there is now no controversy as to the share which goes to the land as rent' (Marshall 1969, p. 192).

17 Expressed in the language of today's new institutional economics, the institution of private ownership of land provides the incentive for productivity-raising innovation and thus for economic growth.

18 The question has been approached from several different angles in the *Review of Social Economy*, which devoted an entire issue to Marshall in 1991, to celebrate the hundredth anniversary of the publication of *Principles of Economics*. I will not go into that debate but will content myself with attempting to clarify what

Marshall has to say about the question in this lecture. This does not mean that the contributions to that issue of *RSE* have not been of great assistance in shaping my own account.

19 See Petrides (1973), McWilliams-Tullberg (1975) and Coates (1967), who all emphasize 'a change in attitude or at least in the tone of Marshall's work, as manifesting itself around 1885'—an opinion which Rima (1990, p. 416) questions. Tullberg and Coates hold that with his manifesto of 1885, Marshall got rid of certain value judgments about socialism and other matters, making a clearer distinction between science and morals and ethics. Rima's view is that after 1885, Marshall attained a higher level of methodological awareness, the primary manifestation of which was the increasing importance he attached to the limitations of economic theory in relation to a complex reality.

20 Foxwell was a representative of the 'historical school' at Cambridge, but a friend of Marshall. In contrast to William Cunningham—Marshall's opponent in the celebrated methodological battle—Foxwell was not wholly out of sympathy with deductive economic theory. See Hodgson (2001, p. 104f.).

21 Marshall (1898, p. 37) writes, 'When the first Volume of a treatise remains for a long while without a successor, it is specially apt to be misinterpreted ... I have preferred as a rule to be silent'. But the criticism of the distribution theory cannot be ignored.

> I propose therefore to take it as the occasion of an attempt to show the place which the account of distribution and exchange given in my first volume holds in the general system of economics ... and in particular to indicate my views as to the nature and the limitations of the so-called "Statical" method.

References

Coats, A.W. (1967). Sociological Aspects of British Economic Thought (1880–1930). *Journal of Political Economy*, 75(5), 706–729.

Coats, A.W. (1990). Marshall and Ethics. In R. McWilliams Tullberg (ed.), *Marshall in Retrospect* (pp. 153–178). Aldershot: Edward Elgar.

Corry, B. (1968). 'Marshall', International Encyclopedia of the Social Sciences, Volume 10. New York: Macmillan.

Foxwell, H.S. (1887). The Economic Movement in England. *Quarterly Journal of Economics*, 2(1), 84–103.

Gray, A. (1980). *The Development of Economic Doctrine. An Introductory Survey*. New York: Longmans, Green.

Harrison, R. (1963). Two Early articles by Alfred Marshall. *Economic Journal*, 73(3), 422–430.

Hodgson, G.M. (2001). *How Economics Forgot. The Problem of Historical Specificity in Social Science*. London and New York: Routledge.

Keynes, J.M. (1933). *Essays in Biography*. London: Macmillan.

Keynes, J.M. (1956). *Essays and Sketches in Biography*. New York: Meridian Books.

Marshall, A. (1898). Distribution and Exchange. *Economic Journal*, 8(29), 37–59.

Marshall, A. (1907). Social Possibilities of Economic Chivalry. *Economic Journal*, 17(65), 7–29.

Marshall, A. ([1890] 1920). *Principles of Economics*. London and New York: Macmillan.

Marshall, A. (1969). Three Lectures on Progress and Poverty by Alfred Marshall. *Journal of Law and Economics*, 12(1), 184–226.

McWilliams-Tullberg, R. (1975). Marshall's Tendency for Socialism. *History of Political Economy, 7*(1), 75–111.

Olsson, C.-A. (1994). *Marshall and Economic History.* Lund: Department of Economic History.

Petrides, A. (1973). Alfred Marshall's Attitude to and Economic Analysis of Trade Unions: A Case of Anomalies in a Competitive System. *History of Political Economy, 5*(1), 165–198.

Pigou, A.C. (1925). *Memorials of Alfred Marshall.* London: Macmillan.

Pigou, A.C. (1956). *Memorials of Alfred Marshall.* New York: Macmillan.

Rima, I. (1990). Marshall's Concern about Poverty: A Hundredth Anniversary Retrospective. *Review of Social Economy, 48*(4), 415–435.

Samuelson, P.A. (1962). Economists and the History of Ideas. *American Economic Review, 2*(1), 1–18.

Schumpeter, J. (1941). Alfred Marshall's Principles. A Semi-Centennial Appraisal. *American Economic Review, 31*(2), 223–235.

Schumpeter, J. (1951). *Ten Great Economists.* New York and Oxford: Oxford University Press.

Staley, C.E. (1991). *A History of Economic Thought.* Cambridge: Cambridge University Press.

Stigler, G.J. (1969). Alfred Marshall's Lectures on Progress and Poverty. *The Journal of Law and Economics, 12*(1), 181–183.

Whitaker, J.K. (1977). Some Neglected Aspects of Alfred Marshall's Economic and Social Thought. *History of Political Economy, 9*(2), 189–197.

8 Knut Wicksell and the causes of poverty

Population growth and diminishing returns

Mats Lundahl

The subject of poverty and population is one of the few areas where the conventional wisdom is that Knut Wicksell failed to produce anything original. The only credit usually given for his writings on these subjects applies to his views of optimum population. Writers on Wicksell tend to pass his other writings on population by, give them a mere cursory treatment, or say that they are doctrinaire and lacking in originality (Lundahl 2005, pp. 1–4).

The only economist who seems to have understood what Wicksell did in the field of poverty and population was Johan Åkerman (1933, p. 114): '... Wicksell gave to the theory of Population a new impulse which proved of capital importance. He demonstrated that for every estimate of an optimum of population a thorough knowledge of the whole economic mechanism is essential.' This is what the present essay is about: Wicksell's views of the causes, consequences and remedies of poverty. It will be argued that there is a great deal more originality in Wicksell than what is commonly realized.

A Swedish Behemoth

Knut Wicksell's entrance into the public population debate was a Behemoth one. Inspired by *The Elements of Social Science*, by the Scottish physician George Drysdale (1876), he gave a speech at the temperance lodge *Hoppets Här* (The Army of Hope) in Uppsala in 1880 on 'The Most Common Causes of Habitual Drunkenness and How to Remove Them' (Wicksell 1880a, 1999a). Wicksell asked why people drink. His answer was that drunkenness was a symptom of poverty, and poverty was caused by population growth. But there was a remedy for poverty. In order to understand it, however, it was necessary to be familiar with 'the view of the causes of poverty that is named after the English clergyman and economist Malthus' (Wicksell 1999a, p. 95): population growth.

The majority of the male population hardly considered celibacy an alternative. Instead, the 1880s had '*poverty, late marriages, drunkenness, prostitution and secret infanticide*' (Wicksell 1999a, p. 104). The alternative was clear '... *every married couple ought to regard it as a sacred duty, indeed, as the most sacred of all duties, not to increase their family to more than two or three children without careful consideration*' (Wicksell 1999a, p. 108).

Wicksell's lecture brought strong reactions (Lundahl 2015). A number of pamphlets condemned his views and he received an admonition by the Lower University Council at Uppsala. The council was especially upset because Wicksell during the second of his lectures had argued that he considered 'no place, not even the pulpit itself, to be too exalted for the preaching of these doctrines' (Wicksell 1999a, p. 110).

Wicksell responded to his critics (Wicksell 1880a, pp. 71–95; 1880b). Poverty was caused by population growth, and the only way to reduce poverty was that of early marriages between spouses educated with respect to the use of contraceptive devices used to limit the size of their families. Only then would it be possible to raise the living standard of the general.

These ideas Wicksell would develop in a large number of writings all the way until his death in 1926. Once you put them side by side it is obvious that together they constitute a coherent general equilibrium theory of the interplay between population growth and poverty in the context of international trade and migration (possibly also capital movements). It is here that his original contribution to the analysis of poverty and population lies. The remainder of the chapter will be devoted to an examination of his theory. We will then begin with its core element: diminishing returns.

Diminishing returns

Since diminishing returns prevail everywhere in the economy, there is an inexorable tendency for population growth to result in a reduction of per capita income and wages (Wicksell 1892, p. 309):

> If, following a too strong population increase, production is displaced to ever more barren tracts, it will not only be the 'pioneers on the frontier of cultivation' that will suffer, but the entire labor force. Wages will fall across the board ...

Diminishing returns are present in other branches as well. In his essay on population for the French *Prix Rossi*, Wicksell (1891, p. 41) dealt with England's problem of securing a coal production that would allow industrial output to grow in the future. He argued that the peak had already been reached. Sweden, he contended, was in equally bad shape, if not worse (Wicksell 1902, p. 548).

The capital stock could be increased, but given its size there is no difference, and besides, it is hardly possible for manufacturing to live a life isolated from agriculture. '... it must necessarily build on agriculture as its foundation and be limited by the extent of the latter' (Wicksell 1914, p. 7). What goes for agriculture must in one way or another be true also for industry.

Diminishing returns are also present in infrastructure. Population growth calls for an increased consumption of foodstuffs, but in the countries of old culture such growth will hardly be possible without infrastructure development (Wicksell 1999c, p. 121). Once the most important infrastructure works are finished, diminishing returns to this activity set in. Thus, these works are undertaken to a lesser extent than before. This leads to unemployment. If the population continues to grow, sooner or later the number of redundant workers, and hence consumers, will increase.

The problem could also be conceived of as a savings problem (Wicksell 1999c, p. 123). Clearly, if the domestic return is low, capital will emigrate, and Wicksell argues that it may be better that emigrating workers are supported by emigrating capital than that they emigrate alone. However, sooner or later, conditions in the recipient countries will resemble those in the countries that they left. The return to capital will then fall, and it will be difficult to obtain a savings rate that can help to sustain the investment necessary to sustain a growing population.

Technological pessimism

One of the most frequently used arguments used to refute stagnation theories is that technological progress will raise incomes. Wicksell, however, argued that this matters little. It shifts the marginal productivity curve upwards, but diminishing returns will continue to take their toll, only from a higher level (Wicksell 1903, p. 173). Most of the time inventions simply lead to an increase of the size of the population, since they make it easier to find work. Sooner or later, some point is therefore reached where all that inventions can do is to sustain a given population (Wicksell 1999a, p. 97).

In his *Lectures on Political Economy*, Wicksell points to how technological progress in agriculture will in general be beneficial, but insufficient, for the workers when the population keeps growing. Technological progress or discovery of natural resources may increase the marginal productivity of labor and the wage rate, but population increases may wipe these increases out (Wicksell 1934, p. 121). Wicksell regarded technological progress as ambiguous from the wage, and hence poverty, point of view (Wicksell 1958, p. 102):

> ... an increase in the total product arising from technical innovations in production need not imply an increase in the marginal productivities of all production factors—and certainly not a uniform increase; it may even happen that the marginal productivity decreases for one factor, while increasing all the more for another. Either the marginal productivity of labour may increase at the expense of that of land, and therefore wages at the expense of rent, or conversely rent may increase at the expense of wages.

As examples of the former sequence, Wicksell cites inventions that increase natural resources, that make it possible to use previously neglected power sources or cultivate hitherto unproductive land. This could make land rents fall and leave the workers with the entire benefit of the production increase. The opposite may occur when an invention renders workers redundant without bringing new natural resources into production (Wicksell 1958, pp. 102–103).

In a celebrated passage in his *Lectures on Political Economy*, Wicksell (1934, p. 164) points to the possibility that labor-saving technological progress may lead to a reduction of wages. For Wicksell, capital was nothing but the 'original production factors', labor and land, saved and embedded in it for a certain time interval, and the rate of interest was '*the difference between the marginal productivity of saved-up labour and land and of current labour and land*' (Wicksell 1934, p. 154). Following Eugen von Böhm-Bawerk, he made a distinction between the 'height' and 'width' of capital. An expansion in height is an increase in the proportion of capital goods invested for longer periods at the expense of those invested for shorter periods, that is, capital deepening. Width refers to the proportion of primary factors annually invested in the replacement of capital goods of various maturity dates, and an expansion in width refers to the proportionate increase in all capital goods of different maturity dates, that is, capital widening (Blaug 1968, pp. 555–556).

Wicksell points out that capital accumulation will generally lead to a wage increase, whereas technological progress may not (Wicksell 1934, p. 164):

> ... the position is different where ... some *technical invention* renders long-term investment, even without a simultaneous growth of capital, more profitable (absolutely) than previously. The consequence must necessarily be – so long as no further capital is saved – a diminution in the 'horizontal-dimension' and an increase in the 'vertical-dimension', so that the quantity of capital used in the course of a year will be reduced; an increased quantity of current labour and land will consequently become available for each year's direct production; and, although this need not necessarily cause their marginal productivity and share in the product to be reduced – since the total product has simultaneously been increased by the technical discovery, yet a reduction may clearly result. The capitalist saver is thus, fundamentally, the friend of labour, though the technical inventor is not infrequently its enemy. The great inventions by which industry has from time to time been revolutionized, at first reduced a number of workers to beggary, as experience shows, whilst causing the profits of the capitalists to soar. [...] But it is really not capital which should bear the blame; in proportion as accumulation continues, these evils must disappear, interest on capital will fall and wages will rise – unless the labourers on their part simultaneously counteract this result by a large *increase in their numbers*.

Knut Wicksell's pessimistic views of technological progress and his insistence on the severity of diminishing returns led him to the conclusion that both Sweden and the rest of Europe were overpopulated.

Overpopulation

The overpopulation concept that Wicksell used was *relative* overpopulation. This is present as soon as the population has increased faster than the available means of nutrition. Wicksell argues that at least a partial relative overpopulation—among the age groups that accounted for most of the emigration—had characterized Sweden in the 1870s (Wicksell 1882, p. 99). He had good reasons for this. From 1850 to 1900, the total population increased from less than 3.5 million to over 5.1 (Hofsten and Lundström 1976, p. 13). Mortality had declined in virtually all age groups, but this decline had not been accompanied by any decline in fertility: The result was that the growth of the population had accelerated to rates never experienced hitherto. Farmers' children were forced to leave the countryside and attempt to make a living in urban areas, where most likely they would find their capital insufficient and be proletarianized. Wicksell was utterly pessimistic with respect to the future (Wicksell 1887a, p. 22) and contended that fertility had to be reduced with at least one-third to arrive at the equilibrium between birth and death rates (Wicksell 1887a, p. 25).

Overpopulation and war

Intimately connected with the growth of the population was war. In his 1880 lectures, Wicksell had emphasized two checks of population growth: war and emigration, and he took the war issue seriously (Wicksell 1979, p. 149). He pointed to Germany, arguing that in spite of all its economic progress that country had not managed to feed its population. 'What will be the end? Some war?' (Wicksell 1891, p. 297).

In 1914, the war was a fact. In his analysis of it, Wicksell states that the strife over territory 'in all periods has constituted the foremost if not the only reason for war', and behind the desire for expansion was always the growth of the population (Wicksell 1978, p. 246). Wars and population growth tended to form a vicious circle since wars were ultimately driven by lack of space to feed the population, but in order to win a war, you need a large population (Wicksell 1978, p. 247). However, if war and population growth form a vicious circle, there is, of course, no reason why peace and population control should not constitute a virtuous one.

Specialization and trade: a non-solution

Wicksell argued that the existence of an industrial sector was a sign of progress in a country beyond the satisfaction of the mere basic needs, and the as yet not finished colonization of overseas territories had led to a division of labor which allowed Europe to subsist on grain and other foodstuffs from overseas and from Eastern Europe (Wicksell 1999d, p. 148). This, however, had its own inherent dangers. The extensive trade of manufactures for food was likely to be just a temporary episode in the economic history. The colonial countries would themselves be running into diminishing returns to labor in agriculture and hence put more of their labor force into industry, and they would become the main consumers of their agricultural produce (Wicksell 1891, p. 180; 1999d, p. 148f).

The process was sped up by the introduction of tariffs on manufactures, making it more difficult for the Western European countries to dispose of their industrial surplus and cover their food needs via imports. The direct cause of protectionism was the growth of the population (Wicksell 1896, p. 64):

> The urge to protect domestic industries will make itself felt as soon as the country has a population large enough to lead to the emergence of rent on a significant scale, with the wage level still appreciably larger than in the old countries.

The introduction of the tariff would increase wages at the expense of rent.

The second danger that Wicksell saw with specialization and trade was that the stocks of mineral raw materials and fossil fuels would be exhausted in the sense that the cost of employing them would increase rapidly, faster than what might be compensated for by material-saving technological progress (Wicksell 1999d, p. 149).

A third obstacle to continued international trade was found on the demand side in the New World. In his booklet on population, Wicksell (1979, p. 148) quoted figures which indicated that at the end of the twentieth century the demand for food imports in Western Europe would amount to three times the figure for 1890. He, however, doubted that this figure would suffice, since in the extreme case where agricultural production in Eastern Europe would remain stationary, while the population would treble its size, the correct figure would be eight to ten times as high as the 1890 one. To satisfy this demand via imports would be impossible since at the same time the population of the food-exporting countries would increase, consume the formerly available food surplus, and in addition cease to demand Western European manufactures.

In 1926, Wicksell noted that the golden age of north-south factor proportions based trade had come to an end. It had been an exceptional episode of the nineteenth century (Wicksell 1926a, p. 265) and he had been waiting for the end of it. The international exchange of manufactured products for food staples constituted a disturbing ingredient in his view of long-run economic development, a view that rested heavily on diminishing returns to a too rapidly growing population (cf. Uhr 1962, pp. 328–329).

Wicksell (1925, p. 10) pointed to the 'artificial economic life' of Western Europe. The population of the regions supplying food to Europe grew, and in the end would reach population densities that would not allow them to produce any exportable surplus. Europe would have to produce its own primary products and that would not be possible unless the density of its population was reduced.

Emigration: a solution of the past

At least 100,000 Swedes left their country in 1880 and 1881, the vast majority for the United States, a figure which Wicksell considered large for a country of 4.5 million inhabitants (Wicksell, 1882). Views diverged on whether emigration was good or bad for Sweden, and Wicksell set out to find the actual effects. Most important quantitatively speaking was the loss of *human capital*—of labor—and this would have consequences in the labor market (Wicksell 1882, p. 19):

> The most certain and most immediate consequence of emigration is that it reduces the competition among the workers and hence increases wages or, if the latter are already on the decrease, counteracts their further reduction. Moreover, even though the workers who remain behind thus get an occasion to increase their consumption, the reduction of the number of consumers should still make the price of all such commodities that are not completely dependent on the position of prices in the foreign market cheaper.

This, from the distributional point of view, would be positive (Wicksell 1882, p. 19). Wicksell was, however, not prepared to endorse the idea that labor migration is an unmitigated blessing. There was still another 'debit' item: the cost of education which accrues to the home country and which does not correspond to any contribution to GDP by the emigrants. This was the most important aspect for Wicksell (1882, p. 23).

To this decidedly long-run view, which assumes that at some point the migrants can be employed at home, Wicksell adds an explicit human capital perspective (Wicksell 1882, p. 24):

> The education and care that is thus bestowed upon the adolescent generation should be regarded as an advance in terms of capital that it must, in its turn, repay some time, mainly by caring for a subsequent generation. For each individual that leaves the realm (or is carried off by death) before he has had the time to repay his share in this debt a loss is obviously inflicted on the country through the capital invested in him but not repaid.

Should it, on the other hand, turn out to be impossible to employ the emigrants at home, their emigration should be regarded simply as a way of writing off a loss that has already been incurred by their home country.

The obvious cause

Wicksell was in no doubt as to what causes emigration (Wicksell 1882, p. 47). He rejected that the conditions in the United States served as a magnet, since the emigration from Sweden received a hitherto unknown boost after the years of severe Swedish harvest failure at the end of the 1860s. The fatal year 1868 sent a shock wave through the country. The ensuing emigration boom lasted for six years, before it began to taper off during the relatively good years 1872–1873, only to pick up again after the turn for worse in 1878, and a new maximum was reached 1880–1882: mainly young people who had difficulties getting a job (Kock 1944, pp. 80–81).

For Wicksell, this was a potentially Malthusian situation, since he could not conceive of any possibility that the growth of agriculture and industry would have been fast enough to accommodate five new families instead of four. He did not deny that both agriculture and manufacturing had taken great strides forward, but not enough to accommodate those who emigrated and their would-be families. The Swedes had to stop breeding emigrants (Wicksell 1882, p. 61).

Besides, in the near future the emigration escape valve would be more difficult to use than in the past (Wicksell 1887a, p. 26). The agricultural frontier extending from north to south in the United States was more or less closed. If in addition emigration to Canada, Brazil, Australia, and Africa was unsuccessful, the livelihood of the population would have to be sought in Sweden itself.

Wicksell's came back to emigration in more favorable terms in 1909 (Wicksell, 1999d), when he made a statement to the Swedish Emigration Inquiry. Not least was he skeptical to the movement hostile against emigration that had served as a trigger of the Emigration Inquiry. Only if the causes were of a temporary nature would such hostility be warranted. Were they of a more permanent nature, it would be a mistake to prevent emigration from taking place. To create new farms would make no sense, since in Sweden, 'a country of old cultivation' (Wicksell 1999d, p. 141), the land most suitable for farming in the long run had already been put under the plow (Wicksell 1999d, pp. 141–142).

Wicksell argued that it was far from certain that technological progress would solve the agricultural productivity problem, since some innovations would simply not be profitable. He pointed to the land as the limiting factor in terms of production per worker, arguing that farm size was often far too small in Sweden. No obstacles should be put in the way of migration (Wicksell 1999d, p. 146). The issue was the optimum size of the population, 'the number that … is best suited to the available natural resources and is therefore most compatible with the achievement of material well-being …' (Wicksell 1999d, p. 157). Wicksell concluded that in the Swedish case the optimum figure was far below the actual one. Here emigration could be of help (Wicksell 1999d, p. 160).

Still, Wicksell argued, emigration is nothing but a palliative. With time the empty and half-empty lands will be filled with people, and then the only solution that remains is to reduce the number of births. Wicksell recommended that the population question 'should be regarded and dealt with as the great national concern it actually is' (Wicksell 1999d, p. 163).

The optimum population

Knut Wicksell (1901, 1926b, 1979) conceived of two different population questions. The first one is (Wicksell 1979, p. 146), '[W]hich is, under given conditions, the optimal density of population in a country?' The optimum is 'the point where an increase of population would no longer in itself lead to any average increase in welfare' (Wicksell 1979, p. 146). When the population grows two opposing forces are at work, on the one hand diminishing returns, which tend to lower per capita income, and on the other hand 'the united human efforts, the division of labor, the cooperation, the organization of industry, etc. ... At the point where these tendencies cancel each other out is indeed the true optimum population' (Overbeek 1973, p. 510). Wicksell was completely convinced that the optimum had been exceeded everywhere in Europe (Wicksell 1979, p. 146). The second population question is, '... [I]n what way should the equilibrium between births and deaths, if it is necessary or desirable, be achieved and maintained?' (Wicksell 1979, p. 147).

According to Wicksell, there are two main reasons why parents limit their offspring: the desire to provide an education and the desire not to divide the inheritance on too many hands. The former simply indicates an imperfection in the way society handles education. The second reason, in turn, builds on the assumption that it is ownership of land and capital that constitutes the main difference between opulent and poor. The situation, however, Wicksell argues, would be completely different in a society with a stationary population, for there, land rents and the return on capital would be drastically reduced whereas wages would be much higher (Wicksell 1999b, pp. 128–129).

The light at the end of the tunnel

Towards the end of his life, Wicksell thought that he saw some progress in the struggle for a smaller population. In one of his last pamphlets, he noted that plenty of progress had been made with respect to the limitation of the size of the individual family (Wicksell 1925, p. 4). He was happy to see that it was seldom that more than two or three children were found, however, mainly in the capital, while 'in the rest of the country it may not be so well ...' (Wicksell 1925, p. 5). Still, he was able to conclude that considerable progress had been made.

The size of the overall population, however, still left a lot to be desired. It was not enough that each individual family managed to bring the number of births down, because pari passu with the declining birth rate there had been a reduction of the death rate, and Sweden may very well have had a tremendous overpopulation were it not for emigration, above all, to the United States. That safety valve was virtually closed in 1925. Still, Wicksell was optimistic, since the reduction of the birth rate had been so substantial 'that a real regulation of the population appears to be in sight, even independently of the possibility of continued emigration' (Wicksell 1925, p. 6).

The one and only remedy

When it came to the methods for reducing the size of the population, Wicksell was opposed to postponing the age of marriage. It was already too high in Sweden, and the Swedes entered fewer marital unions than other Europeans. Postponing the age of marriage further yet would simply breed drunkenness and prostitution. The alternative was celibacy, but in the struggle between celibacy and prostitution, the former in general pulled the short straw.

Wicksell refuted the idea that the sexual instinct was mainly dysfunctional in contemporary society, one of the worst scourges impossible to get rid of in spite of all prayers and efforts. Instead, it was one of 'the richest sources of a harmonious and happy existence. All that we can do is to regulate this instinct so that it does not become an obstacle to the welfare of mankind; this then becomes the aim of rational morality' (Wicksell 1882, p. 73).

The only remedy was the neo-Malthusian one (Wicksell 1979, p. 150). Without it, early marriages were not feasible when they, 'as is too often the case', were 'synonymous with the procreation of an unlimited, uncontrolled number of new individuals' (Wicksell 1887b, p. 49).

Wicksell was worried about the decreasing frequency of marriages, especially among young people. The absence of an orderly family life would simply lead to an increase in the incidence of prostitution and in the number of children born out of wedlock. The only way of getting rid of prostitution was by allowing contraceptive devices to be used within the family. 'Prostitution is *sterile*. This is its only but terribly strong raison d'être' (Wicksell 1921, p. 248). The best way to combat prostitution was by making sexual relations within the marriage possible without risk for unwanted pregnancies (Wicksell 1925, p. 17).

Later in his life, Wicksell would go one step further in his view of how to limit population growth and argue that women should have the right to abortion under reasonable circumstances. Until other means had been developed that were completely effective when it came to preventing conception, *all* punishments for both the physician and the woman in case of abortion had better be abolished (Wicksell 1921, p. 248).

That, Wicksell suggested, also raised the question of whether abortion should be *permitted* (Wicksell 1925, p. 17). He wanted explicit criteria that could be used to determine when abortion should be allowed and not. The simplest rule would be to allow it to take place freely, for example, before the third month of pregnancy when the movement of the fetus begins. The main route to a regulation of fertility, he concluded, should be through the use of contraceptives and the role of abortion should be that of 'an available *last resort*, a safe *guarantee* for the many that absolutely need [it]' (Wicksell 1925, p. 24).

The Wicksellian system

In order to get a complete picture of Wicksell's views on poverty and population, we must pull a number of threads together.[1] In fact, his discussion of the effects of population growth is carried out within an implicit framework that closely resembles the modern specific factors general equilibrium approach to international trade and factor movements, developed in the 1970s (Jones 1971, Samuelson 1971a, 1971b).

Wicksell keeps coming back to the interplay between events in Europe and overseas, two regions that we may label 'The Old World' and 'The New World'. The production structure that Wicksell worked with is almost completely symmetric. We will therefore provide an account of the structure of the Old World and later, when appropriate, simply note where that of the New World differs from it.

The Old World produces agricultural goods using labor, land, and capital, while manufacturing uses labor; a natural resource, for example, forests or mineral ores; and capital. Labor is mobile between the two sectors, and there is full employment. The extension of the land area is given and all land suitable for agricultural production is under the plow. Land is thus a fixed production factor. So is the natural resource. Wicksell kept insisting on the exhaustibility of natural resources everywhere. He did not deal with mobility of capital anywhere in his writings on population and poverty. In fact, the importance of capital in agriculture is played down almost everywhere except in his discussion of technological progress. This makes it natural to treat the two capital stocks as sector-specific. It is thus obvious that Wicksell's production framework essentially corresponds to the specific factors model of Ronald Jones (1971), with a single mobile factor: labor.

With profit-maximizing producers in both sectors all production factors are rewarded with the value of their respective marginal products. (We may choose to measure everything in units of manufactures.) With sector-specific factors there will be no factor price equalization between countries. Assume that the total labor force of the Old World is given. Dividing this between the two sectors so as to equalize the value of the marginal productivity (VMPL) in agriculture and manufacturing yields the Old World wage, given the capital stocks, the land, and the natural resources. Assume next that the New World has exactly the same the same technology and endowments of the fixed factors as the Old World, that is, VMPL schedules that are identical to those of the Old World, but a labor force which is smaller. This will result in a higher wage rate. As long as migration is not free, neither the wages nor the returns to the specific factors will be equalized. We need to operate with one wage rate for the Old World and one for the New. The outputs of the two commodities can also be stated as functions of their relative price (the price of agricultural goods) and a shift parameter that symbolizes exogenous influences on production, like changes in technology.

Wicksell discusses changes in demand and relative commodity prices, that is, he works with the assumption of two 'large' economic regions whose actions together determine international prices. This means that the demand side has to be specified as well. The income of the Old World is equal to the total value of agricultural and manufacturing output. This entire income is spent on consumption of the two goods, and the demand for agricultural (manufactured) goods in the Old World is a function of relative commodity prices, income, and preferences (symbolized by a shift parameter). The economic structure of the New World is completely analogous, but has separate shift parameters (cf., however, below for the case when an agrarian frontier exists).

What remains to be done is to close the system: Wicksell assumes that the Old World trades freely with the New World (while factor movements are regulated). Thus, we may use for example the equilibrium condition for the market for agricultural goods, with the Old World as a net importer and the New World as a net exporter, as is clear from the section on trade. No corresponding equilibrium condition is needed for the market for manufactures, since according to Walras's law, if all markets except one are in equilibrium the last one must be so too.

Population growth and technological progress in the Old World

The trigger that puts the Wicksellian system in motion is the human sex drive which results in the growth of the population and the labor force in the Old World. When the population and the labor force grow, at constant commodity prices, both agriculture and manufacturing increase their employment of labor, but only at a falling wage rate in terms of manufactures, and hence increase their output as well. This increases the returns to the fixed factors, for example, the land rent. That is what Wicksell meant when he stated that the rich in society—the owners of fixed assets—had an interest in maintaining a high rate of population growth, while at the same time this served to depress the living standard of the workers, that is, to increase their poverty and cause drunkenness and other social evils.

Wicksell did not believe that technological progress could serve to overcome the effects of diminishing returns. Provided that marginal productivities are increased in both sectors by technological progress the wage rate must rise at given commodity prices. Whether labor moves in or out of agriculture (manufacturing) depends on which of the two productivity-increasing effects is the stronger one. We can now also compare the effects of diminishing returns on the wage rate with those of technological progress. Wicksell argues that the size of the labor force growth and the strength of the diminishing returns are strong enough to outweigh the productivity-raising influences of technological progress so that the net result is a reduction of the wage rate.

Assuming that the above sequence is generalized to the entire Old World, it is bound to have an impact on relative commodity prices (the price of agricultural goods in terms of manufactures) as well. The price change is determined by the interplay of three different forces. The first is the change in the demand for agricultural goods in the Old World that results from a change in preferences at given incomes and commodity prices when the population grows. Wicksell envisaged an increased demand for food when the population grew. This he made explicit in the case of the New World, and it is clear that he had the same mechanism in mind for the Old World. Hence, this tends to increase the relative price of agricultural goods.

The second force is the increased demand for agricultural goods that emanates from the increase of the total income of the Old World when the labor force grows and more of both commodities is produced at given prices and preferences. Assuming that agricultural goods are not inferior, this as well should exert a positive influence on their relative price.

The third force is the increase in the production of agricultural goods that takes place when the labor force (population) grows. Whether the relative price of agricultural goods rises or falls then depends exclusively on whether the demand for agricultural goods increases faster than the supply of it when the population grows in the Old World. Wicksell assumed that the demand effect was the strongest one. Thus, population growth there tends to turn the terms of trade against the Old World.

Problems of foreign trade

Wicksell did not believe that a specialization according to comparative advantage would contribute to solving the population problem in the Old World. On the contrary, he argued, there were least three problems connected with international trade that would preclude it from working as an engine (Robertson 1938) or 'handmaiden' (Kravis 1970) of growth, to use two latter-day terms: the tendency for manufacturing output to stagnate in the Old World when natural resources were depleted, the tariff policy of the New World, and population growth and demand changes in the New World.

When the natural resource shrinks, the marginal productivity of labor falls in manufacturing, and this sector starts to shed workers, who can only be reabsorbed—some of them in agriculture—at a lower wage rate. This means that manufacturing output must contract while agricultural output expands. At the same time, Old World income must fall at given commodity prices, since the total factor endowment of the Old World has shrunk.

Provided that none of the two goods is inferior, the demand for both manufactures and agricultural goods must shrink as income shrinks, that is, the relative price of agricultural goods, whose production has increased, must fall in relation to that of manufactures. As Wicksell predicted, the depletion of natural resources tends to reduce the demand for imports in the Old World, since this region can now afford to buy less. This interacts with the changes on the supply side to reduce the relative price of agricultural goods in the world market.

The second problem for the Old World when it comes to using international trade to mitigate the consequences of population growth according to Wicksell was the tendency for the New World countries (notably the United States) to use tariffs to protect their manufacturing sectors. Tariffs drive a wedge between relative commodity prices in the domestic market in the New World and world market prices (still adhered to in the Old World).

The introduction of the tariff on manufactured goods raises the relative price of these goods in the New World, that is, it lowers the price of agricultural goods in terms of manufactures. When the tariff on manufactures is introduced, at a constant New World relative price of agricultural goods, their relative price must increase in the world market. Old World producers then react by increasing their production and Old World consumers reduce their demand (while New World consumers and producers, who are facing the New World, not the world market, price do not react at all. An excess supply is created which serves to lower the relative price of agricultural goods in the New World.

The tariff on manufactures in the New World will also lower its relative price in the world market, that is, increase the relative price of agricultural goods. Given the world market price, the relative domestic price of agricultural goods in the New World must fall. New World consumption increases while producers reduce their supply. An excess demand is created in the world market and the international relative price of agricultural goods rises.

This is a standard result: When a tariff is introduced, this serves to increase the domestic price of the good subject to the tariff, while it will lower its price in the world market. The tariff pulls resources out of agriculture into manufacturing in the New World, and hence reduces the worldwide supply of agricultural goods.

The third of Wicksell's obstacles to international trade is the rising demand for agricultural goods accompanying the growth of the population in the New World. At constant commodity prices and incomes, this serves to increase the relative price of agricultural goods in the world market, that is, it tends to turn the terms of trade against the Old World. It should, however, be noted that it does not work in isolation but is a result of the growth of the population in the New World, which means that its effects, and the effects of rising New World income, must be weighed against the effects of increased New World production of agricultural goods when the labor force of the New World grows. Let us next turn to the investigation of these effects, but then we must also introduce emigration from the Old to the New World.

Migration from the Old to the New World

The fall in the wage rate in the Old World when the population there grows is what for Wicksell triggers emigration. The effect of this is to increase the population in the New World instead of in the Old. Hence, it is part of the sequence we have just discussed. In the New World, it increases the demand for agricultural goods at given commodity prices and incomes, it increases the production of agricultural goods and it increases income and hence the demand for agricultural goods at constant commodity prices.

In his discussion of agricultural production in the New World Wicksell kept coming back to the issue of the land frontier. This, he argued, was rapidly being closed, at least in the United States. Our general equilibrium model can be used to examine both situations. Let us begin with the situation where emigrants who arrive in the New World can put virgin land under the plow.

Let us assume that the entire addition to the Old World population can emigrate to the New World. (This allows us to disregard production effects in the Old World.) When they arrive at their new destination they can either work in the manufacturing sector or in agriculture, on the existing agricultural land. They may also, however, extend the land frontier. We may draw on the Findlay (1996) model, of the territorial expansion of empires, where the use of labor (a land-clearing 'brigade') serves to increase the land.

The introduction of an endogenous land frontier in the New World means that labor there now has to be divided between production of manufactures, direct production of agricultural goods and extension of the land frontier. We will assume that on the frontier, land can be obtained only at a rising cost in terms of labor, that is, land clearing is subject to diminishing returns. When the emigrants arrive in the New World they go into all three employments. They can be absorbed, however, only at the cost of a falling wage rate.

What will happen to the land rent on the frontier? Adding labor to a given land area tends to increase the land rent while using labor to develop the frontier with a given 'direct' labor use in agriculture serves to depress it. If the diminishing returns to land clearing are strong, however, the land rent will increase in spite of the existence of an agricultural frontier.

According to Wicksell, the frontier was virtually closed in the United States. Once the frontier is closed we are back in our original general equilibrium system. The structures of the two regions are similar, with the main difference that the New World has a higher endowment of land, which means that the wage is higher there than in the Old World, as pointed out by Wicksell. Emigration should thus be beneficial for the emigrants. Our previous analysis of population growth may be used also for the development of relative commodity prices, substituting the New World for the Old. Presumably, however, the tendency for population growth to increase the relative price of agricultural goods is weaker when the population grows in the New World instead of in the Old, since the additional agricultural output generated should be higher and the shift in consumer preferences weaker. But Wicksell argued that this was only a temporary blessing, since as the population kept growing, the structure of the New World economy would gradually approximate that of the Old World.

The next parameter shift to be discussed is capital movements. We have to compare the effects of a growth of capital stocks in the Old World with the growth of those of the New World, assuming that capitalists can decide where they want accumulation to take place. We then focus on the development of the two wage rates. Let us start in the Old World, with an increase of the two capital stocks at constant commodity prices and a given labor force.

Regardless of which of the two capital stocks that grows the wage rate will increase. Whether labor will move from manufacturing to agriculture or vice versa depends on the differences in capital accumulation on the one hand and on the impact of additional capital on the marginal productivities of labor on the other.

Wicksell implicitly compared the results of capital accumulation in the Old World with analogous changes in the New World, arguing that from the point of view of the prospective emigrants capital formation overseas would be preferable, that is, that the marginal productivity of labor in both sectors would receive a larger boost from capital formation in the latter than in the former.

The only parameter change that we have not investigated so far is war. If we stick to the sequence that Wicksell obviously had in mind, war is triggered by population growth, and the short-run effect of war is a reduction of the population of the nations involved in the war. This would reverse all sequences that we have already dealt with that are triggered by population growth. However, according to Wicksell, war 'solves' the population problem only in the short run, because at some point after the termination of the war activities there will again be a drive to increase the population, possibly triggered by the rulers, politicians, and militaries of the countries that have suffered, and then we are back where we began our analysis.

The result of putting all the bits and pieces of Wicksell's scattered analysis of population growth together is astonishing. Far from confirming the conventional wisdom that what he wrote on the population question was mechanical and simplistic, it turns out that the exercise results in a coherent general equilibrium framework which very much resembles the specific factors model of international trade. Within this setting, Wicksell handled factor growth (population, natural resources, and capital), technological progress, tariffs, and factor movements. In this, he stands out as a precursor of the modern theory of international trade. It is here then, rather than in the use of the optimum population concept, that Wicksell's original contribution to the analysis of population growth lies.

Concluding remarks: the failure of the critics

The critics failed to see the originality of Wicksell's approach. Even disregarding the arguments presented so far, this is understandable. In 1891, when they first appeared in an elaborated version (Wicksell 1891), the modern theory of international trade and factor movements had not yet been worked out. Eli Heckscher had not yet written his pathbreaking article, which would not appear until 1919 (Heckscher 1991); Bertil Ohlin's dissertation (Ohlin 1991) was defended in 1924, and his big treatise on international trade was published in 1933 (Ohlin 1933); Paul Samuelson's (1939, 1948, 1949, 1953, also Stolper and Samuelson 1941) contributions came around World War II; and the specific factors model was not formalized until 1971. It is thus no wonder that Wicksell failed to spell out his model explicitly. Such was the state of the arts when he wrote.

Wicksell's complete views on population and poverty have to be put together from a large number of sources. When this is done, however, the result is an approach that would not be completely developed until some eighty years after the appearance of his long essay in French on population (Jones 1971, Samuelson 1971a, 1971b). It was the analysis of how the interaction between population growth and diminishing returns drove people out of Europe during the late nineteenth century that Wicksell was concerned with, and in the process, he inadvertently became a precursor of modern trade and factor movement theory. In the end, his originality extended into his analysis of poverty and population as well.

Note

1 The explicit model can be found in Lundahl (2005, 2009).

References

Åkerman, J. (1933). Knut Wicksell, A Pioneer of Econometrics. *Econometrica*, *1*(2), 113–118.

Blaug, M. (1968). *Economic Theory in Retrospect*. Second edition. London: Heinemann.

[Drysdale, G.R.] as a doctor of medicine [pseud.] (1876). *The Elements of Social Science; or Physical, Sexual and Natural Religion. An Exposition of the True Cause and Only Cure of the Three Primary Social Evils: Poverty, Prostitution, and Celibacy.* Fourteenth edition, enlarged. London: Edward Truelove.

Findlay, R. (1996). Towards a Model of Territorial Expansion and the Limits of Empire. In M.F. Garfinkel and S. Skaperdas (eds), *The Political Economy of Conflict and Cooperation* (pp. 41–56). New York: Cambridge University Press.

Heckscher, E.F. (1991). The Effect of Foreign Trade on the Distribution of Income. In H. Flam and M.J. Flanders (eds), *Heckscher-Ohlin Trade Theory* (pp. 43–69). Cambridge, MA and London: MIT Press.

Hofsten, E. and Lundström, H. (1976). *Swedish Population History: Main Trends from 1750 to 1970.* Stockholm: National Central Bureau of Statistics.

Jones, R.W. (1971). A Three-Factor Model in Theory, Trade, and History. In J.N. Bhagwati, R.W. Jones, R.A. Mundell and J. Vanek (eds), *Trade, Balance of Payments and Growth: Papers in International Economics in Honor of Charles P. Kindleberger* (pp. 3–21). Amsterdam: North-Holland.

Kock, K. (1944). Nymalthusianismens genombrott i Sverige. In *Studier i ekonomi och historia tillägnade Eli F. Heckscher på 65-årsdagen den 24 november 1944* (pp. 73–88). Uppsala: Almqvist & Wiksells Boktryckeri.

Kravis, I.B. (1970). Trade as a Handmaiden of Growth: Similarities between the Nineteenth and Twentieth Centuries. *Economic Journal, 80*, 850–872.

Lundahl, M. (2005). *Knut Wicksell on Poverty: 'No Place Is Too Exalted for the Preaching of These Doctrines'.* London and New York: Routledge.

Lundahl, M. (2009). Knut Wicksell on Population and Poverty: A General Equilibrium Approach. In D. Basu (ed.), *Advances in Analytical Development Economics* (pp. 29–49). Singapore: World Scientific Publishing Company.

Lundahl, M. (2015). The Reaction to Knut Wicksell's First *Cause Célèbre*: The Chief Cause of Social Misfortunes. In *Seven Figures in the History of Swedish Economic Thought: Knut Wicksell, Eli Heckscher, Bertil Ohlin, Torsten Gårdlund, Sven Rydenfelt, Staffan Burenstam Linder and Jaime Behar* (pp. 20–54). Houndmills and New York: Palgrave Macmillan.

Ohlin, B. (1933). *Interregional and International Trade.* Cambridge, MA: Harvard University Press.

Ohlin, B. (1991). The Theory of Trade. In H. Flam and M.J. Flanders (eds), *Heckscher-Ohlin Trade Theory* (pp. 75–214). Cambridge, MA and London: MIT Press.

Overbeek, J. (1973). Wicksell on Population. *Economic Development and Cultural Change, 21*(2), 205–211.

Robertson, D.H. (1938). The Future of International Trade. *Economic Journal, 48*(1), 1–14.

Samuelson, P.A. (1939). The Gains from International Trade. *Canadian Journal of Economics and Political Science, 5*(2), 195–205.

Samuelson, P.A. (1948). International Trade and Equalisation of Factor Prices. *Economic Journal, 58*(2), 163–184.

Samuelson, P.A. (1949). International Factor-Price Equalisation Once Again'. *Economic Journal, 59*(2), 181–197.

Samuelson, P.A. (1953). Prices of Factors and Goods in General Equilibrium. *Review of Economic Studies, 21*(1), 1–20.

Samuelson, P.A. (1971a). An Exact Hume-Ricardo-Marshall Model of International Trade. *Journal of International Economics, 1*(1), 1–18.

Samuelson, P.A. (1971b). Ohlin Was Right. *Swedish Journal of Economics, 73*(4), 365–384.

Stolper, W.F. and Samuelson, P.A. (1941). Protection and Real Wages. *Review of Economic Studies, 9*(1), 58–73.

Uhr, C.G. (1962). *Economic Doctrines of Knut Wicksell.* Berkeley and Los Angeles: University of California Press.

Wicksell, K. (1880a). *Några ord om samhällsolyckornas vigtigaste orsak och botemedel med särskildt afseende på dryckenskapen.* Upsala: På författarens förlag.

Wicksell, K. (1880b). *Svar till mina granskare. Med ett tillägg: Om ny-malthusianismens nuvarande ställning och utsigter i Europa.* Upsala: Esaias Edquists Boktryckeri.

Wicksell, K. (1882). *Om utvandringen. Dess betydelse och orsaker.* Stockholm: Albert Bonniers Förlag.

Wicksell, K. (1887a). *Om folkökningen i Sverge och de faror den medför för det allmänna välståndet och för sedligheten.* Stockholm: Kungsholms Bokhandel.

Wicksell, K. (1887b). *Om prostitutionen. Huru mildra och motverka detta samhällsonda? Två föredrag.* Stockholm: Kungsholms Bokhandel.

Wicksell, K. (1891). *La population, les causes de ses progrès et les obstacles qui en arrêtent l'essor.* Pièce destinée au concours Rossi, 1891. Manuscript. Paris: Académie des sciences morales et politiques de l'Institut de France.

Wicksell, K. (1892), Normalarbetsdag, dated 1892. In L. Jonung, T. Hedlund-Nyström, and C. Jonung (eds), *Att uppfostra det svenska folket. Knut Wicksells opublicerade manuskript* (pp. 271–313). Stockholm: SNS Förlag.

Wicksell, K. (1896). *Finanzteoretische Untersuchungen nebst Darstellung und Kritik des Steuerwesens Schwedens.* Jena: Verlag von Gustav Fischer.

Wicksell, K. (1901). *Föreläsningar i nationalekonomi. Första delen: Teoretisk nationalekonomi.* Lund: Berlingska Boktryckeriet.

Wicksell, K. (1902). Professor Fahlbeck om nymalthusianismen. *Ekonomisk Tidskrift,* 4, 543–560.

Wicksell, K. (1903). Om begreppen produktivitet, rentabilitet och relativ avkastning inom jordbruket. *Ekonomisk Tidskrift,* 5, 485–507.

Wicksell, K. (1914). *Allvarliga farhågor.* Stockholm: Sällskapet för Humanitär Barnalstring.

Wicksell, K. (1921). Kristen etik och personlig profylax, dated March. In L. Jonung, T. Hedlund-Nyström, and C. Jonung (eds), *Att uppfostra det svenska folket. Knut Wicksells opublicerade manuskript* (pp. 243–249). Stockholm: SNS Förlag.

Wicksell, K. (1924/1925). Befolkningsfrågan och sunda förnuftet, undated. In L. Jonung, T. Hedlund-Nyström, and C. Jonung (eds), *Att uppfostra det svenska folket. Knut Wicksells opublicerade manuskript* (pp. 259–262). Stockholm: SNS Förlag.

Wicksell, K. (1925). *Barnalstringsfrågan: Föredrag, hållet vid Nymalthusianska sällskapet.* Stockholm: Federativs Förlag.

Wicksell, K. (1926a). Befolkningsfrågan och världsfreden, dated 12 January. In L. Jonung, T. Hedlund-Nyström, and C. Jonung (2001), *Att uppfostra det svenska folket. Knut Wicksells opublicerade manuskript* (pp. 262–270). Stockholm: SNS Förlag.

Wicksell, K. (1926b). *Läran om befolkningen, dess sammansättning och förändringar.* Andra upplagan. Med ledning av författarens efterlämnade anteckningar. Utgiven av Sven Wicksell. Stockholm: Studentföreningen Verdandis småskrifter.

Wicksell, K. (1934). *Lectures on Political Economy. Volume One: General Theory.* London: George Routledge and Sons.

Wicksell, K. (1958). Marginal Productivity as the Basis of Distribution in Economics. In *Selected Papers on Economic Theory.* Edited with an introduction by Erik Lindahl (pp. 93–120). London: George Allen & Unwin.

Wicksell, K. (1978). The World War: An Economist's View. *Scandinavian Journal of Economics,* 80(2), 233–235.

Wicksell, K. (1979). The Theory of Population, Its Composition and Changes. In S. Strøm and B. Thalberg (eds), *The Theoretical Contributions of Knut Wicksell* (pp. 123–151). London and Basingstoke: Macmillan.

Wicksell, K. (1999a). A Few Remarks on the Chief Cause of Social Misfortunes and the Best Means to Remedy Them, With Particular Reference to Drunkenness. In B. Sandelin (ed.), Knut Wicksell, *Selected Essays in Economics, Volume II* (pp. 83–116). London and New York: Routledge.

Wicksell, K. (1999b). Can a Country Become Underpopulated? In B. Sandelin (ed.), Knut Wicksell, *Selected Essays in Economics, Volume II* (pp. 125–135). London and New York: Routledge.

Wicksell, K. (1999c). Overproduction – or Overpopulation? In B. Sandelin (ed.), Knut Wicksell, *Selected Essays in Economics, Volume II* (pp. 117–124). London and New York: Routledge.

Wicksell, K. (1999d). From *The Emigration Inquiry*, Appendix 18. In B. Sandelin (ed.), Knut Wicksell, *Selected Essays in Economics, Volume II* (pp. 136–168). London and New York: Routledge.

9 Gustav Cassel on poverty

Growth, not grants!

Benny Carlson

Once upon a time, Gustav Cassel (1866–1945) was very famous. For a while, after World War I, he was even the world's most reputed economist (Carlson 2009). In 1921, he was dubbed 'one of the most brilliant economists in the world' by David Lloyd George, and in 1928, he was lauded before the US House of Representatives (Cassel 1940, p. 315, 1941, p. 195). 'At the beginning of the 1920s he was no doubt the most famous contemporary economist', according to Friedrich von Hayek (*Svenska Dagbladet* 1945), and Joseph Schumpeter (1954, p. 1154) concluded that he was 'the most influential leader of our science in the 1920's'. However, fame may be transient—Gunnar Myrdal (1966) noted that a generation had grown up 'which scarcely remembers his [Cassel's] name'.

Although almost a century has passed since Cassel was in the limelight, his name is still sometimes mentioned in articles and discussions on monetary matters. His writings on other aspects of economic policy are less remembered. This applies not least to his writings on social policy, which have never been much noticed outside of Sweden since they were often delivered in Swedish newspapers.[1] He first appeared as an impatient radical and later on as a grudging conservative. However, as we shall see, there was a good deal of continuity in his life-work.

Cassel's social policy aspirations around the turn of the twentieth century bore clear resemblance to the German historical school's 'sociopolitical interventionism'. He had followed the teachings of Gustav von Schmoller and Adolph Wagner in Berlin in 1898–1899, and according to his own testimony had been particularly influenced by the latter (Cassel 1940). His study trip to England in 1901 had a great impact too: 'I received a very strong impression from the sociopolitical writings of the Webbs' (i.e., the Fabians Sidney and Beatrice Webb), Cassel (1940, p. 45) writes in his memoirs.

Even in Cassel's earliest writings on social policy, the notes of what was to become the great theme song of his latter days could be heard: opposition to grants and subsidies. 'Under the cover of a protective policy, the demands of private individuals for government assistance grow like mushrooms after rain' runs an aphorism from the turn of the twentieth century (Cassel 1900, p. 386). At this time, however, his energies were not focused on cases where the state ought not to intervene but on those where it ought to do so. A policy that sought to protect everybody would lead to universal stagnation. Therefore, the state must form a clear view of the direction in which technical and economic progress was moving and seek to facilitate it. State intervention aimed at raising the level of the working class had a place in the framework of a sound social policy for the very reason that this was a prerequisite for increased production.

A pioneering book

In 1902, Cassel's *Socialpolitik* appeared (Cassel 1902)—the first Swedish book on social policy—which did not fail to make its mark. Social politician Karl Höjer (1952, p. 55) cautiously says that the book 'probably played a certain role in forming middle-class opinion on issues of sociopolitical reform'. Social Democrat Erik Palmstierna (1951) declares that it influenced him in his youth, when he was a radical Liberal. Otto Järte is another sociopolitical heavyweight who sat at Cassel's feet (Andersson 1965). Other writers (Lindeberg 1968, Boalt and Bergryd 1974) cite Cassel's *Socialpolitik* as one of the factors underlying the genesis of the Central Union for Social Work (*Centralförbundet för socialt arbete*, CSA), founded in 1903 and generally credited with having had a great impact on the development of social policy in Sweden. Svante Nycander (2005, pp. 25–26) assumes that Cassel's views on trade unions in the book 'raised concerns among conservative, rich gentlemen', although it was not remarkably radical.

In his book, Cassel did not dig much into the causes of poverty. He discussed inequality and concluded that competition between individuals produces an unnatural economic selection when they start out from different preconditions. He therefore emphasized the importance of excellent education for children of all social backgrounds in order to create equal opportunities for equal talents.

Cassel (1902, pp. 13, 18) sets up as a broad objective '*the highest possible development of all the powers of the personality*'; social policy therefore agrees with liberalism in that the individual is to rely on his own capacities and in opposing all 'policies of greenhouse mollycoddling'. At several points, however, he loftily proclaims his rejection of liberal axioms.

- The formal view of the concept of freedom. True freedom requires the possibility of real choice. 'Social policy does not shrink from using compulsion, whether with the help of government power or of private organizations, whenever such compulsion is designed only to create a greater real freedom' (Cassel 1902, p. 19).
- The atomistic view of society. A society consists not only of individuals but also of social units, just as a building is not only a heap of stones but consists of floor, walls, and roof. 'Social policy therefore strives to achieve the most perfect organization, the most exuberant multiplicity of social

forms. Its ideal is not the atomistic society but the highly-organized society' (Cassel 1902, p. 21).

- The belief that the forces of blind competition lead developments in the right direction. Developments have to be guided along the right course. 'Therefore social policy has to be policy, i.e. a systematic piece of work for the attainment of deliberate objectives, and its very name underlines this' (Cassel 1902, p. 22).

In theory, wages should be sufficient to cover the reproduction cost of labor. But experience showed that wages could fall below this limit and even below the subsistence level. Consequently, some form of intervention was required, some social policy which would on the one hand utilize individual initiative and competition and on the other make use of various social organizations. On the wages issue, Cassel reasoned like this: In a labor market characterized by free competition (free from trade unions), employers tend to be interested more in the cost of labor and less in its competence. Workers underbid each other by accepting poorer and poorer conditions, and their proficiency as workers degenerates. In a market where trade unions set a lower limit to wage competition, employers have to take more interest in competence and less in wages. Workers now overbid each other in terms of competence. The 'bourgeois view' that employers have the right to negotiate individually with every job applicant can thus be liquidated. The ideal is determined by what is expedient from the standpoint of society. If individual wage negotiations bring about competition 'in which inferior elements are victorious', while collective negotiations bring about competition in the service of progress, then there can be no doubt which is right and which is wrong (Cassel 1902, p. 68).[2]

However, trade unions had their weak spots. Certain occupations, into which unskilled labor flowed from all directions, were almost impossible to organize. This raised the question whether the state ought to intervene to establish a statutory minimum wage. Cassel, for his part, considered such a measure economically unworkable. But much could be gained if central and local authorities pursued a proper wages policy themselves (Cassel 1902, p. 96):

> The payment of utterly inadequate wages by private employers, whether because of unwarranted greed or, far more frequently, through the pressure of competition, is no reason for central or local authorities to do the same. If central and local authorities are the organs of the state they must subordinate their interests to the state's, and their policy must form an organic element of an integrated social policy. And when, especially, it involves such a vital social interest as the securing of a given living standard necessary for the efficiency of labor, then it is not fitting for the society's own organs to allow themselves to be dragged blindly and passively into a mechanical competitive struggle ....

Therefore, a minimum wage ought to be introduced, varying according to age, sex, and locality. It should apply not only to workers in permanent employ of state and local government authorities but to everyone engaged in public works and also, if possible, to workers employed by contractors and suppliers to the public service.

That the wage should cover the reproduction cost of labor ought to mean that it should suffice for insurance against those cases where the worker was unable to provide for himself. However, in Cassel's (1902) opinion, the practical solution to insurance questions might vary from case to case.

- Old age insurance was far too big an expenditure for trade unions to handle; neither was it associated with any particular occupation. To collect direct contributions from workers (or employers) would be too complicated. The simplest way would be to finance insurance through taxes on consumption.
- Sickness insurance would require a control which could only be exercised by someone familiar with individuals and their conditions; it ought to be handled by workers' sick benefit societies (*sjukkassor*) supervised and financially supported by the state.
- Unemployment insurance was complicated by the need to take account both of 'voluntary' unemployment, where the trade union did not accept an employer's offer, and involuntary employment, where there was no work to be had. Since the boundary between the two categories was fluid, the entire question should be put in trade union hands.

In a subsequent article, Cassel (1903, p. 280) summarized his efforts in his inimitable fashion by saying that it was a matter of 'fashioning a purposeful and consistent social policy in place of a fumbling philanthropy guided by sentimentality or a cold and blind faith in the dead phrase known as free competition'.

Growth most urgent

A couple of years later, Cassel (1908a) compared the alternatives of welfare assistance policy and efficiency policy with one another. The Swedish nation was still too poor for even the most equal distribution of income to be capable of giving all its citizens an adequate income. 'This is the fundamental economic fact from which the social politician must work, and therefore a wise economic policy is the best social policy'. The object of social policy must be 'the highest development of our productive powers'. This meant that 'the healthy, the strong and the vigorous must be allowed to improve themselves without being hampered by concern for the incompetent':

> To have brought economic policy to bear on this general end is the imperishable contribution of liberalism. Liberalism was mistaken about the

means. Perfect economic freedom, government passivity, the absence of all organization: these were by no means the conditions under which the greatest efficiency could be fostered or the nation's labor attain its highest state of development. Government authorities along with trade unions could do much, as the social policy of a later age has proved in practice, to equalize the extremely unequal power relationships which prevailed especially after the Industrial Revolution, and thus to raise not only the working class but the whole of the nation's work to a higher plane.

Later on that same year, Cassel (1908b) underlined that social and economic questions were now at the top of the agenda, and he mulled over the relation of social policy to economic policy once again:

> The theoretical foundation of all wise social policy is the realization that broadly speaking any improvement of the economic situation of the masses is possible only through increased productivity. Growth of production is therefore always the most urgent object of social policy. In this respect, in other words, its aim coincides with that of economic policy. The roads they take are different: whereas social policy endeavors to strengthen and develop the nation's labor force to the highest level of usefulness and to protect it from unnecessary destruction, economic policy is concerned primarily with the organization of productive work, with the management of the nation's economic life as a whole.

When Hjalmar Branting, the leader of the Social Democrats, argued that the labor movement would never refrain from demanding that the fruits of labor end up in the hands of the working people, Cassel (1908c) did not object but underlined that Social Democrats must understand that the first priority was the 'training and gathering of all productive forces'.

Political scientist Nils Elvander (1961, pp. 467, 482) holds that the Conservatives 'followed a pro-reform course in a spirit of national unity' between 1905 and 1910, when a change of course took place from social conservatism to economic liberalism, and that this reversal most likely resulted from the Conservatives being faced after the franchise reform of 1909 with 'the prospect of the reform policy being further extended by a democratized government under the control of a radicalized liberalism with socialist support'. Even though Cassel portrayed himself as a liberal, he was surely affected by this realignment since he was leaning in a social conservative and nationalist direction.

In an editorial titled 'The Abolition of Poverty', Cassel (1910a) commented on two Social Democrats who had advanced ideas about how to get rid of poverty. Cassel was in agreement with Professor Gustaf Steffen, who wished to combat poverty as a disease. Work could not be given a higher value than it was given on the market and therefore workers had to be educated and trained so that the value of their work increased. Cassel, however, opposed Carl Lindhagen, the mayor of Stockholm, who suggested that the rich should abstain from some of their income so that the whole population could be transformed into a middle class. 'What seems like the road to the one middle class is in reality nothing but the road to general poverty', wrote Cassel. The only road ahead went through 'the struggle of technology, capital and entrepreneurship against poverty'. 'Poverty can never be abolished without making the whole people much richer than it is at present'. However, there should be no quest for wealth of a mercantilist kind. The working classes must not be seen as purely a cost in the quest for wealth. 'They are part of this people, whose economic prosperity is the mission of the national economy'.

In a rejoinder, the signature X.Y.Z. (1910) remarked that Britain's national wealth per capita was much larger than Sweden's, while at the same time poverty was worse in Britain than in any other country in Western Europe. In his reply, Cassel (1910b) on the one hand distanced himself from 'brutal Manchester policy' and on the other hand argued that many within the British working class had achieved quite a high standard of living.

Fight over pensions

Swedish Liberalism, influenced by the new liberalism in England, underwent a sociopolitical radicalization under the leadership of Karl Staaff (Vallinder 1984). During his second administration 1911–1914, a national pension insurance was carried through. The pension proposal was not confined to wage-paid workers alone but was intended to become 'a national insurance scheme', a compromise between insurance and welfare assistance principles, and was thus to be financed both by contributions from those insured and by taxes. The proposal was accepted with a relatively high degree of unity in the *Riksdag* (Parliament).

The proposal however came in for severe criticism from certain groups outside the *Riksdag*, not least political economists. Cassel was the most vocal one and in the spring of 1913 he came up with a series of critical editorials in *Svenska Dagbladet*. In one of them (Cassel 1913a), he argued that pension supplements or benefit payments 'had been awarded to all without distinction... even if they have never performed any socially useful work in their lives'. This would excite 'claims upon the public [purse] on the part of the mass of the people without any corresponding obligations at all'. Instead of this, a pension insurance scheme must be based on personal contributions. 'Broadly speaking, the payment of personal contributions properly made by the individual towards his own pension are undoubtedly a very sound proof of an endeavor on his part to perform his share...' The guiding rule must therefore be 'strict adherence to the conception which must underlie any sound scheme of national insurance: viz. help yourself, then society will help you'. The task was to lift the decent and industrious out of the realm of poor relief; the others must be left there for the present. In the light of these strictures, a harsh verdict on the government's proposal was inevitable:

> That the Swedish government should in this way directly seek to oblite-rate all sense of the importance of individual self-help, thereby doing its utmost to root out of the national consciousness a sentiment which yet must form the deepest foundation of a healthy national economy—this is truly calculated to arouse the gravest misgivings.

Cassel (1913b) agreed that there were good reasons for not confining pension insurance to workers alone but extending it to the nation as a whole. He believed it possible to design a system which would provide both 'labor' and 'national' insurance simultaneously but the principle must be 'that the in-surance is borne to the greatest possible extent directly by productive labor':

> The wage ought to be high enough to provide for the worker's suste-nance throughout his life. Only then does the wage cover the real cost of labor. Intervention by the state is needed mainly to enforce the allocation of an appropriate proportion of the wage for invalidity insurance and for the organization of this insurance. Some minor contribution on the part of the state can be defended as an incentive to those insured.

In other words, the insurance ought to be based on employers' contributions. The argument that these would be reserved for workers alone, to the exclu-sion of other ordinary people, was rejected by Cassel (1913c) as an incitement to jealousy and thus a way of 'calling forth the people's worst instincts'. He knew well enough where the shoe was pinching:

> The object is to save farmers from having to make any contribution to their laborers' pensions. Therefore, the whole of Sweden's working class has to be deprived of the benefit of employers' contributions, and there-fore the whole conception of national insurance is to be distorted and botched up into a welfare benefit. And that is what Mr Branting is going to sit down and sign!

Cassel's voice was also heard in one of the two debates on the proposal ar-ranged by the Swedish Economic Association. He attacked the spirit under-lying the suggestion that society has some obligation to care for the elderly, which had its origins in 'sheer communism' (Nationalekonomiska Före-ningen 1913b, p. 88).[3] The essence of any pension reform must be that the worker should be paid a wage which was high enough for him to afford the premium for pension insurance. If society looked after the elderly, the de-moralizing poor relief label would remain. Knut Wicksell also condemned the proposal as 'utterly misconceived' and demanded that 'national insurance should be based in all essentials on the insured's own contributions' (Nationalekonomiska Föreningen 1913a, pp. 61, 63–64).

On the same day that the *Riksdag* was to consider the proposal, Cassel (1913d) wrote that this was 'perhaps the most fateful issue' ever laid before the *Riksdag*. Hjalmar Branting, who had served on the inquiry into the insurance question, replied to Cassel's criticism when the proposal was introduced in the First Chamber. He (Branting 1928, p. 252) discussed waged-worker insurance versus national insurance and argued that the former would create a multitude of difficult borderline cases. He declared that with respect to this problem 'our theoretical critics of H.M. [His Majesty's] government's proposal' had observed 'a silence such as almost makes one think of a muzzle'. In his newspaper 'philippics' against the proposal, Cassel had evaded discussion of the borderline case and had done the same again when he got up at the Economic Society's meeting 'to decry, and essentially destroy, H.M. government's proposal'. Then Branting (1928, pp. 257–258) let fly with a real salvo:

> But when Professor Cassel says, for example, that 'the people's worst instincts are being called forth' by the government and its supporters to enable politicians to bamboozle this motion through, we are entitled to ask whether the limit has not been exceeded and whether we do not have cause to reject such professorial wisdom, and pretty emphatically too, by taking not the slightest notice of what comes from such overweeningly arrogant quarters.

Fear of a fund

Karl Höjer (1952, p. 132) writes of the early 1920s that in the area of social policy, because of the general economic situation, 'but also because of the lukewarm, or for tactical reasons wary, attitudes of all parties, a mark-time condition prevailed'. Some minor advances were made toward the end of the decade. Proposals for further development of the voluntary sick benefit society movement, involving the provision of state support for 'recognized' societies, were presented by several governments up to 1931, when the *Riksdag* at last found a proposal to its taste.

The Conservative approach to social policy in the 1920s has been characterized by Rolf Torstendahl (1969) as follows: On the one hand, any government worth the name must intervene if the long-term interests of the state are threatened by short-term interests; on the other hand, the will of the individual to provide for himself must not be weakened. Protectionism and social policy both fulfill the aim of protecting different social classes. Protectionism, which gives work to Swedes, is to be preferred to the payment of unemployment benefits to those same Swedes. It is worth noting that Cassel's stance on protectionism was not as principled as that of the other major Swedish proponent of economic liberalism, Eli Heckscher.

If reform policy made a feeble impression during the 1920s, the social policy debates were nonetheless lively. When pension insurance was up for debate by the Economic Association (Nationalekonomiska Föreningen 1924), Gösta Bagge, economist and Conservative politician, brought up the old issue of contributions versus taxes. The contribution system offered psychological and moral advantages and brought about increased capital formation. The tax system was cheaper to administer. Bagge held, however, that the advantages of the contribution system had been overrated. Since contributions were obligatory and thus functioned in principle as taxes, other forms of saving might diminish, and this made it uncertain how large the net increase in total capital formation would be. Bagge also saw certain dangers in large funds being administered by a single authority. His main point was that it was impossible to impose heavy enough premiums on the lowest income groups for them to achieve self-sufficiency. Therefore he proposed that everyone above a certain income level should be covered by compulsory insurance. Those falling below the limit should become cases for the local poor law authorities. As we have seen, Cassel had advocated the same type of boundary-drawing in 1913.

Bagge's proposal met with heavy resistance. Adolf af Jochnick, director-general and head of the National Pensions Board (*Pensionsstyrelsen*), maintained that pension contributions, however small, were a way for the private individual to acquire a social right and gave a sense of independence and self-sufficiency which poor relief could never provide. Two Liberal members of the *Riksdag* testified to the miracle wrought by pension insurance in rural areas, relating how arthritic farmhands and crofters who still had their pride and would not apply for poor relief were now able to collect their pensions with heads held high; they both avowed that any attempt to take insurance away would trigger 'a cry from the soul of the people such as has never before been heard in the land'; so firmly was the reform rooted that not all the united powers of the nation's political economists would suffice to shift it (Nationalekonomiska Föreningen 1924, pp. 35–36).

In an editorial titled 'Pension Insurance Billions Fund', Cassel (1927) argued that a system under which people paid their contributions in advance was not necessary for 'the assertion of the self-sufficiency principle'. 'For that principle can also be applied within the framework of the system hitherto in force, viz. that every generation during its productive years defrays the current cost of caring for the aged and infirm'. The question whether pensions are based on self-sufficiency or the benefit principle is determined, Cassel declared, by whether they 'are paid for by the social classes which actually receive the benefit and not through subsidies from other classes which do not personally receive any benefit from the pension system'. Care of the elderly would still always have to rest socioeconomically on the current national income. In other words, there was no reason to build up funds.

Some years later, Cassel (1930) had abandoned the insurance line of argument more unreservedly in favor of the benefit principle. One reason for this reassessment was uneasiness over the growth of a huge insurance fund whose investments would be placed through a central authority.

When pension insurance came up for renewed debate by the Economic Association, it became apparent that the apprehensions associated with a large-scale insurance fund, which Cassel had been pondering earlier in the year and Bagge as early as 1924, overshadowed everything else. Opening the debate, Bertil Ohlin put his finger on the sore point when he remarked that if 'the fund were allowed to buy stocks and shares, for example, then it is clear that such a fund would have a very big influence on the economy'. Businessmen and industrialists expressed themselves in more vehement terms when they conjectured how possible future dictators might find it 'quite extraordinarily agreeable to be able to play on this instrument, to have at their disposal a fund of thousands of millions of kronor' and 'that if the fund's assets are placed in shares, the nation is thereby socialized'[4] (Nationalekonomiska Föreningen 1930, pp. 153, 161, 163).

Unemployment and degeneration

Unemployment was the headache of the 1920s and formed the subject of a series of inquiries and controversies. The National Unemployment Commission (*Statens arbetslöshetskommission*, AK) had been close to abolition after the war but came in handy during the crisis of 1920–1922. Relief works were organized at a rapid pace, but unemployment—and consequently benefit payments—increased faster still. In 1922, after seven years' work, a committee presented a report containing proposals for unemployment insurance along the lines of the so-called Gent system (state contributions to trade union unemployment funds). The next couple of years, committees of inquiry appointed by both Conservative and Social Democratic administrations pondered on the unemployment insurance question. By the spring of 1928, the 'unemployment experts of 1926' had a report ready. Half were in favor of insurance, half against. Arguments against insurance were primarily to the effect that it would prevent wages from falling to the equilibrium position, thus causing unemployment, and that it would encourage a 'claimant mentality'.

Cassel's (1928) view of unemployment insurance was that a trade union which had to maintain its unemployed members itself would be unable to force wages up beyond a viable market level. There was a corrective inasmuch as excessive wages led to reduced demand for labor, that is, to increased unemployment, which cost the trade union money. Under a state unemployment benefit system, this restraint ceased to operate by virtue of the trade unions' ability to shift the cost on to the state. The unemployment benefit became particularly dangerous when it was exploited by trade unions which sought to limit entry to occupations which were primarily orientated toward the home market. Unemployment must be attributed to lack of labor market mobility and trade union monopoly policy was one of the foremost obstacles to mobility.

When unemployment insurance was debated by the Economic Association, Otto Järte, a former Social Democrat who had turned Conservative, declared that unemployment insurance would put 'a further brake on the mobility of the labor force', and that *'society itself... dislocates free pricing on the labor market in favor of the workers' side'* (Nationalekonomiska Föreningen 1928, pp. 97, 99). Järte also referred to a German doctor who had argued that 'the social insurance system at present simply constitutes a moral danger for the nation at large because of the opportunities it offers for parasitical elements to exploit the benefits provided by social insurance for the malingerers and the work-shy' (Nationalekonomiska Föreningen 1928, p. 106).

These were views redolent of the Cassel spirit. Cassel emerged in the late 1920s as a leading figure in the fight against all 'lax benefit policies', which brought an acid comment from the lips of Professor David Davidson (1928, p. 217): 'Thus Cassel's approach to the science of social policy is that this discipline requires no other criterion than the task of persuading those interested that practical social policy is to all intents and purposes superfluous'. Cassel took no notice, however, and a couple of years later brought out a book bearing the expressive title of *Understödspolitikens urartning* (The Degeneration of Assistance Policy). 'Most dangerous of all', wrote Cassel, is 'that assistance policy which aims to help the unemployed' (Cassel 1930, p. 23).

For the second time (the first time was in 1910), Cassel (1931) wrote an editorial titled 'The Abolition of Poverty'. He argued that the causes of poverty could now be studied in a scientific way. One had to depart from 'the dynamic question, why constantly new masses of people are unable to support themselves'. He praised a Social Democrat, Fabian Månsson, for having raised the issue of youth education in the *Riksdag*. However, he added, Månsson could have started one step before. What followed, in retrospect, was one of Cassel's most controversial statements ever:

> The first and always one of the foremost reasons for the constant regeneration of poverty is the complete lack of the simplest eugenics in present society. As long as we allow the most inferior individuals to stroll freely around and bring children into the world, it will be completely futile to speak about the abolition of poverty through some measures of a socio-economic kind.

When the Social Democrats mustered their forces for an offensive in the late 1920s, this signaled an increased emphasis on social policy. The dream of the coming welfare state—the 'People's Home' (*Folkhemmet*) as the Social Democrats liked to call it—began to be cultivated. Unemployment insurance became the subject of new motions in the *Riksdag*. In 1932, the Social Democrats went to the polls on three broad issues: emergency public works,[5] unemployment insurance, and improved old age pensions. The attitude of the bourgeois left was one of 'wait-and-see', while the right had only 'negative pronouncements' to offer (Höjer 1952, p. 152).

The forming of Per Albin Hansson's first government set Gustav Möller on his long career path as Minister of Social Affairs. As is well known, he came to play as forceful a role in the area of social policy as Finance Minister Ernst Wigforss did in that of crisis policy, tax policy, and economic planning. In Conservative quarters there was fear of the consequences of a more aggressive social policy. 'A somewhat excited debate flared up during these years over what was called by the new vogue term of the "claimant mentality"', writes Höjer (1952, p. 182).

Cassel (1932) remarked right away that a Social Democrat government would bring the unemployment insurance issue to the fore. This 'insurance' was still fundamentally a benefit which would entail 'exorbitant and incalculable claims on the public purse' as well as grave dislocations of the labor market. 'Unemployment is the natural corrective against excessive wage claims'. State-assisted unemployment insurance would make it easier for workers to keep wages exorbitantly high, and unemployment would rise in consequence. Nor was the time right—in the midst of a crisis—for introducing insurance. 'One insures oneself against a future risk; no one takes out fire insurance just when the house is burning down'.

Sure enough, the government's crisis package of 1933 included voluntary unemployment insurance involving state assistance to trade union unemployment insurance funds, provided they fulfilled certain conditions. This meant they could be 'recognized' just like the sick benefit societies.

Life or death

As time went by, the fear among Conservatives that assistance policies would lead to parasitism became more subdued. The debate over population policy probably contributed to this. The Conservatives found it difficult to simultaneously advocate assistance for families with children and criticize the perils of assistance policies in general. In 1934, the population issue became a national topic as a result of Gunnar and Alva Myrdal's book *Kris i befolkningsfrågan* (The Population Crisis) (Myrdal and Myrdal 1934a). According to Höjer (1952, pp. 205–206),

> The nonsocialist camp evinced a particularly intense interest in this question. The approaches adopted ranged from those of elements of the bourgeois left, whose views with respect to the current measures which ought to be examined scarcely exhibited any noticeable difference from those presented by the Myrdals, to those of the extreme right, where nationalistic stances predominated. The view that the family as a unit also ought to receive financial assistance from public funds seems to have been embraced, at least to a certain extent, even in circles which very recently had been vigorously upholding the high moral importance of strengthening the individual's will to provide for his family without burdening society ...

Cassel grappled with the population question in a series of editorials in 1934, published in the book *Liv eller död* (Life or Death). He could not (Cassel 1935a, pp. 197, 204) adequately express how important it was that the Myrdals had brought this, 'the great life-or-death issue for our nation', under the spotlight, but at the same time he accused them of exploiting the issue in order to make propaganda for their 'communist society'. Cassel (1935a, p. 206), in fact, had no other recipe for population increase than economic growth: 'With the standard of living which the Swedish people are now beginning to set as a prerequisite for having children, the only chance of rescuing our population lies in very brisk economic progress'. The Myrdals (Myrdal and Myrdal 1934b) declared themselves at one with Cassel on the importance of growth—but sociopolitical reforms focused on families with several children were necessary as well. Cassel's approach was described as one where 'he stands empty-handed as far as practical proposals are concerned and tends to confine himself simply to repeating ancient conjurations'.

The proposals for improvements in pension insurance presented to the 1935 *Riksdag* session were classed by Cassel (1935b) as 'economically preposterous'. Even if the money could be found, it ought to be invested in children, not in old folks—the Social Democratic government ought to be well aware that the Myrdals had 'set these two interests in the sharpest opposition to one another'. Cassel (1935c) also made the prediction that the number of occupationally active people would diminish over time in proportion to the number pensioners and drew the conclusion that this dilemma could only be resolved by making use of the remaining working potential of old people to support themselves.

Claimants versus taxpayers

In the election campaign of 1936, welfare policy became the watchword above all others in the Social Democratic agitation. After the elections, Social Democrats and Farmers formed a coalition government and a period of relaxation of tension in domestic politics—including social policy—ensued.

Even after the election of 1936, however, the Conservatives embraced a very negative approach to social policy. Bagge (1937) spoke of a social policy race which went faster than growth permitted and risked leading to inflation, which, in turn, would reduce social policy to ruins; to unemployment, since people would be unable to find work on the conditions fixed by statute; and to tax hikes, which would hit the broad segments of society.

When Gustav Möller launched ideas about increasing the purchasing power among the poorest households in order to eradicate unemployment, Cassel (1936a) wrote an editorial on 'Socialist Welfare Magic'. 'The state can after all do nothing more than take purchasing power from one place and use it on another'. In Cassel's (1936b) eyes, the flora of welfare benefits now seemed to have grown wild. He announced to the new coalition government that it would have to abandon the idea that universal prosperity could be attained through large groups of society living on assistance payments. 'If the collaboration of the government parties is to be based on their political power to vote subsidies to each other at the expense of society as a whole, then we are treading a most perilous path'. Public assistance was necessary when there was real distress, but its present tendency was to burst the bounds of distress. At this point, a balancing of claimants' against taxpayers' interests became necessary. In this connection, Cassel (1937, p. 45) believed himself to have discovered a 'bias' in state actions: The state is usually 'liberal and considerate towards its claimants', but 'towards the taxpayers, on the other hand, it is harsh and inconsiderate'.

Cassel (1938) once again attacked the notion that a more equal distribution of income could end poverty and emphasized the importance of incentives:

> For primitive thought it may seem as a simple calculation to take from the richer and give to the poorer. This idea is footed on the notion that income is something given in advance. This presumption is essentially wrong. People's incomes are to a large extent dependent upon the efforts they make to earn an income. If society grabs the result of these efforts, they will not be made and the income will disappear.

The social security state

During the 1940s, the spirit of mutual understanding which had crept into social policy in the late 1930s developed further. This is a description to which Bertil Ohlin (1975) gladly subscribed on behalf of the Liberal party. He declared that his chief ambition as party leader—aside from preventing any socialization—was to secure a policy of social reform. The same opinion is echoed in the comments of Social Democratic leaders. 'In the mid-1940s we on the Social Democratic side could see that social policy was no longer a great point of dispute between the parties', writes party leader 1946–1969 Tage Erlander (1972, p. 152). In 1946, the *Riksdag* decided with a large majority on a new national pension statute in which for the first time pensions were to cover the elementary necessities of life and where the size of pension was made independent of the size of contributions, as well as on universal compulsory health insurance.

The increased mutual understanding in the field of social policy naturally meant that an economic liberal such as Cassel found the rug to some extent pulled from under his feet. In a series of editorials in 1943–1944, he discussed the conceivable consequences of the Beveridge Plan, which, with its aspiration for the state to guarantee all citizens a minimum standard of life, came to occupy a key position in social policy around the world. It goes without saying that he had many objections against this 'social security state'. The incentive to work would diminish, since people would not need to exert themselves in order to earn the official minimum standard, and sundry expert committees would have to decide what was to be included in the minimum standard. 'The State would thus come to exercise extensive control over consumption' (Cassel 1944, p. 56).

Cassel's fame subsided but his character was unbending. Only economic progress could lead humanity from poverty to prosperity (Cassel 1943, p. 35):

> The creation of social security is a concern of extreme importance for the whole world. But the goal can be attained only by a development of the world economy which will give every people an increasing national prosperity and which will give work a steadily increasing economic value. This value must be doubled, nay increased many times over, before we can speak of general prosperity and security, based thereon, for the economic subsistence of the individual.

Concluding remarks

Social policy played a key role in the arsenal of growth-promoting weapons wielded by the younger Cassel. The position of workers must be improved in order to raise their efficiency as factor of production. The general principle was that wages should cover the workers' cost of reproduction, in other words should suffice for them to insure against old age, sickness, and unemployment, situations where they might otherwise end up in poverty. Cassel was pragmatic with respect to the organizational solutions which might be utilized, whether trade unions or the state could achieve the best results. However, even in his early writings, he warned the state not to encourage welfare dependency, and as time went by, his interest in sociopolitical issues took the purely negative form of a struggle against the 'degeneration of assistance policy'.

From the 1920s on, Cassel was thus involved in an endless fight against the 'claimant spirit'. On the question of pensions, however, he, like so many others in the non-socialist camp, shifted from contributory to tax financing because of fear of a huge insurance fund in the hands of socialists. He warned against unemployment benefits being exploited by 'trade union monopolism'. Unemployment must be attributed to lack of labor force mobility and trade unions were obstacles to mobility. At the end of his life, Cassel argued against a 'social security state' of the Beveridge type.

Cassel's stance on social policy had changed in a drastic way over the years. Social Democrat Rickard Lindström (1940), in a review of Cassel's memoirs, pointed to Cassel's earlier contributions and continued, 'It does no harm to recall all this, because Professor Cassel is now regarded in many quarters as an inveterate "reactionary". But he has made a great positive contribution to economic and social progress'. Gunnar Myrdal's (1972, pp. 305–306) verdict is that Cassel's 'later personal development ran directly contrary to historical tendencies in Sweden and the world' and step by step he became 'a mouthpiece for negative criticism of the welfare policy actually being pursued'. Cassel himself considered the situation to be that his opinions held firm with

162   *Benny Carlson*

the passage of time. It was events that got out of step with Cassel, not the other way around. When he was criticized in Social Democratic quarters in the 1920s for having moved in a negative direction since the publication of *Socialpolitik* in 1902, Cassel (1928, p. 113) inquired by way of reply 'whether this is not the old question cropping up again, viz. whether it is the sun or the earth that moves'.

Cassel had a point. There was continuity in his thinking. Economic progress (growth) was always at the top of his agenda. The younger Cassel's interest was aligned toward labor, whose efficiency seemed threatened by the dominance of capital, and toward the role which the state ought to play. The older Cassel's interest was directed toward capital, whose efficiency seemed threatened by the onward march of the working class, and toward all the roles which the state played but ought not to play.

Notes

1 Cassel wrote 1,500 editorials and articles in the conservative daily *Svenska Dagbladet* over the years.
2 Cassel's reasoning is reminiscent of the 'wages solidarity' policy launched in Sweden during the 1950s, under which restraint in their wage claims was urged on higher-paid workers in the interests of the lower-paid. The introduction of minimum wages would wipe out 'dirty competition'. Backward employers who were unable to pay full wages would go bust, and this would favor growth.
3 The proceedings of Nationalekonomiska Föreningen (The Swedish Economic Association) cited in the present essay can be found at https://www.nationale-konomi.se/NEF-forhandlingar.
4 These concerns were not unjustified, as the introduction of wage earners' funds by a Social Democratic government half a century later demonstrated.
5 For Cassel's fight against public works, see Carlson (1994, Chapter 12).

References

Andersson, I. (1965). *Otto Järte – en man för sig*. Stockholm: Bonniers.
Bagge, G. (1937). *Politiska tal år 1937*. Stockholm.
Boalt, G. and Bergryd, S. (1974). *Centralförbundet för social arbete: Ett kapitel svensk socialpolitik*. Stockholm: Bonnier Fakta.
Branting, H. (1928). *Tal och skrifter VII: Ekonomisk och social arbetarpolitik*. Stockholm: Tidens Förlag.
Carlson, B. (1994). *The State as a Monster: Gustav Cassel and Eli Heckscher on the Role and Growth of the State*. Lanham, New York, and London: University Press of America.
Carlson, B. (2009). Who Was Most World-Famous – Cassel or Keynes? The Economist as Yardstick. *Journal of the History of Economic Thought, 31*(4), 519–530.
Cassel, G. (1900). En socialpolitik på afvägar. *Ekonomisk Tidskrift, 2*, 385–416.
Cassel, G. (1902). *Socialpolitik*. Stockholm: Hugo Gebers Förlag.
Cassel, G. (1903). Det sociala värdets problem. *Ekonomisk Tidskrift, 5*, 258–280.
Cassel, G. (1908a). Riktlinjer för vår socialekonomiska politik: II. Försörjningspolitik eller effektivitetspolitik. *Svenska Dagbladet*, 22 January.

Gustav Cassel on poverty 163

Cassel, G. (1908b). Det liberala partiet och vår närmaste uppgift. *Svenska Dagbladet,* 18 June.

Cassel, G. (1908c). Arbete eller delning. *Svenska Dagbladet,* 6 September.

Cassel, G. (1910a). Fattigdomens afskaffande. *Svenska Dagbladet,* 22 October.

Cassel, G. (1910b). Välståndspolitik. *Svenska Dagbladet,* 30 October.

Cassel, G. (1913a). Folkförsäkringens grundtanke. *Svenska Dagbladet,* 29 March.

Cassel, G. (1913b). Arbetareförsäkring och folkförsäkring. *Svenska Dagbladet,* 10 April.

Cassel, G. (1913c). Folkförsäkringen. *Svenska Dagbladet,* 17 May.

Cassel, G. (1913d). Inför afgörandet. *Svenska Dagbladet,* 21 May.

Cassel, G. (1927). Pensionsförsäkringens milliardfond. *Svenska Dagbladet,* 22 October.

Cassel, G. (1928). *Socialism eller framåtskridande.* Stockholm: P. A. Norstedt & Söner.

Cassel, G. (1930). *Understödspolitikens urartning.* Stockholm: P. A. Norstedt & Söner.

Cassel, G. (1931). Fattigdomens avskaffande. *Svenska Dagbladet,* 22 February.

Cassel, G. (1932). En farlig illusion. *Svenska Dagbladet,* 27 September.

Cassel, G. (1935a). *Liv eller död.* Stockholm: Bonniers.

Cassel, G. (1935b). Folkpensioneringens ekonomi. *Svenska Dagbladet,* 8 April.

Cassel, G. (1935c). Ålderdomsförsörjningens problem. *Svenska Dagbladet,* 12 April.

Cassel, G. (1936a). Socialistiskt välfärdstrolleri. *Svenska Dagbladet,* 11 April.

Cassel, G. (1936b). Välståndspolitik. *Svenska Dagbladet,* 8 October.

Cassel, G. (1937). Understöd, beskattning och framåtskridande. *Sunt Förnuft,* 17(2), 45–46.

Cassel, G. (1938). Fattiga och rika. *Svenska Dagbladet,* 28 August.

Cassel, G. (1940). *I förnuftets tjänst. Vol. 1.* Stockholm: Natur och Kultur.

Cassel, G. (1941). *I förnuftets tjänst. Vol. 2.* Stockholm: Natur och Kultur.

Cassel, G. (1943). The Economic Basis for Social Security. *Skandinaviska Banken Quarterly Review,* 24, 31–35.

Cassel, G. (1944). The Social Security State. *Skandinaviska Banken Quarterly Review,* 25, 45–48.

Davidson, D. (1928). Aktuella problem. *Ekonomisk Tidskrift,* 30(10/12), 201–222.

Elvander, N. (1961). *Harald Hjärne och konservatismen: Konservativ idédebatt i Sverige 1865–1922.* Uppsala: Almqvist & Wiksell.

Erlander, T. (1972). *1901–1939.* Malmö: Tidens Förlag.

Höjer, K. (1952). *Svensk socialpolitisk historia.* Malmö: Norstedts.

Lindeberg, S.-O. (1968). *Nödhjälp och samhällsneutralitet: Svensk arbetslöshetspolitik 1920–1925.* Lund: Bokförlaget Universitet och skola.

Lindström, R. (1940). I förnuftets tjänst. *Social-Demokraten,* 12 December.

Myrdal, G. (1966). Gustav Cassel. *Svenska Dagbladet,* 20 October.

Myrdal, G. (1972). *Vetenskap och politik i nationalekonomin.* Stockholm: Rabén & Sjögren.

Myrdal, A. and Myrdal, G. (1934a). *Kris i befolkningsfrågan.* Stockholm: Bonnier.

Myrdal, A. and Myrdal, G. (1934b). Avfolkning eller samhällsreform. *Svenska Dagbladet,* 6 December.

Nationalekonomiska Föreningen (1913a). *Nationalekonomiska Föreningens sammanträde,* 4 April, Förslaget till lag om allmän pensionsförsäkring.

Nationalekonomiska Föreningen (1913b). *Nationalekonomiska Föreningens sammanträde,* 5 May, Förslaget till lag om allmän pensionsförsäkring.

Nationalekonomiska Föreningen (1924). *Nationalekonomiska Föreningens sammanträde,* 18 January, Pensionsförsäkringen.

164   Benny Carlson

Nationalekonomiska Föreningen (1928). *Nationalekonomiska Föreningens sammanträde*, 10 May, Arbetslöshetspolitiken i anledning av arbetslöshetssakkunnigas betänkande.

Nationalekonomiska Föreningen (1930). *Nationalekonomiska Föreningens sammanträde*, 27 November, De nationalekonomiska verkningarna av ålderdomsförsärkingens finansiering enligt fondprincipen.

Nycander, S. (2005). *Från värdeteori till välfärdsteori*. Stockholm: SNS Förlag.

Ohlin, B. (1975). *Socialistisk skördetid kom bort*. Stockholm: Bonniers.

Palmstierna, E. (1951). *Ett brytningsskede: Minnen och dagboksanteckningar*. Stockholm: Tidens Förlag.

Schumpeter, J. (1954). *History of Economic Analysis*. London: George Allen & Unwin.

Svenska Dagbladet (1945). Gustav Cassels livsgärning, 16 January.

Torstendahl, R. (1969). *Mellan nykonservatism och liberalism: Idébrytningar inom högern och bondepartierna 1918–1934*. Uppsala: Svenska Bokförlaget.

Vallinder, T. (1984). Folkpartiets ideologiska och organisatoriska bakgrund 1866–1934. In *Liberal ideologi och politik 1934–1984* (pp. 12–79). Falköping: Folk & Samhälle.

X.Y.Z. (1910). En fråga till professor Cassel. *Svenska Dagbladet*, 27 October.

10 Eli Heckscher on poverty

Causes and cures

Benny Carlson

Anyone curious to know what Eli Heckscher (1879–1952), the Swedish economist and economic historian, 'world-famous' for the Heckscher-Ohlin theorem and his great work on *Mercantilism*, has to say about poverty and its causes and cures will need to refer to a lecture of 1913 dealing with that very question, namely: *Varpå beror det, att några människor äro rika och andra fattiga?* (Why are some people rich and others poor?). This lecture dates to the transitional period during which Heckscher was changing direction from social conservatism to economic liberalism, a change which signified a shift of emphasis away from belief in the capacity of the state for farsighted and forcible intervention so as to raise the national social and economic standard, and towards the belief that individuals have the capability to take responsibility for themselves and that their actions—aided by the free price mechanism which guides them to the place in the market where they are most needed—generate the best result for society. Such a shift of emphasis ought to have had an influence on the way in which Heckscher—or, indeed, any other thinker on social issues—regarded the responsibility of state and individual, respectively, for the existence of poverty. It is therefore wise to begin by scrutinizing Heckscher's lecture on poverty closely, then to take one step backward in time and another step forward so as to see the extent to which his ideological change of direction actually did affect his view of poverty.

Why should anyone in our era want to know what Heckscher in his era had to say about poverty? There are several reasons. First, as we will see in a moment, he regarded the abolition of poverty as the prime purpose of all economic and social labor. Second, on and off over a long lifetime, he was interested in questions of income distribution, and this long lifetime coincided with the construction of the modern social state. Third, his views often cut across the ideology which was predominant during this epoch. It is true that he said his goal was a more equal distribution of incomes, but he was stressing the responsibility of the individual and the importance of incentives and economic growth at the same time as his Social Democratic opponents were speaking of society's responsibility and equalization of incomes without much reference to incentives. His approach therefore ought to be of interest in our time, when interest in the problems of both distribution and growth is widespread. However—fourth—his views on poverty have, in fact, not attracted very much attention (perhaps for the very reason that in his own era he did not dance to the tunes of political fashion), as we can discover by sifting rapidly through the few grains which float upwards out of the stream of reports describing his life and works.

Earlier assessments

Arthur Montgomery (1953, p. 158) has summarized the liberal Heckscher's standpoint on the distribution question as follows: He adopted 'an approach which in principle was sympathetic' to efforts to create a more equal distribution of incomes but found 'the margin [to be] rather narrow'. 'He was most inclined to the view that progressive taxation and special charges on unearned incomes had by this time already gone much too far in Sweden. In these circumstances the scope for measures of social policy was somewhat limited'.

Heckscher's iron self-discipline and work ethic are well vouched for, and in his attitude to the poor and jobless, they probably reflected the demands he made on himself. Axel Hirsch's (1953) memoir of him sheds an interesting background light on that attitude. Hirsch devotes a certain amount of space to Heckscher's mother, Rosa. She took the view (in words) 'that poor relief must never be allowed to appear attractive in any respect; people ought to manage as far as possible without having recourse to poor relief' (Hirsch 1953, p. 203). When Heckscher warned, as he did from time to time, against the development of a poorhouse spirit, it may be surmised that the message had been imbibed by him with his mother's milk, or as the Swedish proverb has it, 'had been in the sack before it found its way into the bag'.

It seems to have amused Gunnar Myrdal that Heckscher, when proclaiming his liberal programme at the beginning of the 1920s, enthusiastically presented John Stuart Mill's century-old reservation against the laissez-faire doctrine to the effect that intervention in the distribution of incomes is legitimate, but nonetheless had 'a tendency to arrive at a conservatively passive standpoint' with regard to most issues of distribution policy (Myrdal 1972, p. 273).

Finally, Bertil Ohlin (1972, p. 77) states that for 50 years he had clung steadfastly to Heckscher's aim of an income distribution as equal as can be achieved without damaging the growth-creating forces, but with the proviso that he (Ohlin) uses the 'more radical' wording 'without *vitally* damaging'. So *that* is the difference between economic and social liberalism!

The lecture on poverty

Let us, then, dive head first into Heckscher's lecture on poverty.[1] Heckscher (1913, p. 3) begins by declaring that his aims are to pursue a discussion in terms of economics, that is, 'without partiality as far as possible' and with no moral or emotional overtones, of the distribution of income on an individual and not class basis. He then rejects the socialist view that the rich only have unearned incomes and the poor only earned incomes. Many small farmers have incomes from land and many small savers have incomes from capital. The very poorest individuals often only have unearned incomes because they are no longer fit to work. Many of those receiving large incomes—managing directors for example—have earned incomes only.

Heckscher (1913, p. 14) goes on to say that if you want to explain why income is unequally distributed, it is necessary to study 'how it comes about *firstly* that unearned income, i.e. wealth, is unequally distributed, and *secondly* that earned income too differs as between one individual and another'. He suggests four reasons why wealth is unequally distributed. First, some people get a better start in life than others as a result of inheritance. This explanation carries most weight in economically stagnant countries, whereas in countries enjoying rapid economic growth large fortunes are usually newly created. In this connection, Heckscher (1913, p. 20) notes that 'wealth is acquired during one generation, is frequently enlarged during the next, is stationary during the third and disappears during the fourth'. Second, people's economic aptitude differs. Their talent may be negative, manifesting itself in saving, or positive, expressing itself in enterprise. In economically progressive societies, large fortunes are founded by enterprise and enlarged by saving, but it is unusual for anyone to amass a great fortune by saving. That not everyone can create a fortune by enterprise is obvious—otherwise anybody would do it. Third, income disparities lead to wealth disparities. Fourth, pure chance plays a part.

As regards the reasons for uneven distribution of labor incomes, Heckscher adduces the same factors as in the case of wealth but attaches somewhat different importance to them. First, economic aptitude (talent) varies. Economic talent means 'the capacity to satisfy and draw utility from the market's needs' (Heckscher 1913, p. 27). Talent is always scarce and is rewarded accordingly. Regarded from the opposite angle, lack of economic aptitude leads to low incomes, and what Heckscher (1913, p. 27) is saying—though he admits it may sound heartless—is, 'that in the *majority* of instances an unemployed worker is less competent than another worker in the same trade who has a job—otherwise the employer must have misunderstood his own interest quite badly when he kept the latter on and dismissed the former'.

Second, people's start in life varies. In some cases, society fails to secure its members' physical, intellectual and moral development into people being ready to work. Certain individuals may receive an education not enjoyed by all, giving them an exceptional position with high incomes as a result. 'The most fundamental—but also the most difficult—and truly democratic of tasks, therefore', says Heckscher (1913, p. 29), 'is to give every member of society the education best corresponding to his or her gifts, without reference to the parents' financial standing'. Third, chance plays its tricks. Heckscher thus arrives at the conclusion 'that the causes of unequal income distribution are essentially three: differences of economic aptitude, inequalities at the starting point and—probably in a relatively small number of instances—pure chance' (Heckscher 1913, p. 29).

Heckscher next turns to the question of what should and can be done to equalize the distribution of incomes. That something should be done—provided that the national income is not diminished thereby—is self-evident since 'a given national income yields a greater sum of satisfaction the more evenly distributed it is' (Heckscher 1913, p. 30). Whether anything can be done is harder to say because the unequal distribution of incomes corresponds to 'profound national economic needs'. 'The obvious risk is that if people are no longer remunerated according to what their activity is worth to the national economy, they are encouraged to contribute less to the national economy' (Heckscher 1913, p. 31). This is not to say that all equalization must lead to stagnation. If a particular income or fortune is acquired in such a way that it makes no addition to the national economy, then blocking these private sources of income will do no damage to any forces of value to the national economy. Even if some particular income or fortune constitutes an addition to the national economy, society can still appropriate part of it as long as the individual concerned is not robbed of the incentive to increase his own and thus the national economy's incomes.

Having demonstrated the woolliness of the term economic justice, Heckscher declares that the political economist has to make up his mind about 'economic expediency' and that the most expedient distribution of income is the one which produces the best response to the needs of the people as a whole. And this is by no means the absolutely equal distribution of incomes but *'an income distribution as equal as can be achieved without weakening the wealth-creating forces'* (Heckscher 1913, p. 34).

Social reforms

Heckscher does not examine any of the ways in which it might be possible to equalize the distribution of incomes without impairing the incentives for people to exert themselves, apart from underlining the importance of education as we have seen. However, he does make reference to an article on social reforms in *Svensk Tidskrift* in 1912. In this article Heckscher proposes the abolition of poverty as the highest goal of all economic and social work, or, more correctly, 'the abolition of poverty for all persons who have the will to perform that function to which society assigns them' (Heckscher 1912b, p. 411). For those who do not wish to perform these tasks there is no hope: 'Society's dregs, its antisocial element—the unemployables—will never be able to escape poverty …' Large incomes and fortunes are no problem as long as they do not consist of purely speculative profits which bring no benefit to society—these items may according to Heckscher with advantage be treated as 'sponges, which the government first allows to fill up and then squeezes out into its coffers'

(Heckscher 1912b, p. 413). Heckscher (1912b, pp. 414–415) is prepared to allot a socially reformative role to taxation but underlines at the same time that poverty cannot be abolished through distribution: 'It has been demonstrated time and again … that the present national income, even if divided up equally, is too small to abolish poverty …. In any discussion of the abolition of poverty, in fact, the expansion of production is the be-all and end-all'.

Nor is Heckscher hostile to other forms of state intervention to reduce poverty. He can conceive of legislation dealing with maximum working hours and (with some hesitation) minimum wages and social insurance. However, care must be taken not to undermine the sense of personal responsibility. Heckscher states, 'that each and every one of us is "the architect of his own future", that poverty … must never appear to the individual as not of his own making as long as he has had some opportunity of avoiding it'. Therefore, every responsible-minded person must strive to ensure that the forthcoming social reforms 'do not lead to the pauperisation of the people, to the creation of a poorhouse mentality in the whole of society' (Heckscher 1912b, pp. 415–416).

From social conservatism …

We can now go on to consider the question of whether Heckscher's opinion concerning the causes of poverty looked different some years before and after the lecture of 1913, respectively.

In his early contributions to political economy, in the years 1906–1910, Heckscher went vigorously on the offensive against both the old liberalism and the old conservatism. At this time, he represented a social conservatism which called for a strong and active state capable of incorporating the workers into society and organizing the national economy in a more efficient fashion.

By 1910, Heckscher was advocating some form of state socialism, but a year after that, his enthusiasm began to cool. Now he plunged into controversy with the Social Democrats as he grappled with the question of poverty. When Social Democrats emphasized more and more that the aim of socialism was to abolish poverty, Heckscher (1911) posed two questions: Can socialism increase economic growth? Can socialism prevent pauperization of the people? By the latter he meant that talk of society's guilt and the individual's innocence in the matter of individual poverty risked undermining the spirit of personal responsibility and creating a poorhouse mentality.

In the following year Heckscher (1912a) struck a blow against what in time would come to be termed the Wigforss doctrine (after Ernst Wigforss, the Social Democratic ideologue and finance minister), namely, the view that poverty, or at least the sense of poverty, will disappear if only inequality disappears. In 1912 this idea was championed by a statistician, Isidor Flodström, who asserted the following in a lecture: 'Poverty and wealth are correlative terms; without poverty there is no wealth, and vice versa'. Heckscher's acid comment on this proposition was, 'The abolition of poverty, the common goal of us all, thus becomes amazingly easy of achievement—simply abolish wealth, and you banish poverty from the earth at a stroke' (Heckscher 1912a, p. 270). The risk was of course that after any such operation everyone would become poorer, and Heckscher criticized Flodström for not having given a thought to the 'wealth-creating forces—wealth-creating in the sense of enhancing the prosperity of the people' (Heckscher 1912a. p. 270).

Whether Heckscher during his state-activist period up to 1910 saw the causes of poverty in any other and less individual-oriented light than he would do later is difficult to say, because at that time he had still not begun twisting and turning over the poverty question. At any rate, we can say that in 1911 his emphasis was primarily on the risk that the talk of society's responsibility for individual poverty would create a poorhouse spirit, whereby the individual would seek the succour of the state rather than try to lift himself out of poverty by his own exertions. Nevertheless, he was not afraid to let the state intervene if the efficiency of the labor force was at risk of being undermined by starvation wages, a bad work environment and long working days. This attitude was manifested in his lectures on *Industrialism* in 1906, for example. Here Heckscher (1906, p. 10) expresses his social conservative approach in the following words: 'It is *society's* interest which shall dictate the rules. That is the meaning of the expression *social* legislation, which is neither charity nor sympathy for the workers; it is not class legislation but social legislation; it is the means for a better organisation of society'.

... to economic liberalism

Experience of the 'wartime socialism' of the First World War confirmed Heckscher's scepticism with regard to state intervention. His grand entrance as the prophet of economic liberalism in Sweden came with *Gammal och ny ekonomisk liberalism* (Economic liberalism old and new) in 1921. This work is our prime source of knowledge of the liberal Heckscher's view of poverty. It is scarcely necessary to rely on his subsequent writings, because he maintained his economic liberal approach with great consistency throughout his life,[2] and also because as time went by he devoted less of his interest to questions of poverty and distribution.

In a chapter on the equalization of income distribution, Heckscher argues that large parts of the incomes produced under free competition are not needed to stimulate economically useful activity. An entrepreneur earning several millions a year is scarcely going to twiddle his thumbs in idleness just because his remuneration diminishes (Heckscher 1921, p. 51):

> He does not derive his gigantic income from working like a slave but from being the fortunate possessor of specially highly esteemed natural gifts, the employment of which usually affords him a kind of satisfaction; therefore he is unlikely to reduce his work performance or work product in the least, even if his remuneration decreases very considerably.

Matters are different for an employee who can only increase his income through extra work; if you take a substantial proportion of his increased income away from him he will reduce his work performance. The situation is similar with interest on capital. A multi-millionaire will certainly save almost as much even if the interest rate is lowered. But he who perceives saving as a tangible sacrifice will save less. The content of Heckscher's reasoning thus far is that 'a part of society's income is *freely disposable* in the sense that it is not necessary as remuneration to those whose work performances are valued especially highly' (Heckscher 1921, pp. 51–52).

Ought this freely disposable income to be used for the purpose of reducing economic inequality? Here Heckscher reverts to the view 'that to a large extent total income creates greater aggregate satisfaction in a society the more evenly distributed it is'. Since the rich man's human value is no greater than the poor man's, 'then the conclusion in fact is clear: the *most equal* distribution of income is intrinsically the best' (Heckscher 1921, p. 52). But at the same time, an unequal distribution of income is necessary largely for the purpose of sustaining socially requisite behavior such as diligence and thrift. The goal which Heckscher sets is therefore the same as the one he formulated in 1913: *'an income distribution as equal as can be achieved without weakening the wealth-creating forces'* (Heckscher 1921, p. 53).

The instrument for attaining this end, Heckscher continues, is progressive taxation, which is 'a means of gaining access to income which has no impact on its recipient's willingness to exert himself in the interests of society' (Heckscher 1921, p. 55). Caution ought to be exercised in taxing groups for which an increase in income results from an increase in labor, but less caution is necessary when taxing the really high incomes which are the fruit not of increased but of especially profitable labor.

For what purposes ought 'freely disposable income' to be used? Heckscher's answer is: for capital formation, for society's necessary expenditure (the judiciary, defence, administration, etc.) and for cost-free education. However, this income probably does not suffice for these expenditures. In that case the broad masses of the population must be taxed, and, Heckscher concludes, 'thus, in principle, all justification for imposing special measures to equalize incomes disappears, for they would then be paid for, so to speak, by the broad masses of the population themselves' and therefore 'the new liberalism has very little cause to look favorably on government action aimed at equalizing incomes' (Heckscher 1921, p. 83).

In his discussion of social policy, Heckscher argues that 'the market's pricing of labor must be accepted as it actually is' (Heckscher 1921, p. 62). Measures such as compulsory minimum wages can therefore scarcely achieve any good purpose, for such a statute would either confirm the pricing of the market, and thus be meaningless, or else raise wages above it, creating unemployment. Social policy could, however, influence the market price of labor through vocational education and by facilitating occupational choices that fits in with the needs of the market. Labor exchanges are of great importance for oiling the equilibrium machinery of free pricing. Heckscher contends that as regards the scope for intervening on the labor market, the new liberalism must 'retain somewhat more of the old liberalism's reserved standpoint than is now fashionable' (Heckscher 1921, p. 64).

What justification is there, then, for social policy? Well, Heckscher does not think it is to be found 'in the endless and not infrequently pretty worthless sociopolitical literature' (Heckscher 1921, p. 67), but in *Das nationale System der politischen Oekonomie* by Friedrich List (1841), namely in List's remark that the classical theory is a doctrine of value-in-exchange and not of productive forces; it is a case where the parties to the exchange make a profit for the moment but the future impact of the exchange is ignored. 'This line of thought has its most irrefutable validity ... for such future interests as lie outside the parties' own lives but are nevertheless affected by their action' (Heckscher 1921, p. 68). A palpable example is child labor, which yields a temporary private and national economic return but in the long run prevents the individual from becoming an efficient worker and member of society; the short-term profit is then, in Heckscher's (1921, p. 68) words, achieved 'by consuming human capital'. With respect to the parties' own future interests, intervention is less called for. If we believe that legislators and officials comprehend the future interests of the acting parties better than they do themselves, then we are entering the realm of tutelage over mature adults.

Nevertheless, Heckscher accepts that the state, through the medium of social insurance, forces people to think about the future risks of old age, invalidity and accidents. Here, the inability to look after one's own interest is so palpable and the harm resulting from the risk of remaining uninsured so extensive 'that there can scarcely be any doubt of the desirability of the state's intervening and enforcing provision for the purpose' (Heckscher 1921, p. 85); but such intervention must take the form not of a mere support system, but of 'real social insurance, in which the state's intervention compels those insured to save against the contingency of future insured events' (Heckscher 1921, p. 70).

Heckscher's principal message, however, is that the field must be left open to the forces of economic growth (Heckscher 1921, p. 95):

> even at the risk that a considerable number of extravagant, unenterprising, lazy, uneconomically-inclined individuals and groups will fall into difficulties from which an all-regulating state would have been able to rescue them. These are the very ones who, in the long run, will suffer most if material progress should go definitely into reverse ...

In other words, Heckscher represents the point of view which in modern-day America is commonly summed up in the motto that the tide of economic growth lifts all boats.

Inheritance tax and equalization

Our puzzle still has a piece missing. The fact that Heckscher regarded the individual's start in life as an important explanation of wealth and poverty, respectively, makes one wonder what line he took on inheritance taxes. Three articles in *Dagens Nyheter* in 1927 set out his views on 'Inheritance from the Economic Point of View'. In one of these articles Heckscher (1927) discusses whether the right of inheritance is necessary for economic growth and concludes that such is the case—for it is a fact 'that people exert themselves more and save more when they have others to provide for than just themselves', so it is 'clear right away that national income and national wealth would diminish if the right of inheritance were removed'. But people in modern society save mostly for their children and hardly at all for subsequent generations. Thus, Heckscher is able *in principle* to support the Italian Eugenio Rignano's plan: the usual inheritance tax on transfer to the children, deduction of half on transfer from children to grandchildren and deduction of everything on the death of the grandchildren. However, he rejects the plan as unworkable in practice because by the time of the latter transfers it is impossible to work out what the original bequest consists of.

During Heckscher's time in the hothouse atmosphere of economic policy, the inheritance tax was put in the frontline twice by the Social Democrats, namely, in the run-up to the so-called Cossack election of 1928 and again when *kvarlåtenskapsskatt* (estate duty) was introduced in 1946. On the former of these occasions, Heckscher took no part in the battle, even though his articles from 1927 seemed to foreshadow his doing so. On the second occasion, he found himself at the center of the controversy, delivering a 'classical' address, followed by polemical exchanges with Finance Minister Wigforss, at a meeting of the Swedish Economic Association in 1947. Let us summarize some of the main arguments deployed in this address.

Heckscher begins by declaring that the motive underlying the tax proposals was to accomplish a far-reaching equalization of incomes and capital even though there was no dangerous tendency calling for counter-measures, because 'the income distribution is much more even at the present time than it has been during most previous periods of history', and without taking into consideration that income equalization is the most difficult of all social reforms (Nationalekonomiska Föreningen 1947, p. 2). The example of Soviet Russia demonstrated how matters could turn out—there, all they had got for their pains was a new ruling class along with larger income differentials than in the capitalist societies.

No surprises so far. However, to the increasing astonishment of his listeners, Heckscher then declared that he would by no means abandon the idea of equalization of incomes: There was no reason why 'the particular class which has sat at the flesh-pots over the past centuries ... should always sit there'. Admittedly it might happen that the broad masses would profit more by 'letting things rip' than by seeking to equalize incomes, since growth will then be maximized. But—and here Heckscher made a concession to Wigforss—the fact cannot be ignored 'that large parts of the broad masses regard inequality of income distribution as an injustice in itself, regardless of whether it would afford them material benefits which they would not otherwise receive' (Nationalekonomiska Föreningen 1947, p. 4).

Heckscher then reverted to his agenda and declared that he stuck to the goal which he set in 1913, to the effect that the highest possible degree of income equalization should be sought that would not impair the wealth-creating forces. As regards the estate duty proposal Heckscher considered it 'self-evident that what we have here is a clear tendency towards socialization' and that this conflicted with the Social Democratic program which only proposed socialization in cases of market failure and not across the entire spectrum (Nationalekonomiska Föreningen 1947, p. 11).

In his final contribution to the income distribution question Heckscher (1949) considered the demand for income equalization to be so strong that it had to be addressed for fear of otherwise inviting revolution or dictatorship. Nevertheless, equalization must, Heckscher (1949, p. 190) maintained, be effected with 'the least possible damage to prosperity-creating forces' by encouraging saving, rising incomes and new enterprise. His longer-term forecast was that progressive taxation would have to dig deeper among the broad masses so as to plough up the vast tax revenues needed by the modern state—and that then the working class too will react against the pressure of taxes.

Conclusions

It is difficult to discern that any major changes occurred over time in Heckscher's view of the causes and cures of poverty.[3] He did not really begin to write about poverty, unequal incomes and social reform until the period 1911–1913, and by then he had already commenced his reorientation from social conservatism to economic liberalism. This dating of Heckscher's change of direction is not in fact uncontroversial. Some observers consider that Heckscher's reorientation began with his appointment as professor of economics in 1909. Others think—in line with Heckscher's own intimations—that his conversion came during the First World War. My own view—based on his writings on how the state can and should act in various respects—is that his shift of emphasis began in the years 1910–1911, coinciding with the Conservative party's loss of both reforming zeal and political power, and that the principal effect of the experiences of the First World War was to reinforce his new economic-liberal world view.[4]

Heckscher's explanations of wealth and poverty deal with varying aptitude or talent, different starts in life (inheritance and education) and random chance. As regards aptitude the individual receives the remuneration he merits in terms of the value put on his efforts by the market and/or society. In other words the poor man is poor because he has little to offer that other people value, and therefore—Heckscher seems to be arguing—he is himself to be blamed. One feels that a distinction would be in order here. He who is born 'untalented' cannot help that, for even individual qualities are a matter of inheritance. That he who is born 'talented' but cannot be bothered to make use of his talents is at fault is hardly a controversial opinion, and here Heckscher does not pull his punches—the term he uses is 'dregs'. As to one's start in life, there are factors at work here which the individual cannot control, wealth or educational traditions which are inherited. In the case of chance, it is of course impossible to speak in advance about either individual or social factors underlying poverty.

When it comes to what can be done about poverty, the main thrust of Heckscher's approach is that adult persons who have intelligence enough to act in their own interests do not need the state or anyone else as a guardian. The responsibility for avoiding poverty should rest as far as possible on the private individual. If too much responsibility is laid on society (the state) there is a risk of implanting a poorhouse spirit.[5] But protective measures by the government are needed when an agreement between two parties affect a third party (here Heckscher has the market failure external effects in mind), especially if this third party is under age and 'human capital' is consumed (here Heckscher is anticipating the human capital theory). Heckscher further argues that people do not always attend to their own interests in a sufficiently long perspective and that the state must therefore compel them to save through the medium of social insurance so as to provide against future risks. He also accepts equalization of income and wealth by means of progressive taxation and inheritance taxes but does not believe it possible to get very far along the progressive route before being compelled to tax 'the broad masses', and he sees practical problems in trying to prevent transfers of cash between several generations. His formula for dealing with the imbalance between the inequality of income, which is the consequence when people are rewarded for their efforts in the market (and which is necessary to get them to make those efforts), and the increase of aggregate satisfaction, which results from a more even distribution of income, is expressed as an income distribution as equal as that which can be achieved without damaging the wealth-creating forces.

Heckscher's primary recipe for reducing poverty is genuinely liberal: free education to reduce the impact of a poor start in life, vocational training to raise the value of the workforce and job-finding services to improve the efficiency of the labor market. These measures are, of course, all aimed at increasing the economic growth which is needed if poverty is to be eradicated in the long term. Socialist conceptions about poverty vanishing if only wealth is eradicated were simply the philosophy of the madhouse in Heckscher's eyes. But, at some point, he did recognize that unequal distribution of income can be regarded as 'an injustice in itself', even though, in the long run, it affords greater opportunities for eliminating poverty than absolutely equal distribution.

Notes

1 Heckscher explains in a footnote that his lecture to a large extent coincides with (which perhaps should be interpreted as meaning that it is inspired by) two works, namely, William Smart's *The Distribution of Income* (1912) and Edwin Cannan's *The Economic Outlook* (1912) (Heckscher 1913, note, p. 35).
2 Ohlin (1972, p. 269) contends that Heckscher's approach to economic policy after *Gammal och ny ekonomisk* liberalism 'seemed remarkably unaffected by the course of events'. Kurt Wickman (2000, p. 15) takes the same view: 'Heckscher would retain the economic policy programme of 1921 with relatively small changes until his death in 1952'.
3 Thus, for example, the causes of unequal income distribution which Heckscher identified in 1913 are repeated unchanged (though considerably abbreviated) in his lecture notes (Heckscher 1926).
4 See Carlson (2006). Elvander (1961) and Sundell (1989) have concluded that there was a change of direction from social conservatism to economic liberalism in the conservative camp around 1910.
5 In the 1920s and 1930s the term used was 'a spirit of dependency'. Today, as we know, we speak of welfare dependency.

References

Cannan, E. (1912). *The Economic Outlook.* London: Fisher Unwin.

Carlson, B. (2006). When Heckscher Changed Direction. In R. Findlay, R.G.H. Henriksson, H. Lindgren, and M. Lundahl (eds), *Eli Heckscher, International Trade, and Economic History.* Cambridge, MA and London: MIT Press, 505–524.

Elvander, N. (1961). *Harald Hjärne och konservatismen: Konservativ idédebatt i Sverige 1865–1922.* Stockholm, Gothenburg, and Uppsala: Almquist & Wiksell.

Heckscher, E.F. (1906). *Industrialismen: Tre föreläsningar.* Stockholm: Oskar Eklunds Boktryckeri.

Heckscher, E.F. (1911). Socialismen och fattigdomens afskaffande. *Svensk Tidskrift,* 1, 231–235.

Heckscher, E.F. (1912a). Fattigdom och rikedom. *Svensk Tidskrift,* 2, 269–272.

Heckscher, E.F. (1912b). Sociala reformer. *Svensk Tidskrift,* 2, 409–420.

Heckscher, E.F. (1913). *Varpå beror det, att några människor äro rika och andra fattiga?* Lecture at Föreningen Heimdal, 17 April 1913. Stockholm: Albert Bonniers Förlag.

Heckscher, E.F. (1921). *Gammal och ny ekonomisk liberalism.* Stockholm: P.A. Norstedt & Söner.

Heckscher, E.F. (1926). *Nationalekonomiens grundvalar: Grundlinjer till föreläsningar.* Stockholm: Centraltryckeriet.

Heckscher, E.F. (1927). Arvsfrågor ur ekonomisk synpunkt. III. Arvsrättens upphävande. *Dagens Nyheter,* 28 August.

Heckscher, E.F. (1949). Inkomstutjämning och beskattning. *Balans,* 1, 189–192.

Hirsch, A. (1953). *Minnen som dröjt kvar.* Stockholm: Hökerberg.

List, F. (1841). *Das nationale System der politischen Oekonomie.* Stuttgart and Tübingen: J.G. Cotta'scher Verlag.

Montgomery, A. (1953). Eli Heckscher som vetenskapsman. *Ekonomisk Tidskrift,* 55(3), 149–185.

Myrdal, G. (1972). *Vetenskap och politik i nationalekonomin.* Stockholm: Rabén & Sjögren.

Nationalekonomiska Föreningen. (1947). *Nationalekonomiska Föreningens sammanträde*, 14 January, De nya skatteförslagen.

Ohlin, B. (1972). *Ung man blir politiker.* Stockholm: Bonniers.

Smart, W. (1912). *The Distribution of Income: Being a Study of What the National Wealth Is and of How It Is Distributed According to Economic Worth.* London: Macmillan.

Sundell, Å. (1989). *Den svenska högerns assimilering av ekonomisk liberalism. Studier kring en ideologisk förändringsproblematik.* Lund: BTJ.

Wickman, K. (2000). Eli Heckscher – pionjär utan efterföljare. In E.F. Heckscher. *Om staten, liberalismen och den ekonomiska politiken. Texter i urval av Kurt Wickman.* Stockholm: Timbro, 11–49.

Index

Note: Page numbers followed by "n" refer to notes.